IMAGES
of America

MODESTO

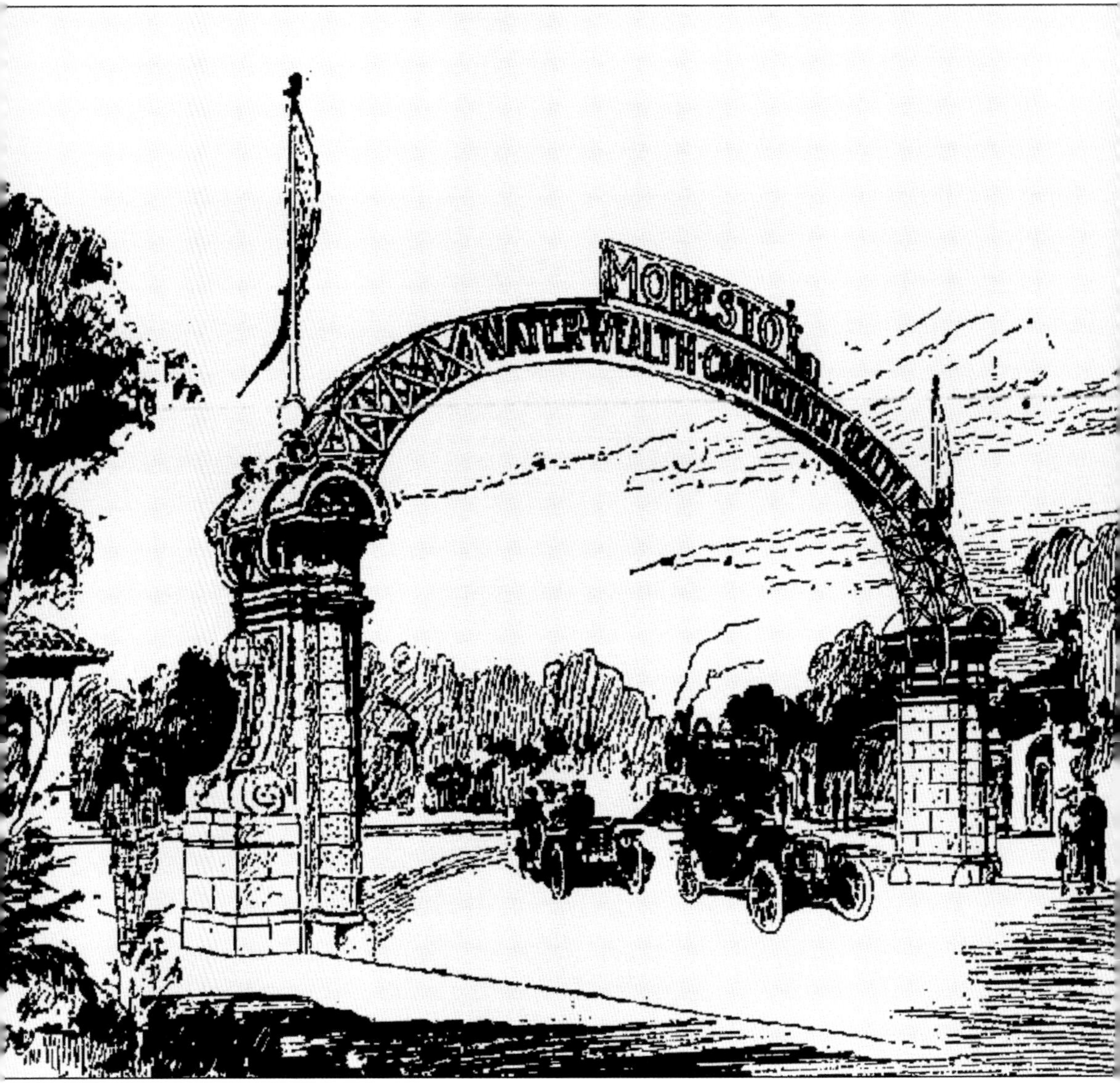

ARCHITECT'S SKETCH, C. 1911. Pictured above is San Francisco architect Bernard J. Joseph's sketch of the Modesto Arch as printed on the front page of the *Modesto News* in 1911. With the acceptance of his plans came a comment from the architect's assistant, Clarence Dakin, who explained, "We purposely made this arch elaborate. We believed that Modesto should have something that any city might be proud of. Paris itself would not sneer at an arch such as this. You intend to place the word 'wealth' on the arch. Therefore you do not want something that looks like it cost a nickel." (Author's collection.)

ON THE COVER: The Modesto Arch is pictured in its original location at Ninth and I Streets, before being moved several feet to the west in the 1930s to accommodate increased traffic. The motto on the arch was actually the second-place winner in the original contest. First place went to "Nobody's Got Modesto's Goat." The arch was funded by the public and dedicated in 1912 when a bottle of canal water was broken over the foundation site and construction begun. Completed the same year, it cost $2,000. (J. Broome, Camera Center Collection.)

IMAGES
of America

MODESTO

Carl P. Baggese and the McHenry Museum

ARCADIA
PUBLISHING

ISBN 978-0-7385-7150-8

Published by Arcadia Publishing
Charleston, South Carolina

Printed in the United States of America

Library of Congress Control Number: 2009928049

For all general information contact Arcadia Publishing at:
Telephone 843-853-2070
Fax 843-853-0044
E-mail sales@arcadiapublishing.com
For customer service and orders:
Toll-Free 1-888-313-2665

Visit us on the Internet at www.arcadiapublishing.com

To my mother and father, Peter and Antoinette Baggese, who both came from a long distance to settle in Modesto and raise their family.

Contents

ACKNOWLEDGMENTS

The photographs in this book come from various sources, including the McHenry Museum Collection; J. Broome, Camera Center Collection; and Raeann Bittleston, Clem Baker Collection.

In addition, the unique "Faces of Stanislaus Collection," made available by coordinator Dan Onorato, was sponsored by Community College Humanities Association, National Endowment of the Humanities, Modesto Junior College, the *Modesto Bee*, the Stanislaus County Office of Education, the International Festival, and the Stanislaus County Board of Supervisors. Contributors to the "Faces of Stanislaus" collection whose photographs are used in this book include Jerry Starr, Irene Angelo, Mary Caswell Bucknam, Jacqueline Foret, Beverly Hammon, Francis Landini, David Orth, Robert Smith, Joyce Scaglione Turner, Nancy Lee, Samuel E. Courtney, Mike DeFerrari, Robert Courtney, Loren Case, Karen Skelly, Gary Ard, and Helen McBride. Their photographs brought a human face to Modesto's history.

Individuals who helped with the creation of this book and to whom I owe a debt of gratitude include Wayne Mathes, director of the McHenry Mansion and McHenry Museum; museum exhibit coordinator, Laura Mesa, and museum volunteer, Janet Lancaster, whose combined knowledge of the extensive photograph collection in the museum basement was instrumental in completing this book; Janie Meily, longtime friend, old school chum, McHenry Mansion docent, and Modesto native, for her continued encouragement and assistance; Kari Volonte, who assisted in procuring the Camera Center Collection; Anthony Housewright, who used his inestimable talents to restore some of the very old photographs; John Broome, a photograph collector with an eye for Modesto history; Derek Waring and Bob Pinheiro, who have encouraged continued interest in early radio with www.ModestoRadioMuseum.org; Bruce Stearns for adding a new source of information to my book collection; Jeff and Sherry Vail, who provided a help with the hospital and churches section; Norman Ham, who shared his collection of historical publications; and Jim and Leslie Beggs, who helped with photograph research. Special thanks to the Arcadia Publishing staff, including John Poultney, Devon Weston, Lynn Beahm, Julie Rivers, and Ryan Easterling.

Of course, I owe very special thanks to my wife, Judi, who spent hours listening to historic anecdotes, assisted in choosing photographs, and helped me organize the final book (without her none of this would have been possible).

Most images in this book appear courtesy of the McHenry Museum. Images from other collections are indicated in photograph captions. Excerpts from writings of Colleen Stanley Bare are used by permission of the museum.

INTRODUCTION

In late February, a little bit before spring arrives, the peach and almond orchards begin their showy appearance of pink and white blossoms in and around Modesto. Rushing water released from the foothill reservoirs fills the concrete waterways of the irrigation district, and farmers prepare for another year of growth and harvest. The perfumed scent of the air can take one back to early days, when the agriculturally rich Central Valley of California beckoned with the wealth of the soil. The farms and ranches of the Modesto area are fewer now, and most of the once plentiful processing plants have closed or moved elsewhere, yet the rich heritage of the city deeply reflects the days when prosperity was counted by how many acres a person owned.

Modesto's motto comes from a time when the town was the center of everything in Stanislaus County. Still emblazoned on the city's arch, its sentiment exhibits the attitude of unbridled success felt by the citizens of the town in 1912: "Modesto—Water, Wealth, Contentment, Health." When the Modesto Businessmen's Association chose San Francisco architect Bernard J. Joseph's design in August 1911, they were seeking something grand to greet travelers passing through Modesto, giving them, perhaps, a reason to stop. What they achieved may have proved longer lasting than even the architect and the association could have imagined. The arch still stands at Ninth and I Streets, an iconic backdrop for modern photographs, writings, and worldwide news reports, good or bad, about Modesto.

The arch has survived through the years because no one here can envision Modesto without it. (Talk of moving or removing the arch in 1966 was met with a firestorm of protests.) The rest of the downtown core has not been as fortunate. Once a bustling city where daytime trade gave way to nighttime frolic and teenaged drivers embraced the craze of cruising Tenth and Eleventh Streets in their hot rods, Modesto is no longer the commercial hub of an earlier time. The deepest cut may have occurred in 1973, when Modesto native George Lucas decided to make a movie that took place in Modesto in 1962, just 11 years earlier. *American Graffiti* was filmed in Petaluma, however, because Modesto no longer looked as Lucas remembered it from his youth.

While it is easy to speculate about what has happened to Modesto, it may be more important to look at the past and think about what the town's citizens accomplished over the years. As voyeurs of history, we are able to watch the story pass at an accelerated pace, as H. G. Wells's Time Traveler did in *The Time Machine*. Roads will be paved, sidewalks and gutters poured, buildings constructed and torn down, and people will live and die. While Modesto may have started out as a "modest" city, its accomplishments were something to boast about as it grew from infancy to adulthood.

Before the region became Paradise Valley, tribes of Native Americans called Yokuts inhabited the area. Historian Sol P. Elias says that there were 4,000 Yokuts living in the Stanislaus area. The county and the river were both named after a one-time mission Native American, Estanislao, who left the protection of the padres at Mission San Jose in the late 1820s. He banded together with others from this mission and fought Spanish soldiers in a river area north of what would become Modesto. By the time gold was discovered in 1849 and California became a state, the valley tribes were decimated by the influx of settlers. According to Elias, "After the discovery of gold, the Indian was treated as an intruder in his own ancient habitat and as a common enemy by the whites."

When the Central Pacific Railroad stretched its iron rails across the Stanislaus River into the county in October 1870, it staked out a simple village with streets running north and south to be numbered and those running east and west to be lettered. Modesto was founded a year and six months after the transcontinental railroad was completed. The coming of the railroad sounded the death knell for Paradise City and Tuolumne City, two towns located on the river, whose time had passed. Riverboats would no longer ply the waters, moving goods from one port to another; instead, the railroad would spread the agricultural wealth of California throughout the nation. So the populace of these two towns moved their buildings and themselves to the new village where they prospered. Within a year of its founding, Modesto bested Knights Ferry for the role of county seat of Stanislaus County.

Modesto became as wild as any Western frontier town depicted in books and films. Saloons, dance halls, and brothels lined Front Street, and violence prevailed for the first few years. Chinatown boasted opium dens and laundries as well as joss houses where indigenous religious practices could be retained. It was vigilante justice that finally cleaned up old Modesto when the San Joaquin Regulators took over law enforcement in the early years. Eventually growing out of its rowdy adolescence, Modesto welcomed new growth and new families with names such as McHenry, Beard, Cressey, Hatton, Schafer, and Stoddard, among many others. These were the names that would build the foundations of Modesto's history. Through their efforts, business flourished. Modesto incorporated as a charter city in 1884.

As the city grew, droughts plagued the area, and farmers sought an alternative to depending on nature to keep their crops alive. There was a fight for the right to divert the mountain runoff into reservoirs and send it cascading down to water new crops in the fertile valley through irrigation. The great system of dams and canals was hailed as a monumental feat that other parts of the country should emulate. With the water came electricity and growth and people. Modesto had begun its historic journey to the present.

One

The Railroad Arrives in Paradise Valley

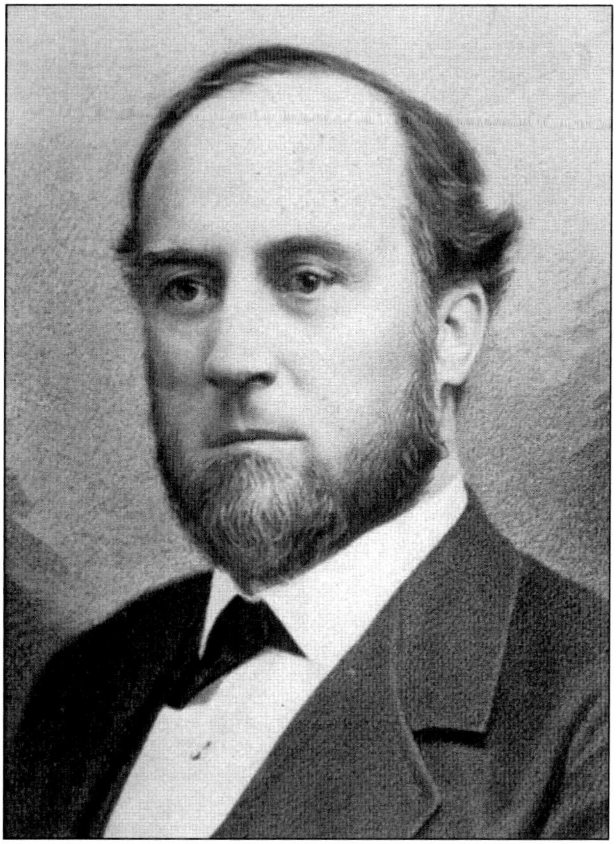

William Chapman Ralston, c. 1870. It all seemed so simple. The new village laid out by the Central Pacific Railroad would be named for San Francisco banker W. C. Ralston, but he declined. So a convention of citizens was called to name the village. Ralston was present and again modestly refused. A suggestion was made that the Spanish word for modest be used, so the name Modesto was adopted with great acclaim. (Author's collection.)

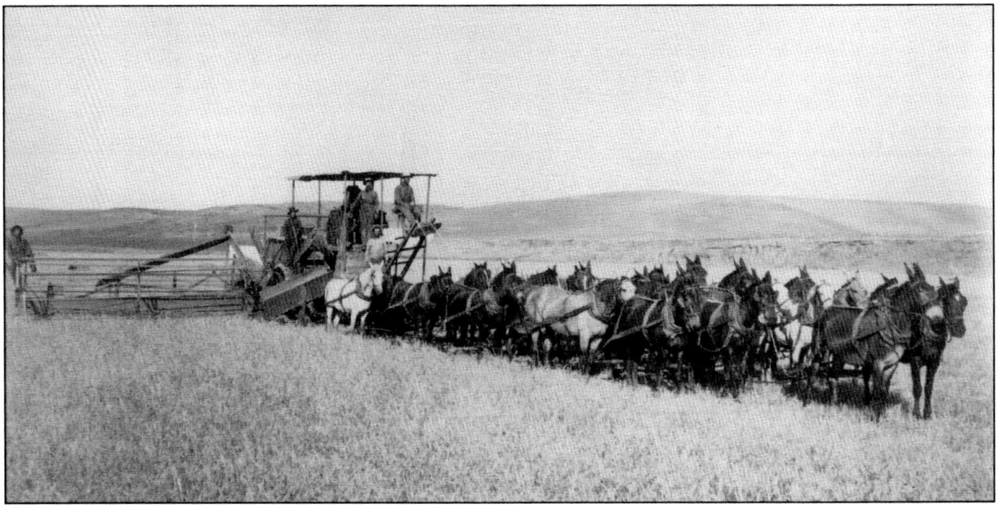

Harvesting Wheat, Late 1800s. Wheat was the "prime staple crop of the county," according to early historian Sol P. Elias. In the photograph above, it is at least a 20-mule and -horse team pulling the thresher to harvest the wheat. When the new village came into being, wheat was being shipped by boat, a practice that soon became obsolete because of the railroad.

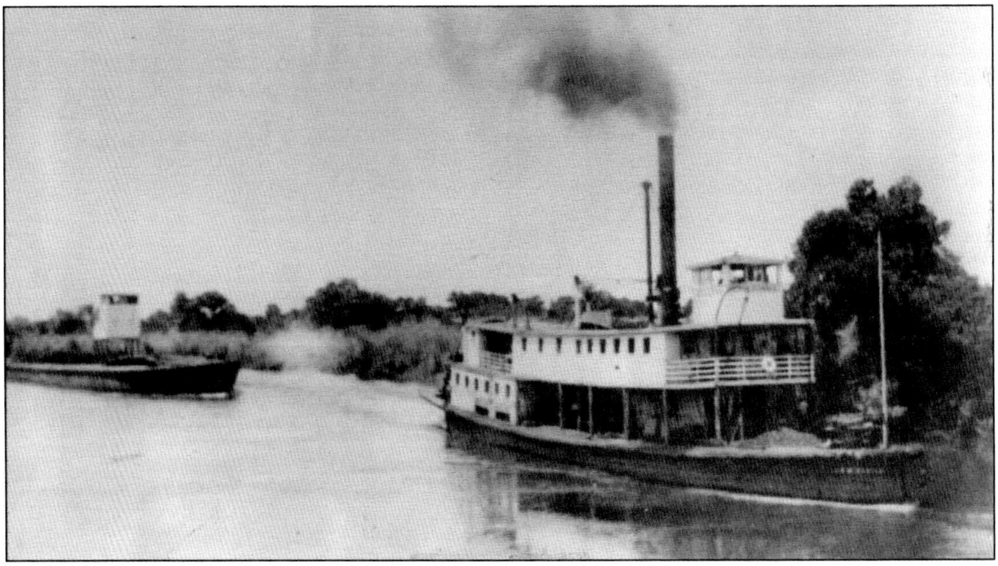

Wheat Boat, Mid-1800s. Along the Tuolumne River, boats plied the water, picking up sacks of grain harvested and milled in Paradise Valley. Tuolumne City and Paradise City had prime locations along the river. The flour mill at Paradise City could turn out 200 barrels a day. In 1870, when the railroad established the village of Modesto, citizens of the two ports moved buildings and belongings to the new town.

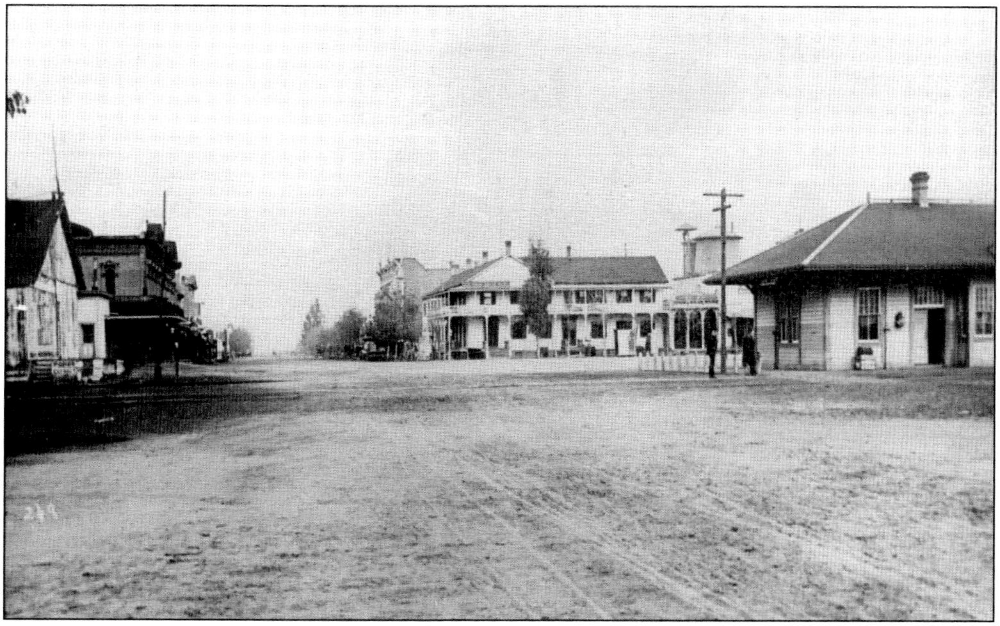

I Street at the Front, c. 1885. I Street was designed by the railroad to be Modesto's broadest avenue; it was 100 feet wide. This view shows the Ross House in the center background, moved in two sections from Paradise City. The railroad depot is at right, and the Art Gallery building is in the left background. The city water towers can be seen rising above the Modesto Bank to the right of the hotel.

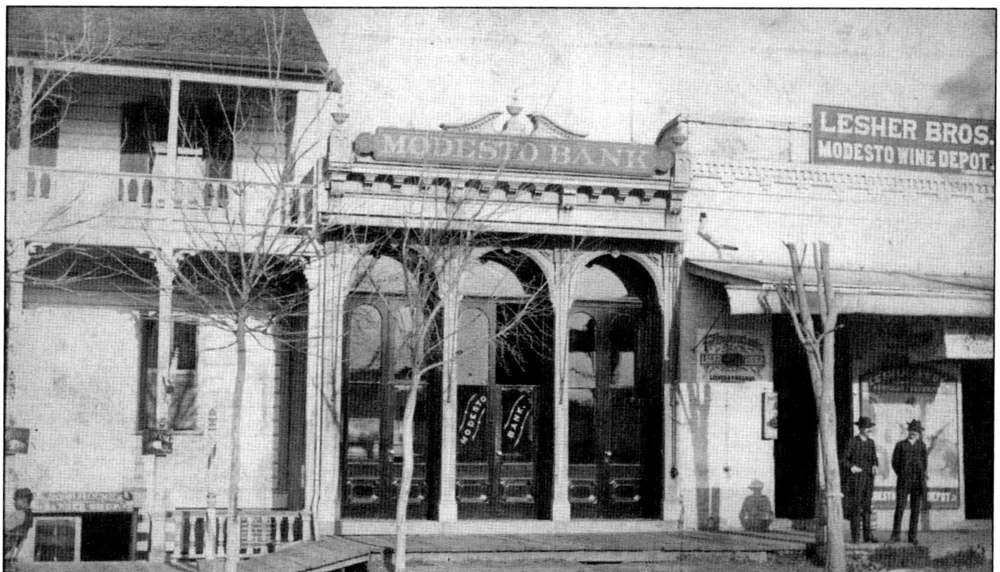

Modesto Bank, c. 1885. This was the town's first bank. This closer photograph by local photographer William Brown shows the detail of the bank's windows and arches. Ross House is on the left with the basement door to the barbershop open. As Modesto's finest hotel, it featured many period refinements. Interestingly, at right is Lesher Brothers Modesto Wine Depot, where Frederickson's Lager Beer was also sold.

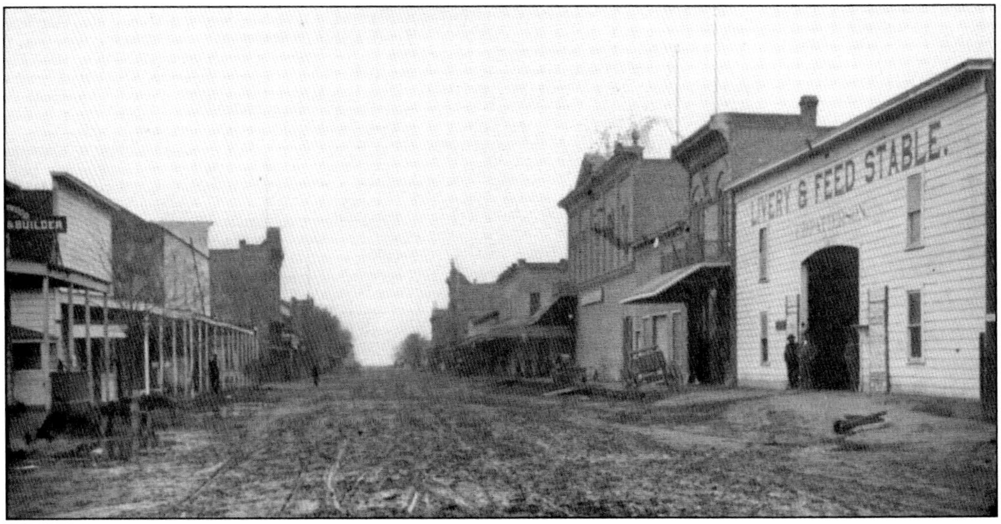

MODESTO STREET VIEWS, 1880S. The above photograph shows Tenth Street looking south. To the right is C. D. Patterson Livery and Feed Stable. Below is I Street near Tenth Street, looking toward Front (Ninth) Street. During this period, Modesto was a rough and rowdy Western town. Shootings occurred regularly in the saloons along Front Street, and not many decent citizens would venture beyond these blocks. The streets were muddy in the winter and dusty in the summer. Perhaps early historian Sol P. Elias put it best: "Like every frontier village that grew up with a rush . . . Modesto, in its infancy, suffered its period of open lawlessness, its era of unbridled gambling, its reign of brutal thuggery, its sway of the malign saloon influence, and its season of brazen, flaunting vice."

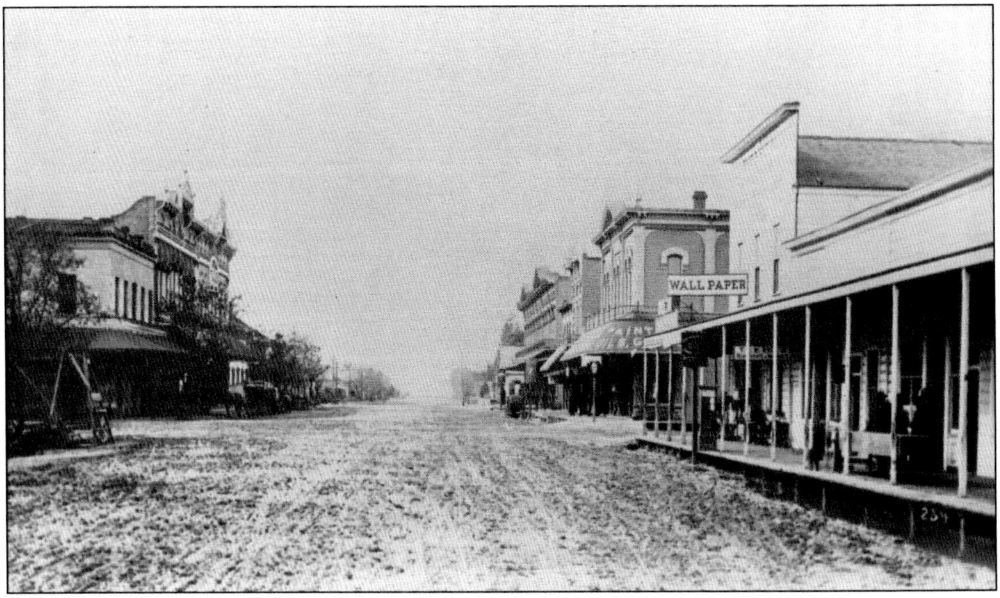

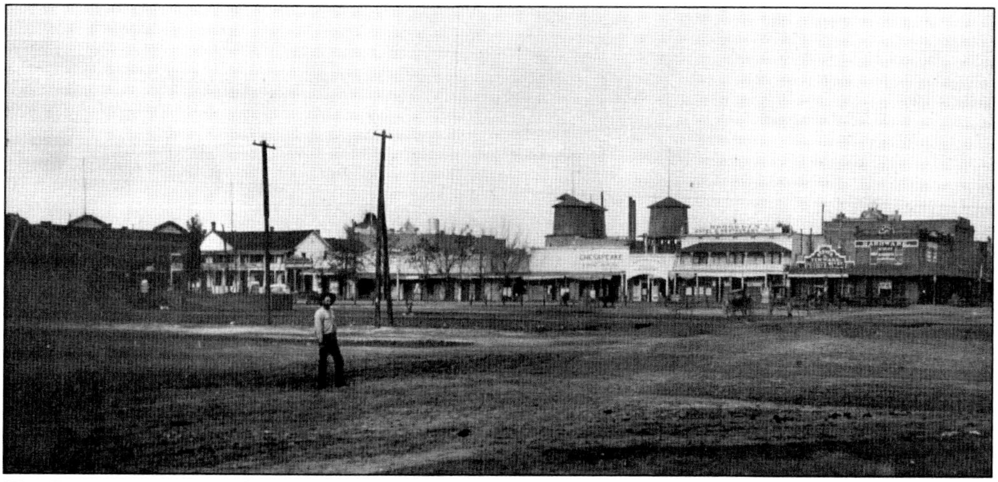

The Front, c. 1880. This was the rowdiest part of town. Taken from the middle of H Street, west of the railroad tracks, this photograph shows Ross House, the two-story white building at left. A hardware store anchors the right corner; Rogers Hall is on the extreme right. Signs along Front Street include Chesapeake Chop House, Brooklyn's Hotel and Restaurant, and Stover Tinware. This photograph was taken a year after the San Joaquin Regulators started doling out justice.

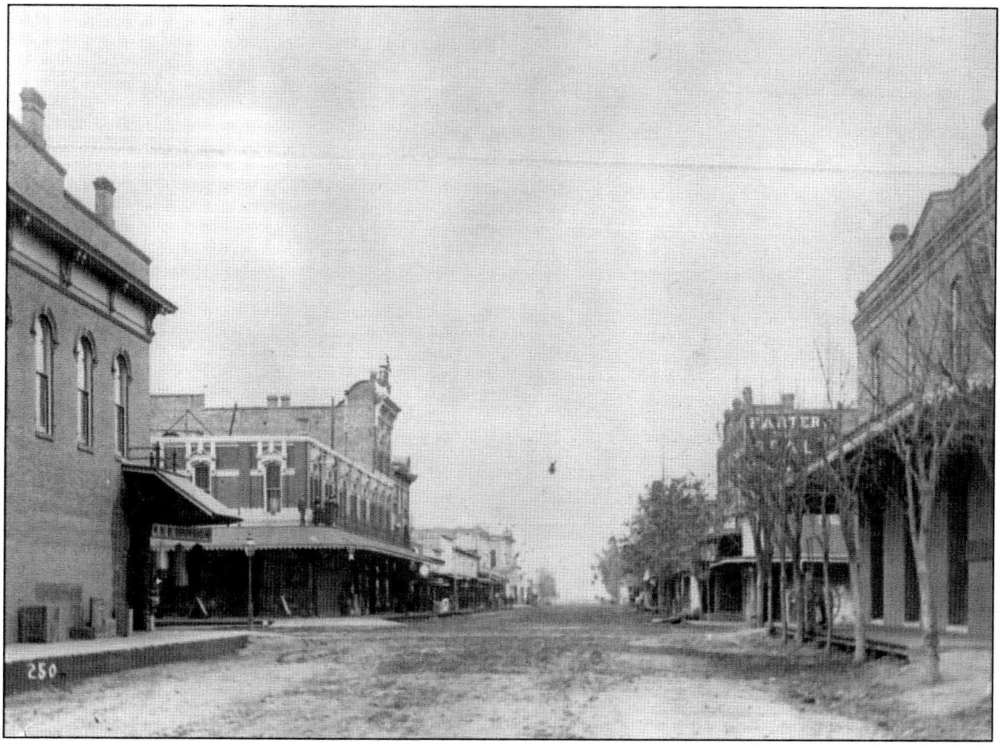

Tenth and H Streets, c. 1890. This view became very popular in postcards and photographs through the years as Modesto grew. In this photograph, the Tynan Hotel, one of the first major hostelries built in the city, is under construction. The IOOF building at left housed H. and B. Grunbaum's general store on the first floor. At right is the Braun building. The *Modesto Herald* was upstairs.

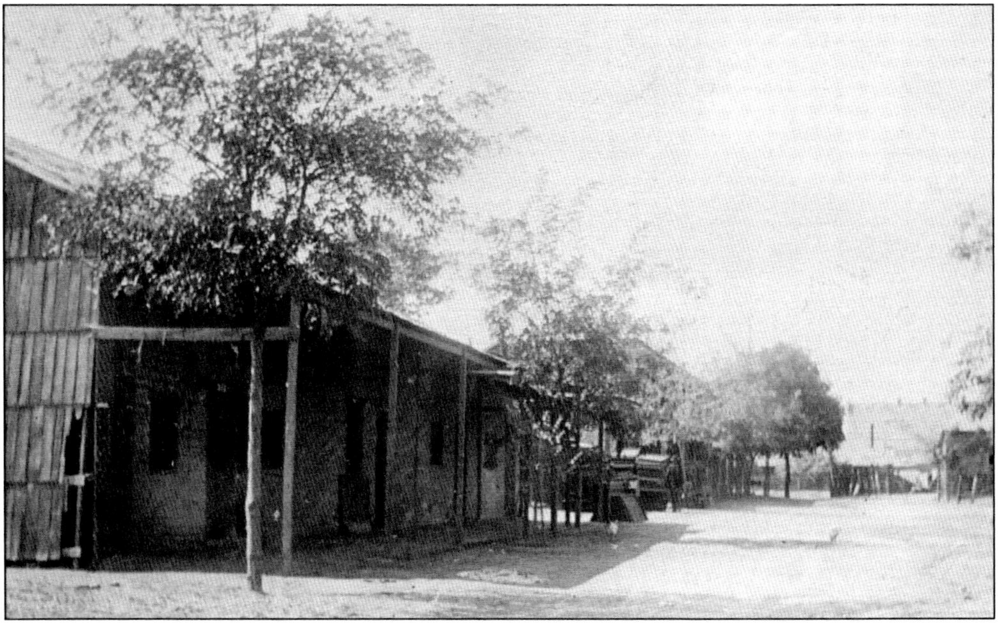

CHINATOWN, C. 1900. Chinatown was located in the block of F and G and Seventh and Eighth Streets, according to historian Colleen Stanley Bare. Modesto's red light district was an extension of the same area in an alley between G and H Streets near the Front. The San Joaquin Regulators, a vigilante group that sought to clean up Modesto's unsavory elements, targeted Chinatown's opium dens and joss houses.

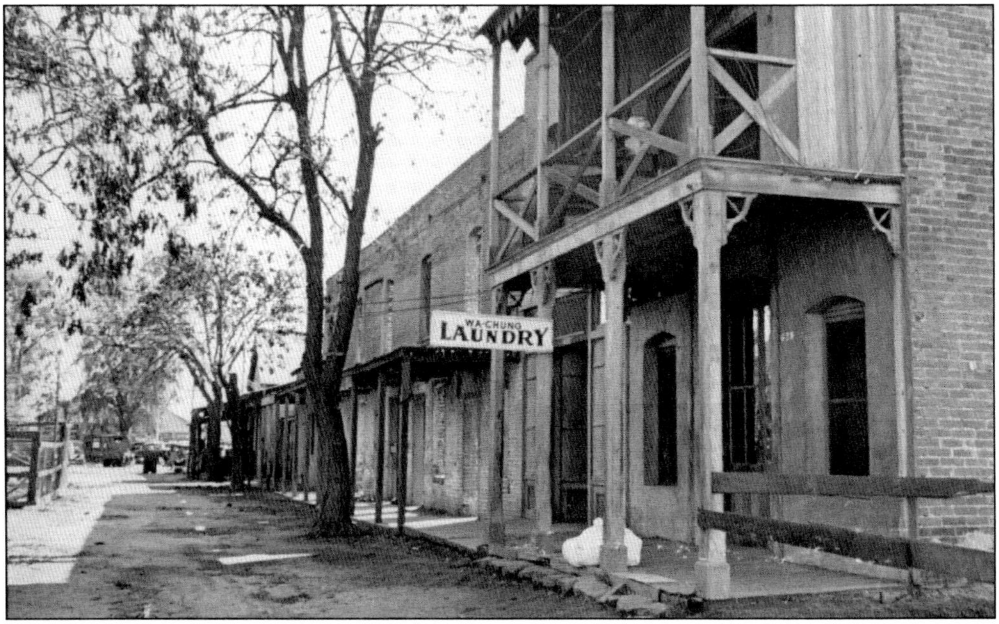

CHINA ALLEY. The Chinese community continued with their businesses even after destructive raids by the San Joaquin Regulators in 1879 and 1884. This photograph of the Chinese area was taken in the 1920s, as indicated by the vehicles in the background. It was located between Seventh and Eighth Streets, south on G Street. Businesses in this area were often connected by tunnels 14 feet underground.

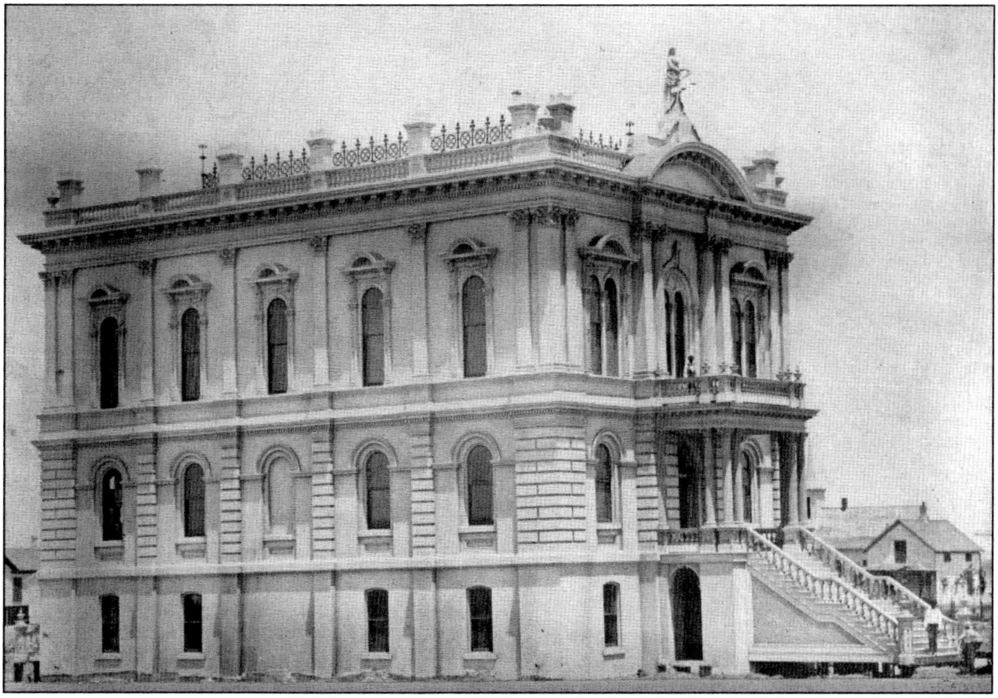

Stanislaus County Courthouse, c. 1873. In 1871, Knights Ferry lost its status as county seat to Modesto after a contentious election. A new courthouse was necessary, so in 1872–1873, this building was erected at a cost of $60,000, including furnishings. The land was donated by the railroad. A. A. Bennett of San Francisco was the architect and Robinson Brothers of Stockton the builders. This building stood until the late 1950s.

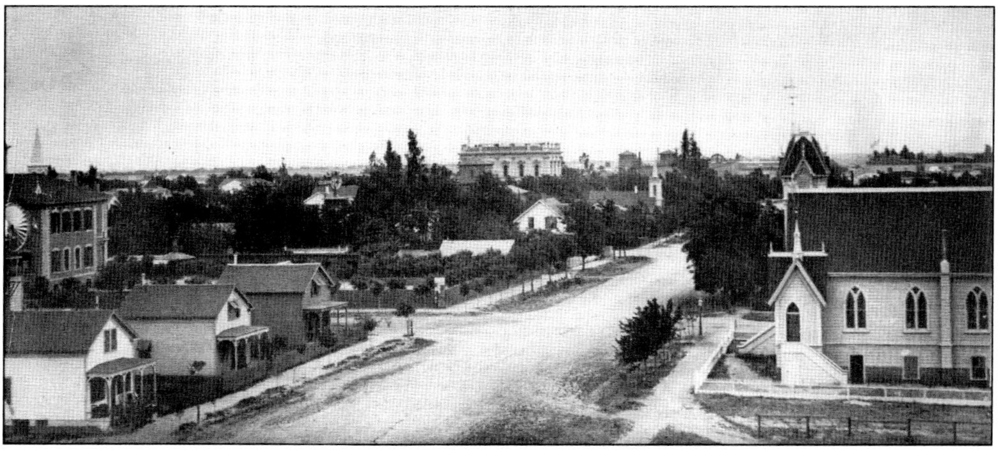

I Street at Fourteenth Street, c. 1885. Trees dot the landscape along I Street with homes and churches taking their place in the growing town. In the center of this photograph is the Stanislaus County Courthouse, its third floor towering above everything else. In the left foreground is a corner of the Fourteenth Street School, also called the Brick Schoolhouse.

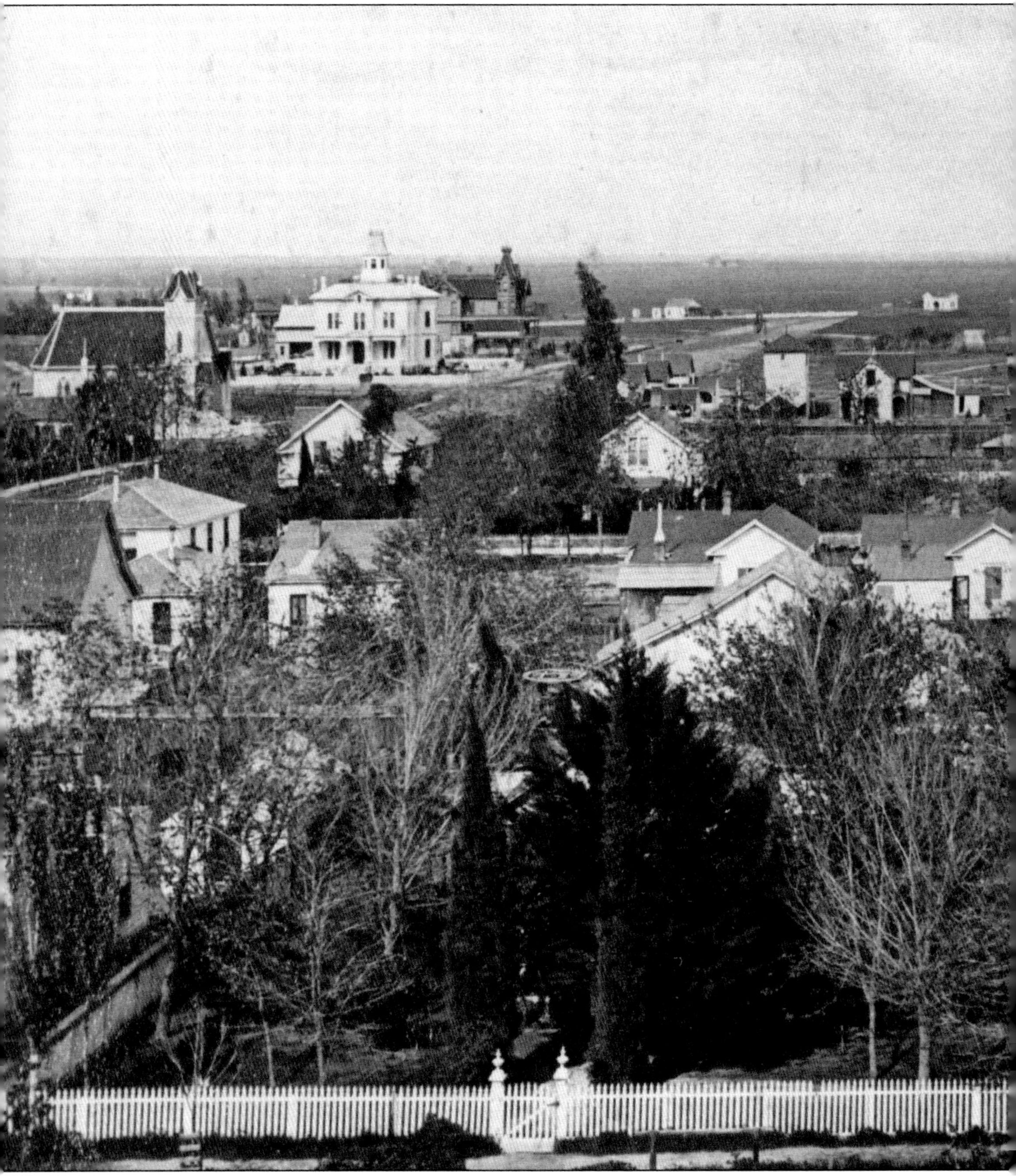

Northeast View of Modesto, c. 1885. The city has developed a Victorian-era influence in its appearance in both public and private structures. This photograph was taken from the roof of the Stanislaus County Courthouse. In the center is the back of the Fourteenth Street School or the Brick Schoolhouse. To the left in the distance are, from left to right, the First Presbyterian

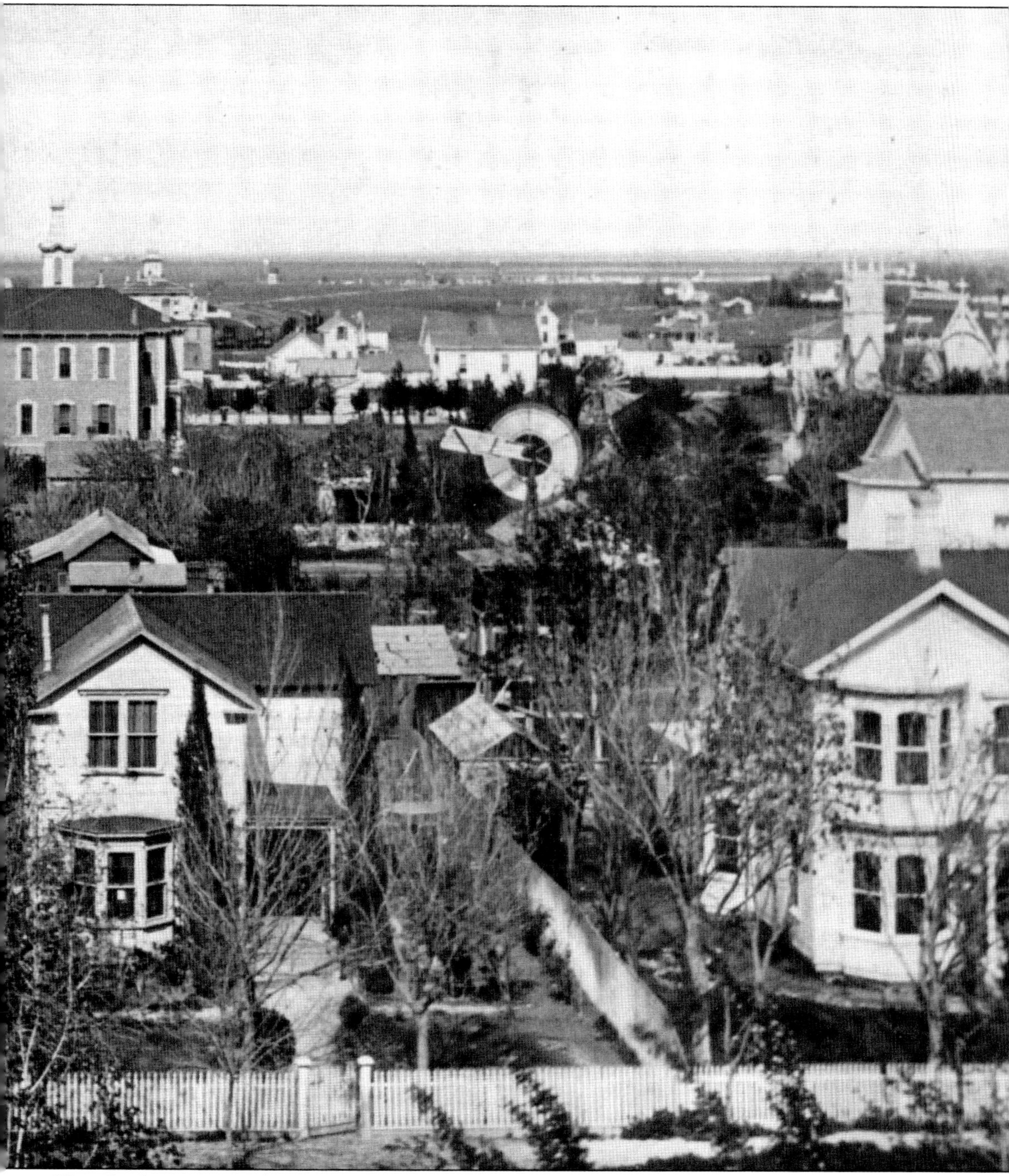

Church, the McHenry home with its cupola standing tall above the elegant structure, and the Bledsoe home directly behind it. At the far right is the First Methodist Episcopal Church, North. The Wood home can be seen in the right foreground.

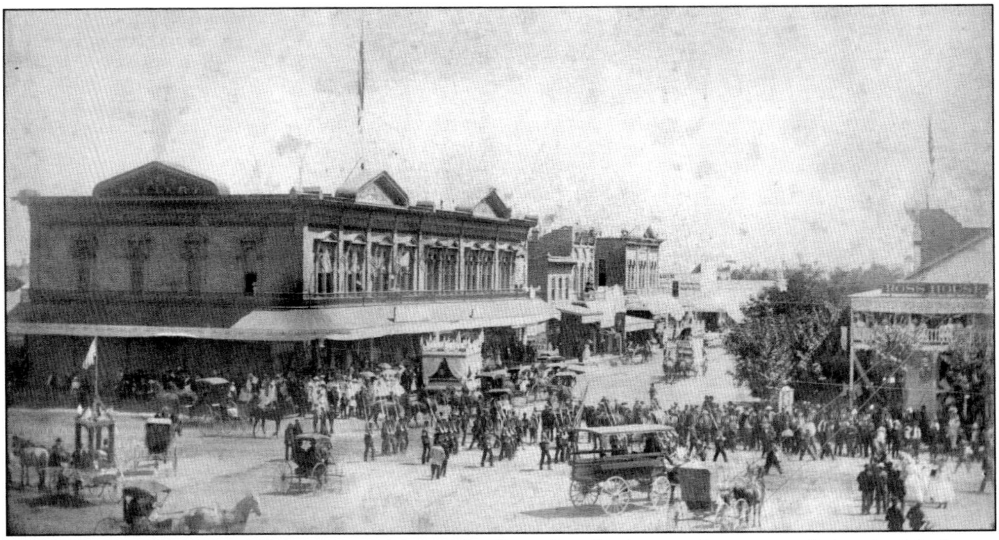

First Fourth of July Parade, c. 1874. The Fourth of July parade is a tradition in Modesto, which began with this parade four years after the village was founded. Taken by photographer William Brown, this photograph shows Ninth and I Streets, with the Ross House to the right. A military unit and horses and buggies join citizens of the town who are celebrating the country's 98th birthday.

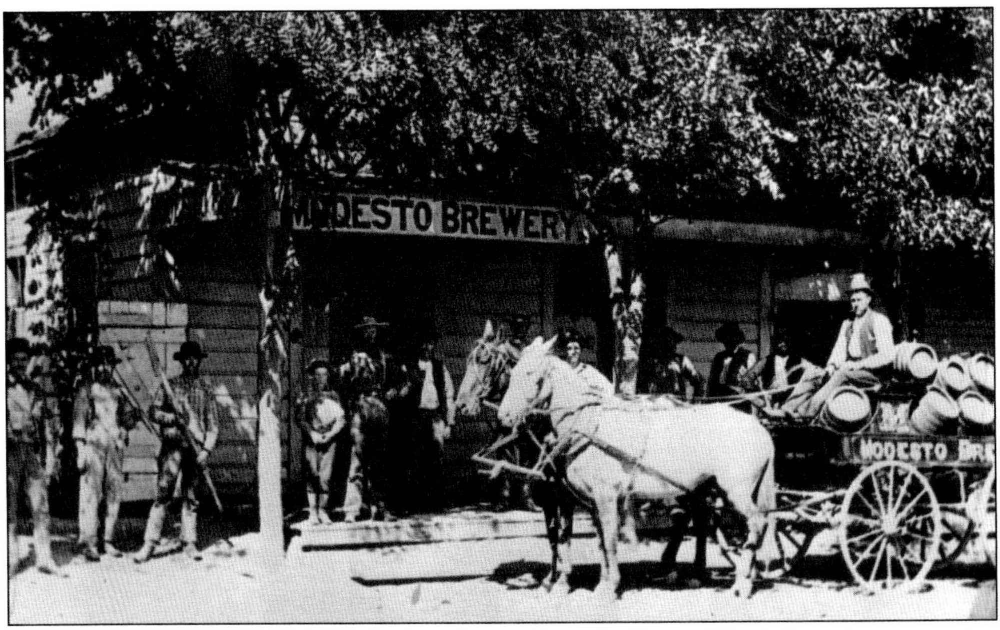

Modesto Brewery, c. 1885. While the saloons along the Front (Ninth Street) were causing anxiety among the proper citizens of Modesto, this brewery was supplying barrels of alcohol to the locals without much concern for the results. The photograph shows quite a bit of activity around the brewery building, which was located at 708-10 Tenth Street. Delivery by horse-drawn wagon was part of the brewery's service.

Robert McHenry, Undated. Born in 1827 in Vermont, Robert McHenry came west in 1849 (depending on which historical biography is being quoted). He mined and then settled in Stockton before "acquiring 2,640 acres of land along the Stanislaus River that later came to be known as the Bald Eagle Ranch," according to historian Colleen Stanley Bare. Robert married Matilda M. Hewitt in 1859 and became a wealthy wheat farmer, a banker, and a strong advocate of irrigation. Their son, Oramil, was born in 1861.

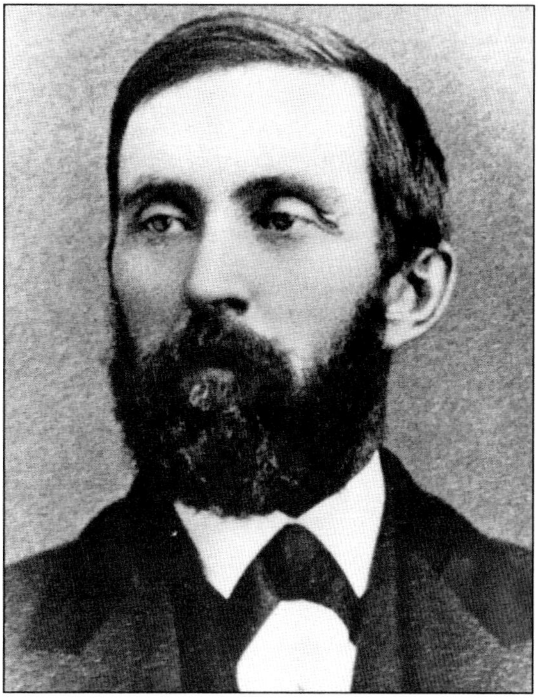

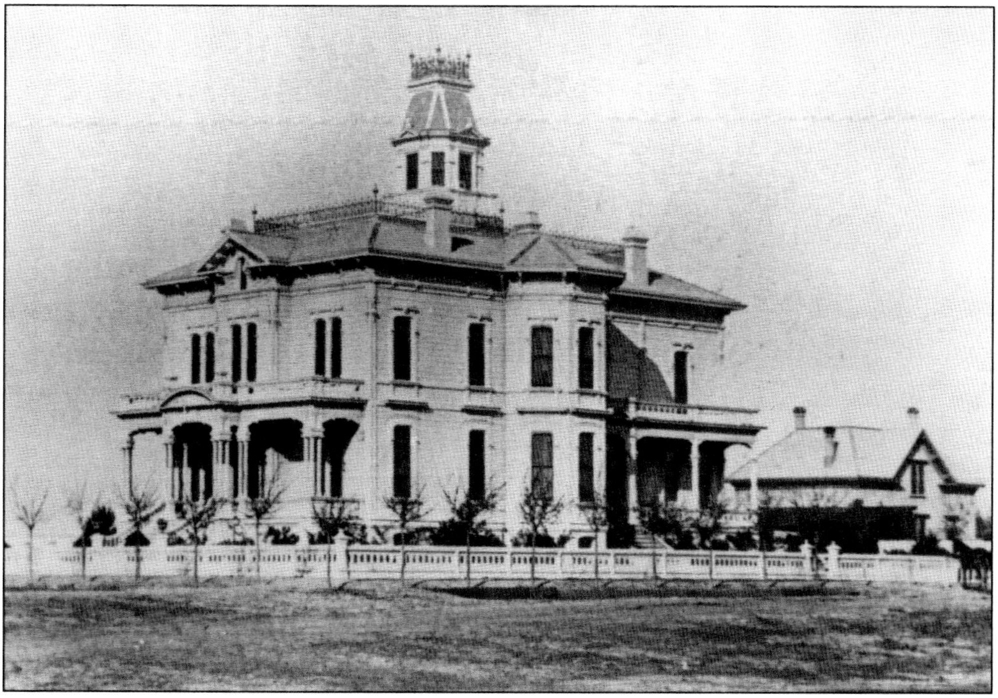

McHenry Home, c. 1885. This is the earliest photograph of the McHenry house at Fifteenth and I Streets. Robert bought the property in 1880 from Charles Crocker. The home was designed and built in 1882–1883 by Jeremiah Robinson, of the Robinson Brothers who built the county courthouse. Designed in Victorian Italianate style, the home had 10,080 square feet of interior space. Most notably, the house was topped with an eight-windowed octagonal cupola.

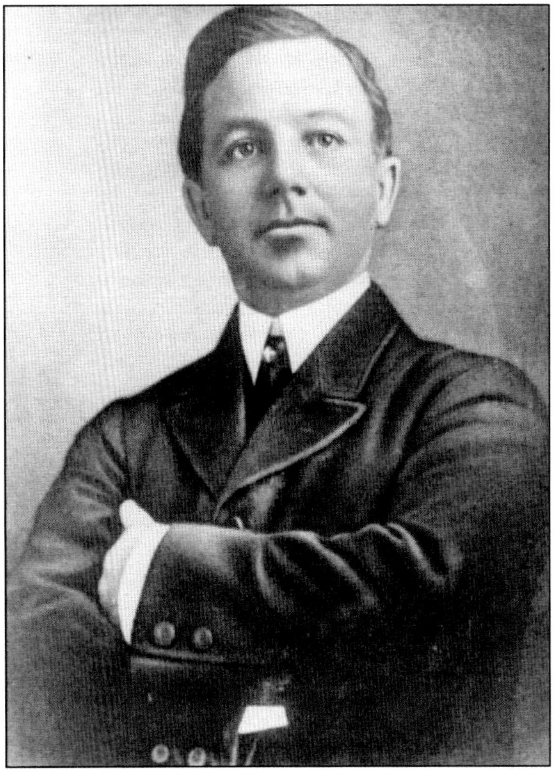

ORAMIL MCHENRY, UNDATED. When Robert died in 1890 and Matilda in 1896, Oramil inherited the house and estate. He increased the family fortune, and at his death in 1906 at the age of 44, he owned the McHenry Packing Company, the Bald Eagle Ranch, and vast acreage in Fresno and Kern Counties. By bequest, he donated Modesto's first public library, now the home of the McHenry Museum.

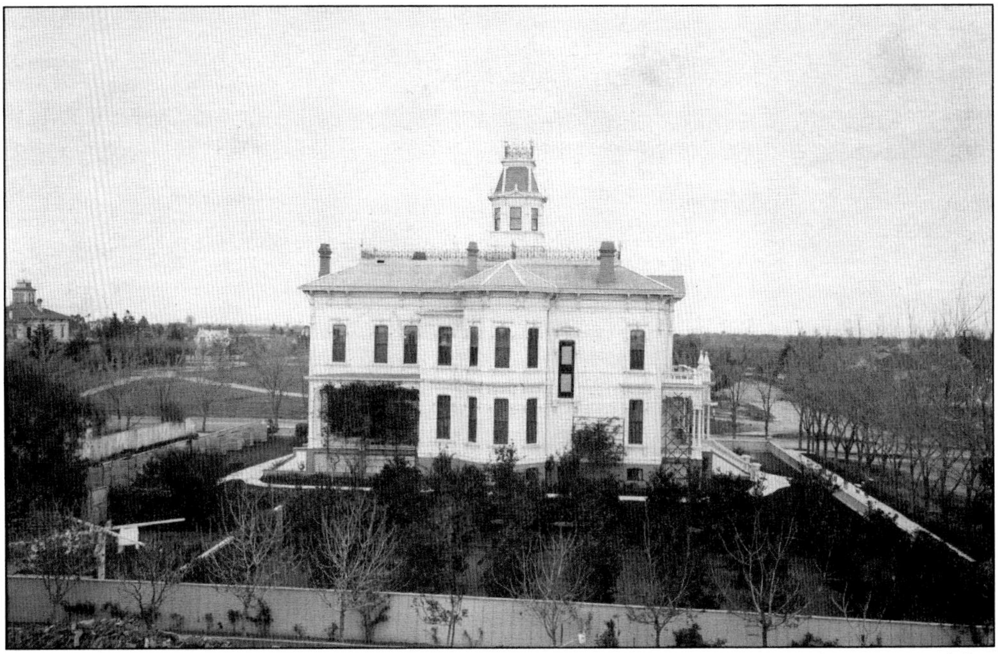

ELEGANT SIDE VIEW, LATE 1880S. This view of the mansion shows the parklike setting of this area of Modesto. The trees in the side yard are most likely citrus, while elms line Fifteenth Street. Legend has it that Robert McHenry bet a friend that his home could be constructed for less than $10,000. Robert won. Notice at the bottom left corner a clothes drying device is visible.

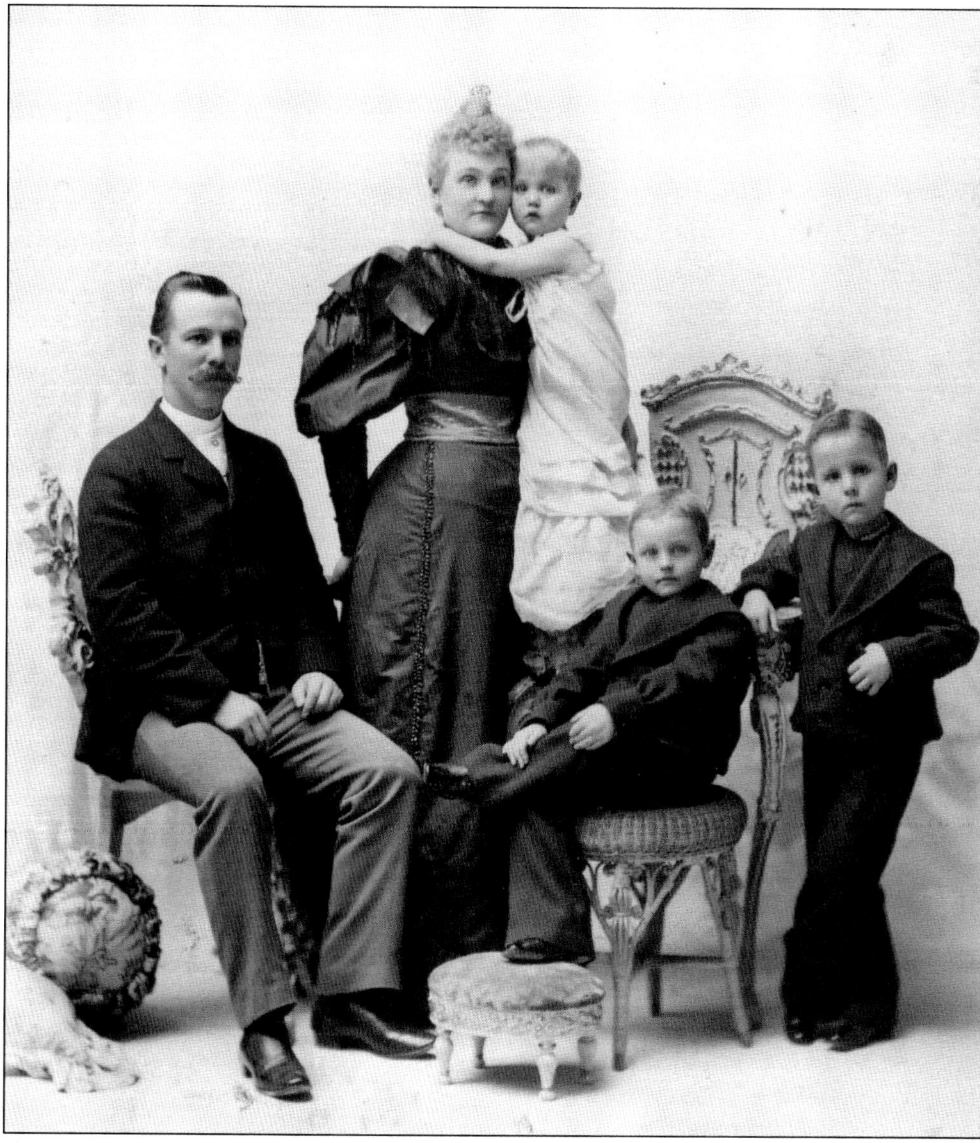

HAPPIER TIMES, C. 1894. This family portrait shows Oramil; wife Louise; daughter Ora Louise; and sons Albert and Robert. On March 29, 1901, a divorce announcement appeared in local newspapers. Louise was given a yearly allowance of $2,100 and $600 a year support for Ora Louise. Albert and Robert stayed with Oramil at the McHenry house. A few months later, Ora Louise died from burns caused by an alcohol lamp while staying at a hotel with her mother in Los Angeles.

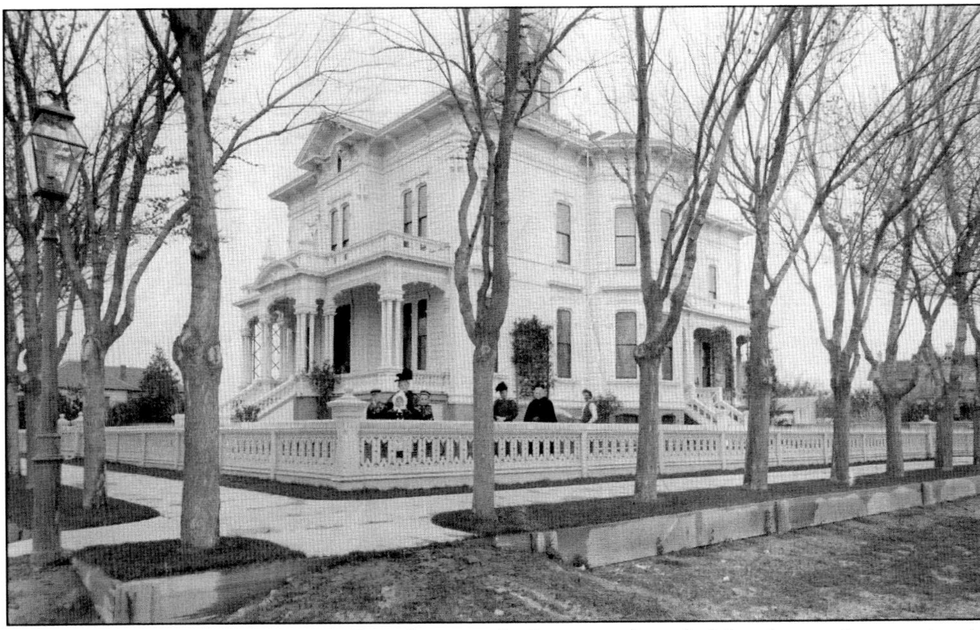

Mansion Gathering, c. 1895. This photograph shows unidentified family members posing in front of the mansion. There are three children, three women, and a gardener. The children may be Ora Louise, Albert, and Robert. The woman with the child is probably Louise, Oramil's first wife. The older ladies may be Matilda McHenry and Louise's mother, Caroline Bilicke. Matilda died in 1896, and Ora Louise died from burns in July 1901.

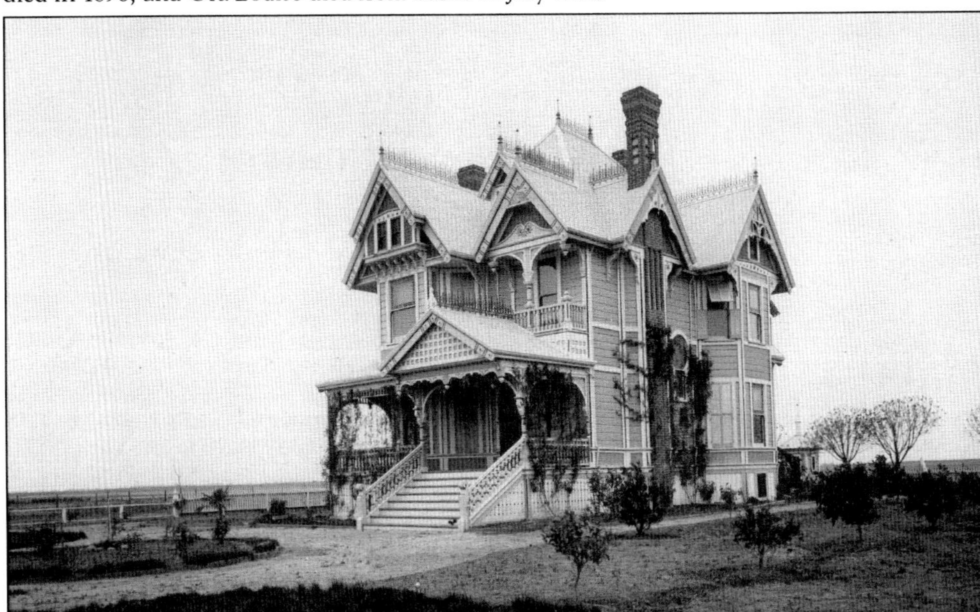

Bald Eagle Ranch House, c. 1891. A dirt road (now McHenry Avenue) led from town to the Bald Eagle Ranch. Ora's house was the beginning of an expansion at the ranch, which included a raisin dry-house and a two-story packinghouse. The latter was also used for parties. The Bald Eagle Ranch was innovative for its day, with crops "irrigated" by use of centrifugal pumps, pulling up water from 90 feet below ground.

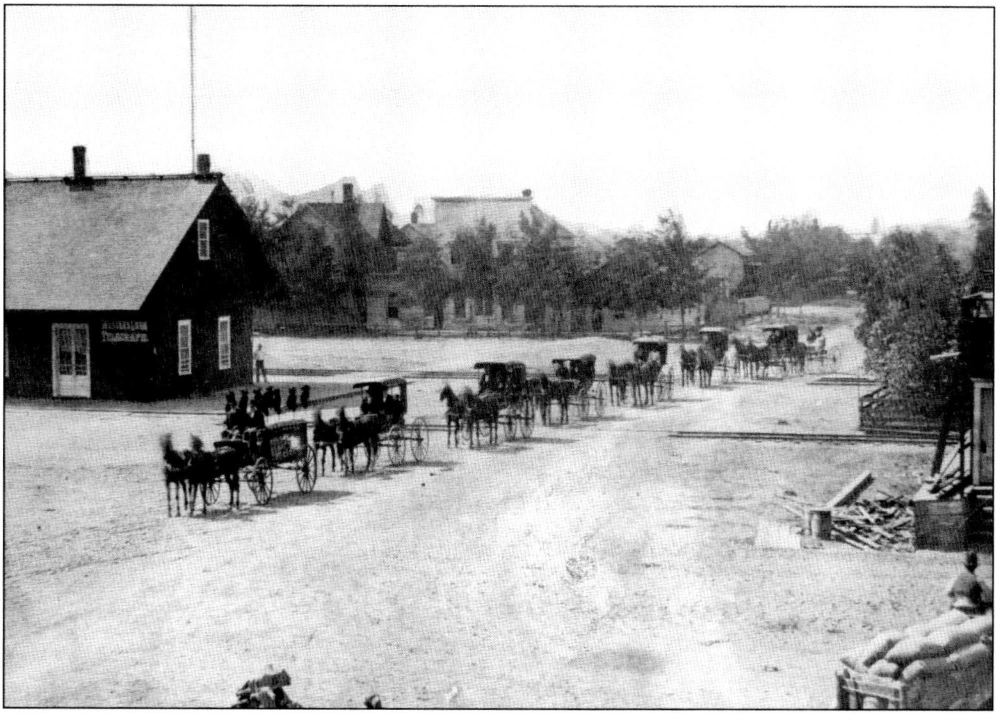

FUNERAL, c. 1881. This funeral cortege is heading east on I Street near Front Street (between Eighth and Ninth Streets). Frank Henry Fischer drives the hearse in what is believed to be the first funeral in Modesto with a hearse, in 1881. The undertakers listed on the photograph are Cleveland and Hardesty. (Faces of Stanislaus, Jerry Starr.)

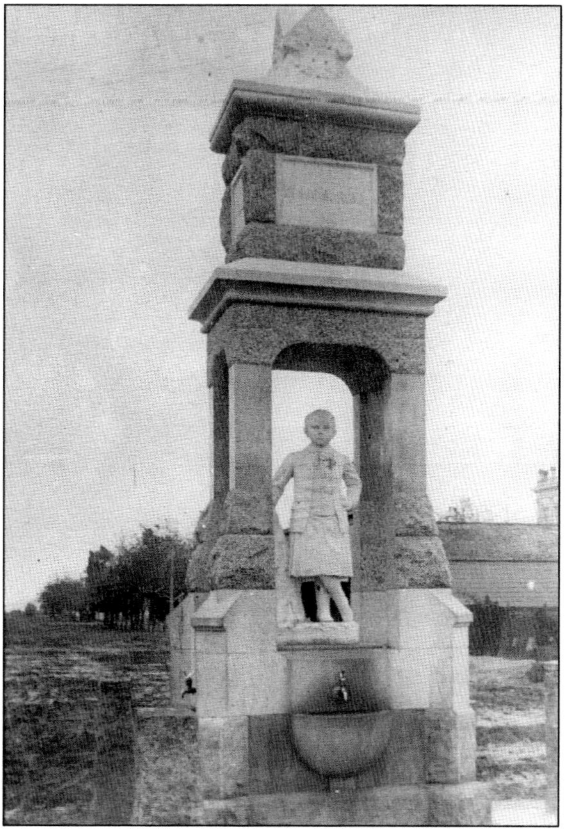

THE ROGERS DRINKING FOUNTAIN, c. 1893. Caroline Rogers DeYoe commissioned this $1500 memorial in memory of her husband, her son, and her grandson (Stephen R.), whose statue is on the fountain. Located originally at the intersection of Tenth and I Streets, it was eventually moved to Courthouse Park when city traffic increased in 1906. Later it was dismantled and placed in the city corporation yard where it remains, sans statue.

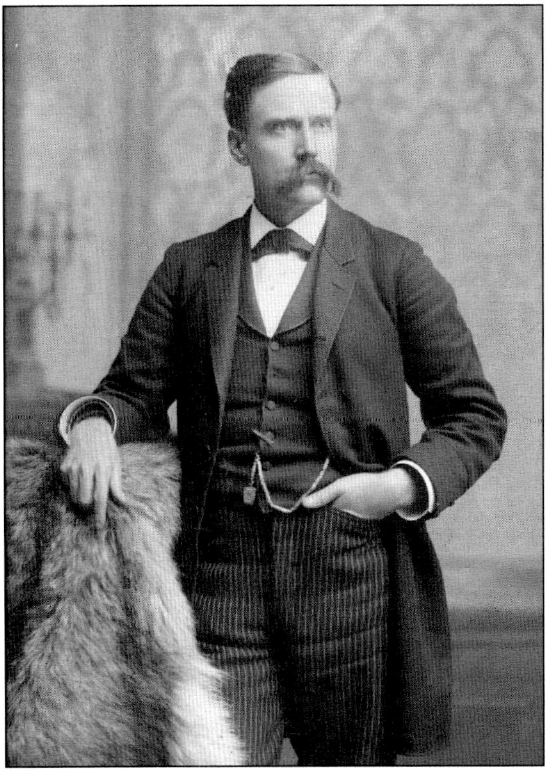

C. C. Wright, c. 1887. Known as "the father of irrigation," Modesto assemblyman C. C. Wright was given a first draft of the bill that allowed the formation of local irrigation districts owned, financed, and managed by the people. He rewrote the bill, which was passed by the state legislature as the Wright Irrigation Act and signed into law on March 7, 1887. The Modesto Irrigation and Turlock Irrigation Districts (MID and TID, respectively) were formed that year.

La Grange Dam, c. 1893. Construction began on the 28-foot, 6-inch overflow dam in 1891. Known as the "Niagara Falls of the West," it cost the MID and TID $550,000 to build. Even though the dam was completed in 1893, construction of the lateral canals had been stopped by lawsuits. It would be over 10 years before water would actually flow to the valley.

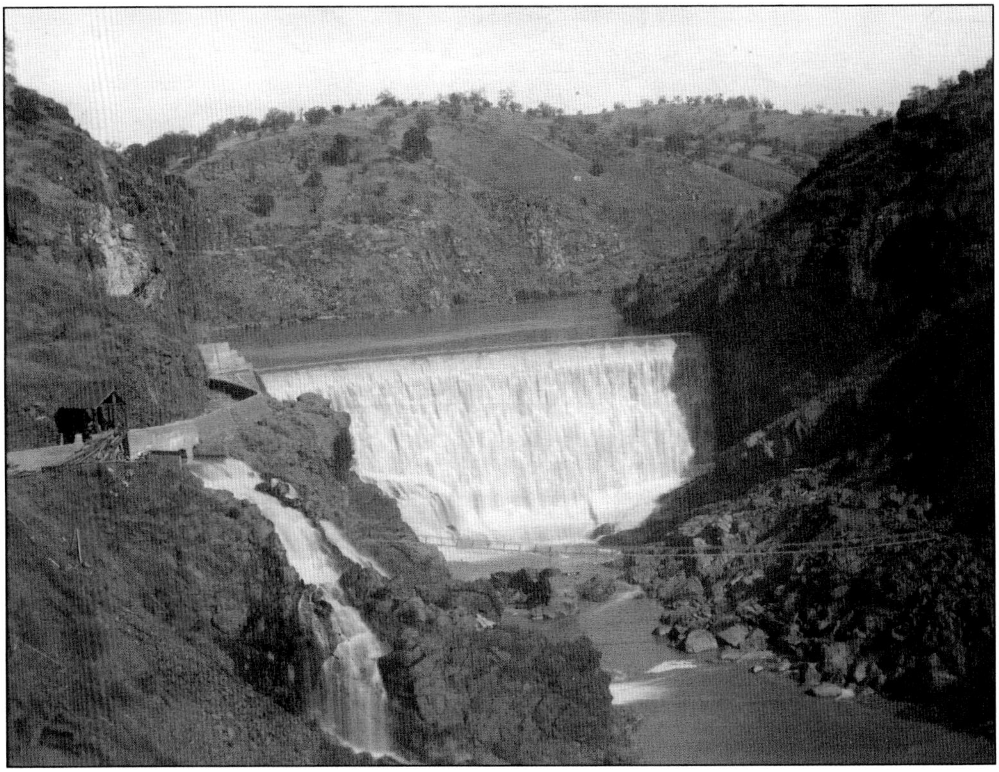

Two

COMING OF AGE IN A NEW CENTURY

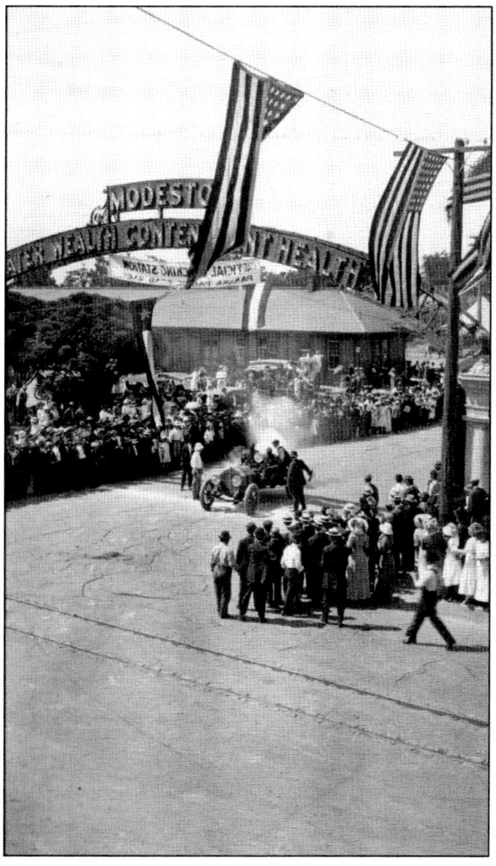

PANAMA PACIFIC ROAD RACE, C. 1913. The new century saw Modesto grow into a center of great activity for the county. Statewide events made their way to town. Coinciding with Modesto's Fourth of July celebration, participants in the 444-mile Panama-Pacific Road Race from Los Angeles to Sacramento "whizzed" through Modesto's official checking station with throngs of people watching. The race ended in the capital and was won by Frank Verbeck driving a Fiat for Barney Oldfield, also in the race, who said he reached speeds of 110 miles an hour. The crowd here is pictured under the year-old arch at I and Ninth Streets.

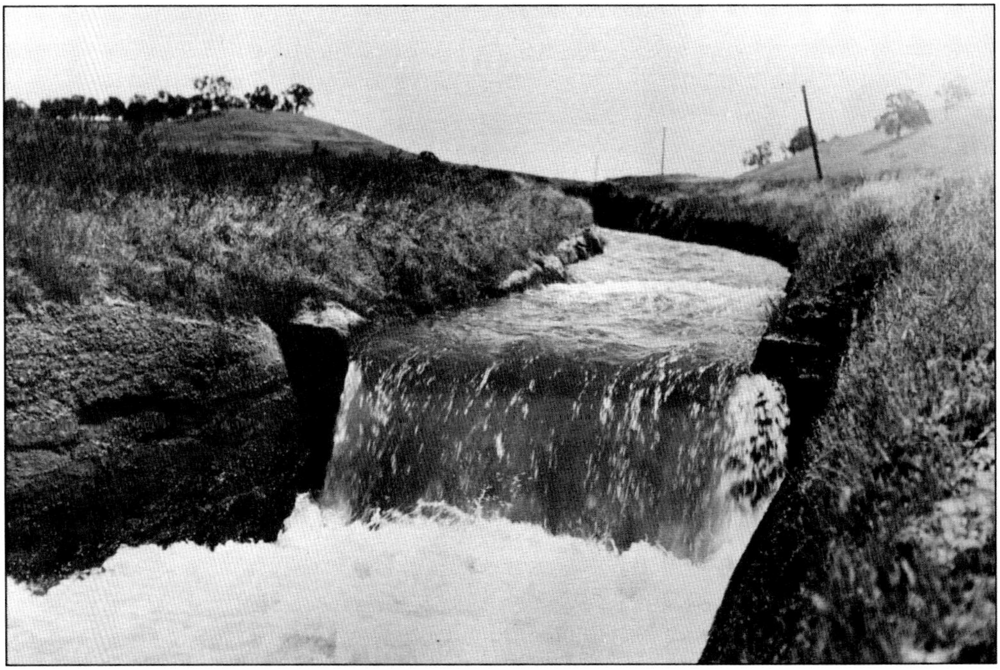

First Water, c. 1903. After a 20-year battle to irrigate the fields of Stanislaus County, water finally coursed through the canals in 1903. The photograph shows the beginnings of a great era of growth for the county and the city of Modesto. Both the Modesto and Turlock Irrigation Districts would provide water for the dry farmlands of the area and electricity to light streets, businesses, and homes.

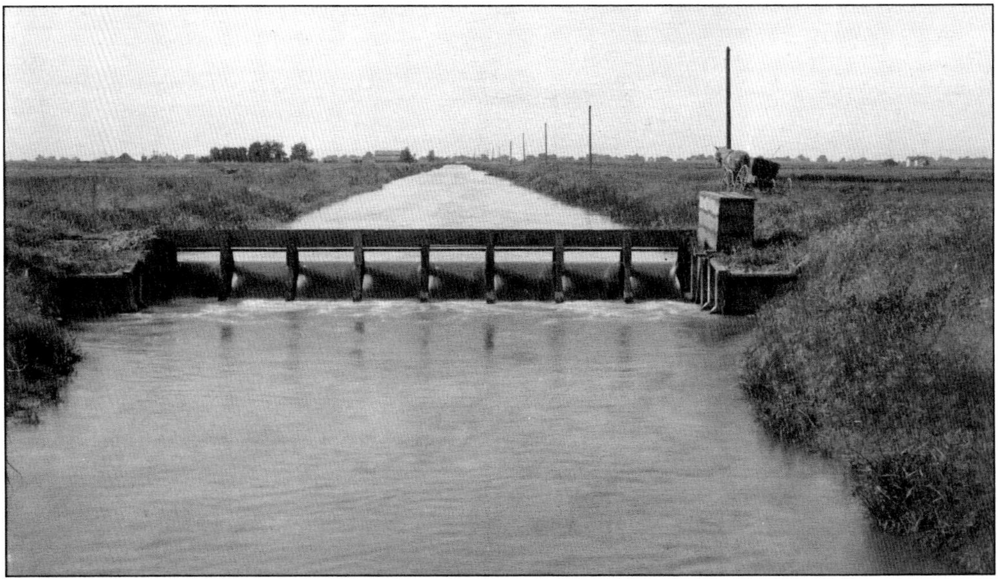

MID Main Ditch, c. 1903. The district's main canal is filled with water as far as the eye can see. The contractors and farmers who helped build the canals were "rendered valuable financial aid and assistance" by Ora McHenry, according to historian Sol P. Elias. April 21–22, 1904, Modesto held a "jubilee" to celebrate the completion of the irrigation system. Some 5,000 visitors joined Modesto's 2,500 citizens in celebration.

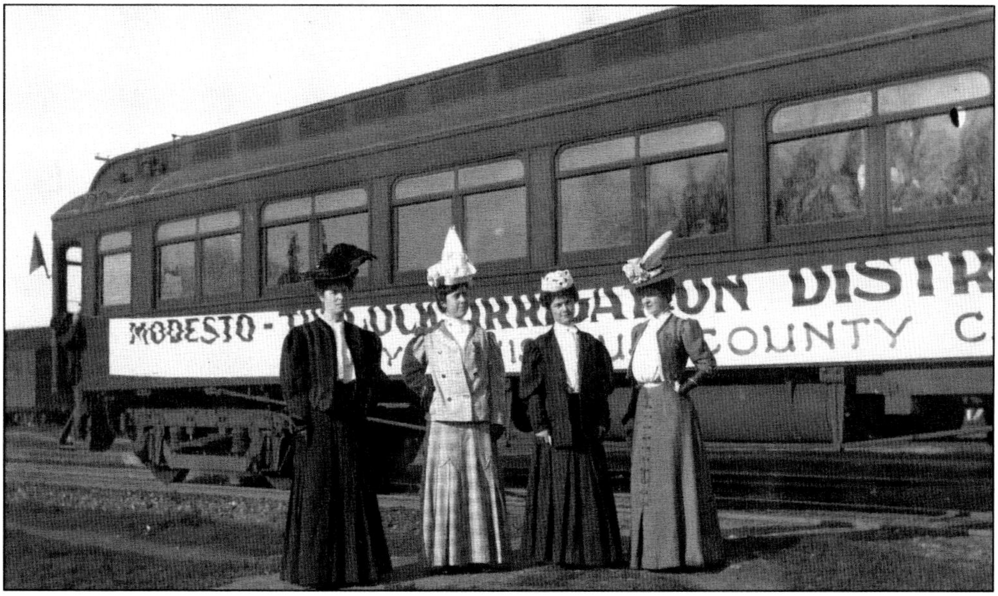

JUBILEE EXCURSION TRAIN, C. 1904. Four unidentified women are part of the many people who took a 30-car excursion train to explore the "twin districts, which are divided by the two main canals and their laterals into great rectangles of Eden-like fertility." The battle for irrigation was over and the result, according to the same visitor, "was an eloquent tribute to the accomplishments of money, faith, and dauntless labor."

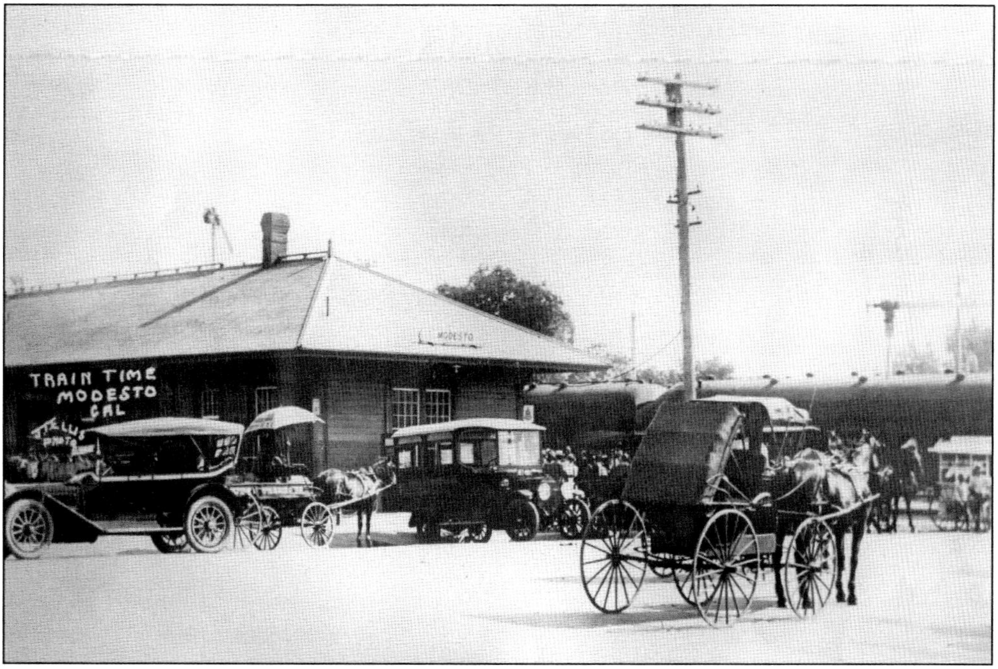

SP TRAIN STATION, 1900S. It is a varied group of vehicles that have driven out to greet the train at the original Southern Pacific Depot in this photograph. At the far right is the "peanut wagon," which used to be seen in various locations around Modesto for years. There is a hotel carriage picking up arriving guests and even an early taxi. Train time was an event every day in town.

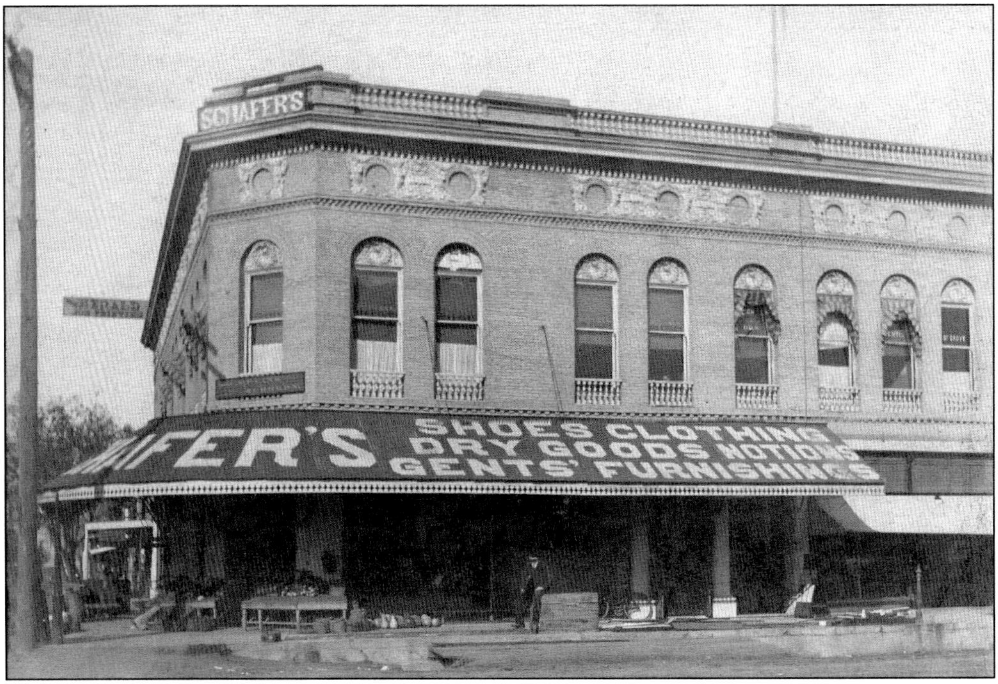

SCHAFER'S STORE, C. 1900. Originally built by Ora McHenry at the corner of Tenth and I Streets for I. E. Gilbert and Company's General Store in 1898, it became Schafer's in 1900. The store, owned by McHenry and managed by his brother-in-law, George Schafer, was the largest mercantile establishment in the Central Valley, according to historian Colleen Stanley Bare. It remained in business until 1927.

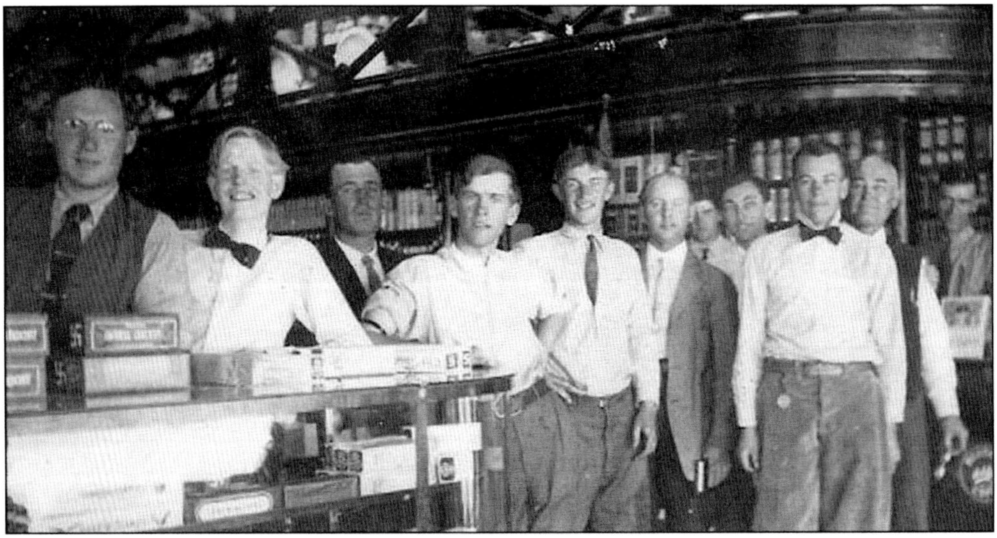

SCHAFER'S STAFF, C. 1911. A group of mostly young staff members poses for the camera inside Schafer's. Note the boxes in showcase with the swastika logo. It was not uncommon for this ancient symbol to be used in advertising prior to its association with Germany beginning in the 1930s. This photograph was taken by Clem Baker, who lived in Modesto for a number of years and left a legacy of photographs of the time period behind. The only person identified in this photograph is the second from the left; the smiling young man is Horace Steele. (Clem Baker Collection.)

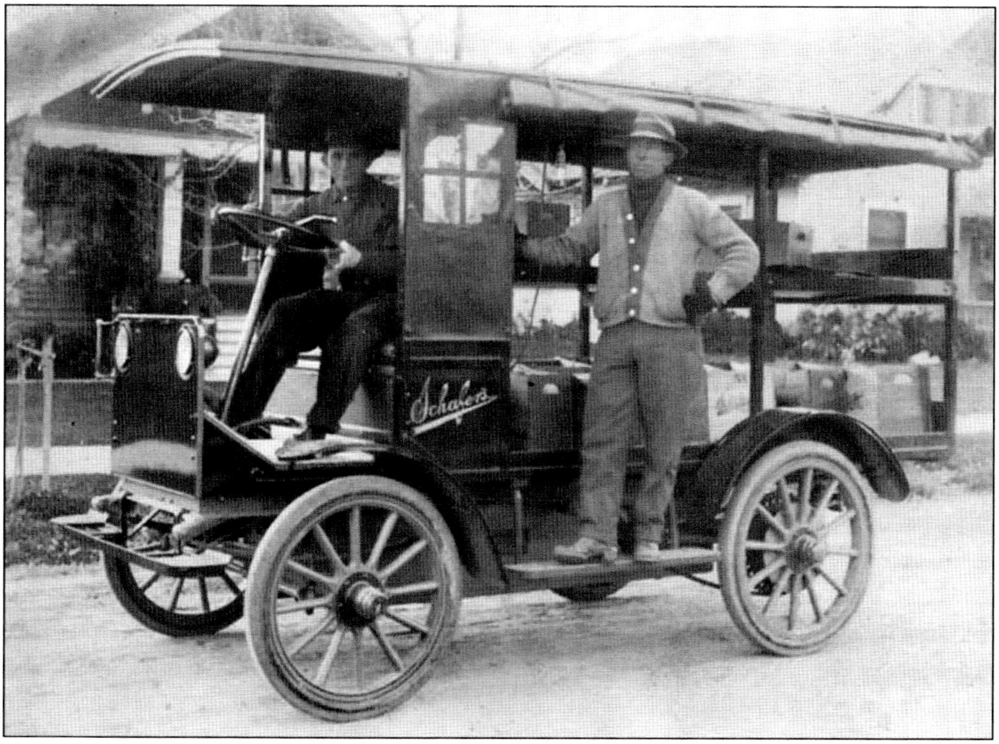

NEIGHBORHOOD DELIVERIES, c. 1911. Clem Baker sits behind the wheel of a Schafer's delivery truck in a Modesto neighborhood in the photograph above. The other person is unidentified. In the photograph below, delivery trucks loaded with numbered boxes are ready to set out for Modesto homes with requested items. Deciding what the numbers stood for on the boxes would be a guess, but since they are all in the same range, they could be street addresses, with both trucks headed for the same area of town. Schafer's carried a wide variety of items from groceries to dry goods to clothing and the first ready-to-wear women's clothing sold in Modesto. (Above, Clem Baker Collection; below, McHenry Museum.)

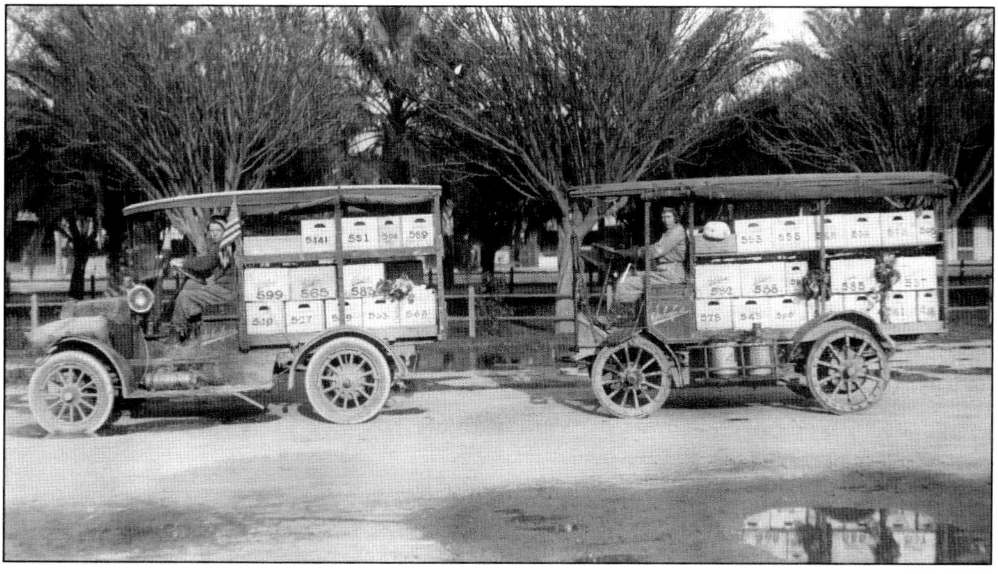

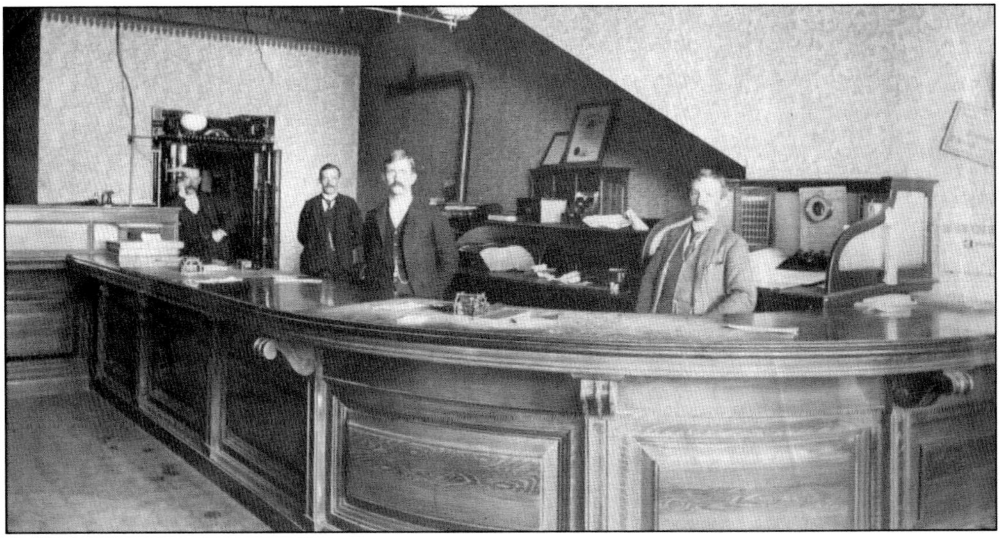

Modesto Bankers, c. 1904. Some of the town's most influential citizens are shown running the First National Bank of Modesto. Pictured from left to right are G. R. Stoddard, assistant cashier; G. P. Schafer, bookkeeper; J. E. Ward, cashier; and Ora McHenry, president. The four men had been elected to their positions in January at the bank's annual meeting. That same year, the bank moved to the northwest corner of Tenth and I Streets.

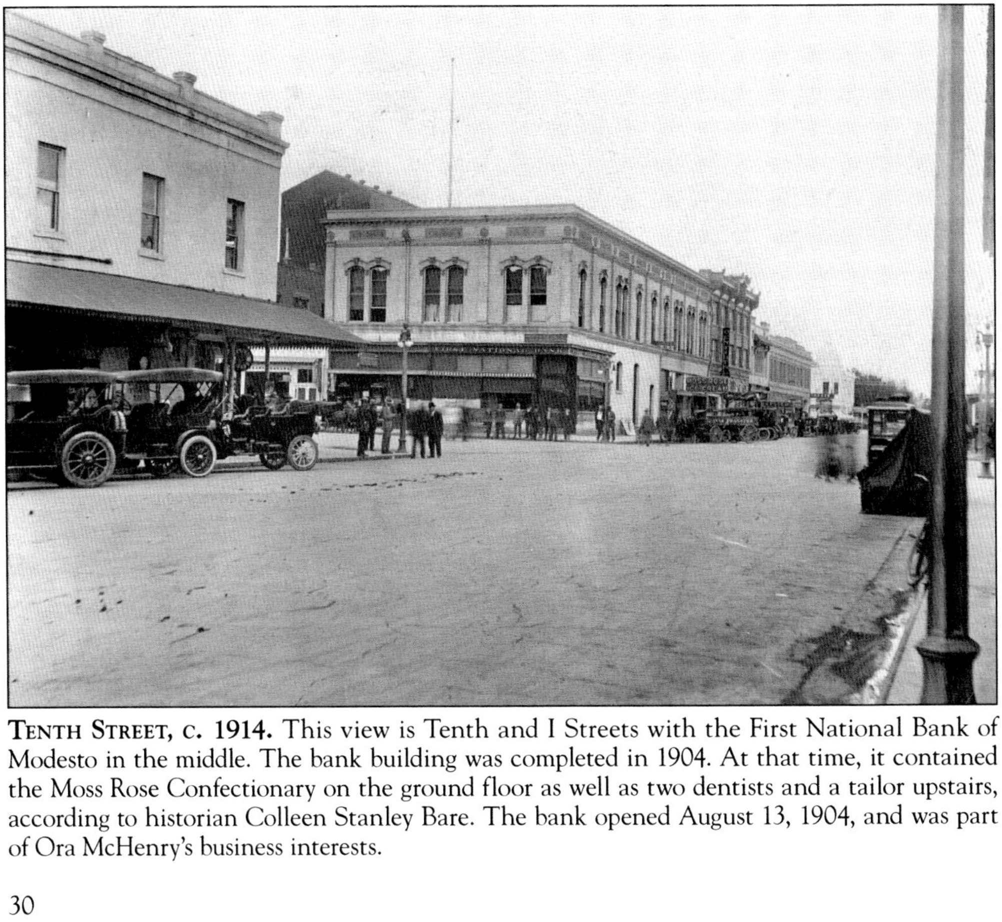

Tenth Street, c. 1914. This view is Tenth and I Streets with the First National Bank of Modesto in the middle. The bank building was completed in 1904. At that time, it contained the Moss Rose Confectionary on the ground floor as well as two dentists and a tailor upstairs, according to historian Colleen Stanley Bare. The bank opened August 13, 1904, and was part of Ora McHenry's business interests.

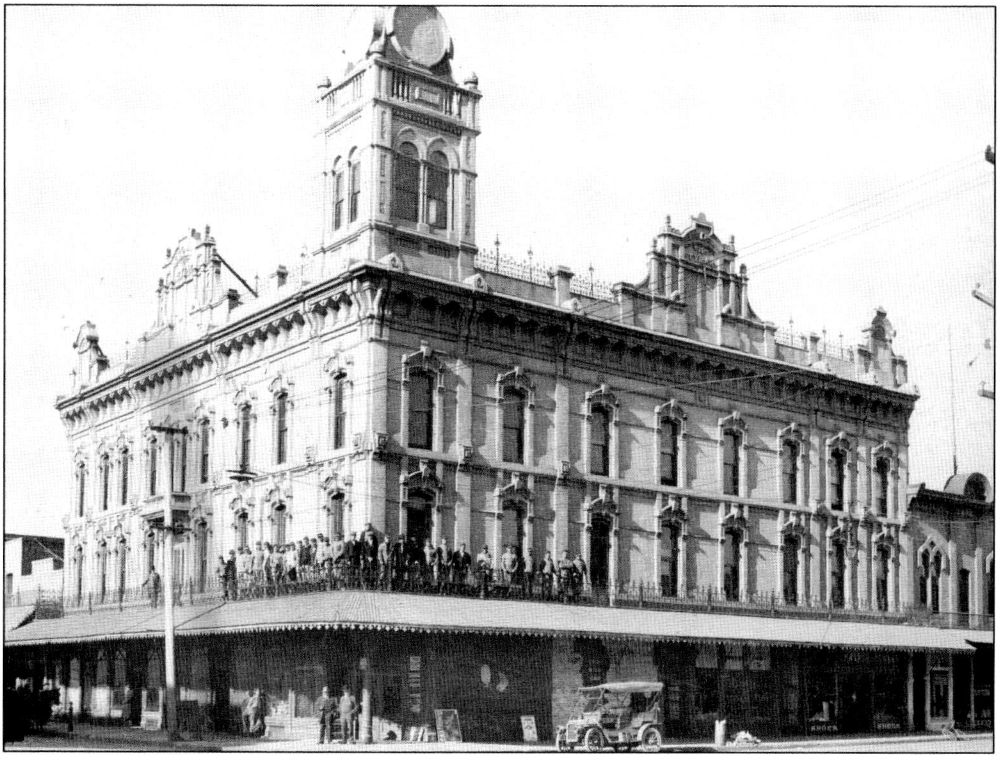

Tynan Hotel, c. 1911. In the above photograph, the San Francisco Seals baseball team is shown standing on the second-floor balcony of the Tynan Hotel, located at 923 H Street. The team was in Modesto to train for the 1911 Coast League Pennant. The hotel was built in 1890 by Thomas Tynan and was said to rival the best hotels in San Francisco. Rooms featured fireplaces, electric lights, elevator service, and speaking tubes from rooms to the main desk. The only thing it lacked was a clock in the clock tower. The photograph below shows the main desk at the hotel, with unidentified employees behind the cash register. On the counter, in the center, is a register for visitors staying the night, and a mailbox is at left. (Above, McHenry Museum; below, Clem Baker Collection.)

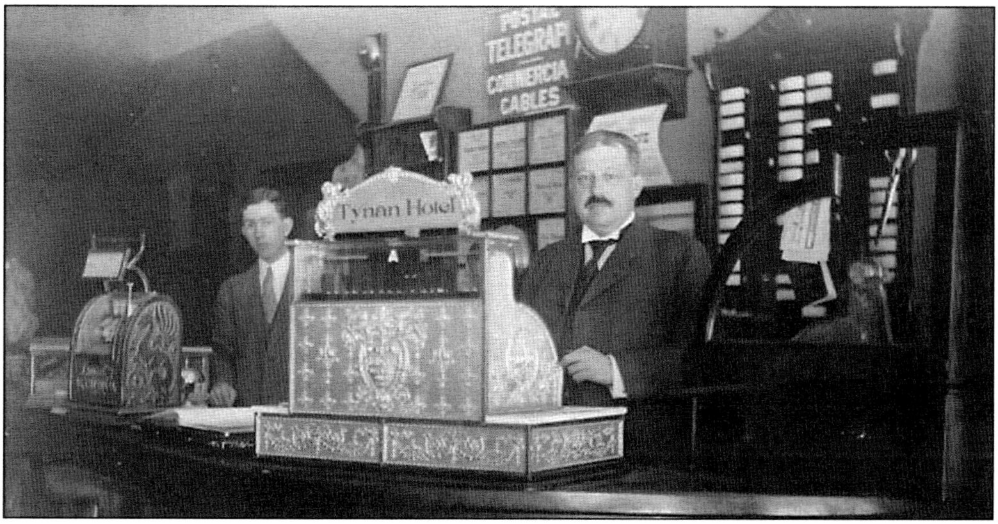

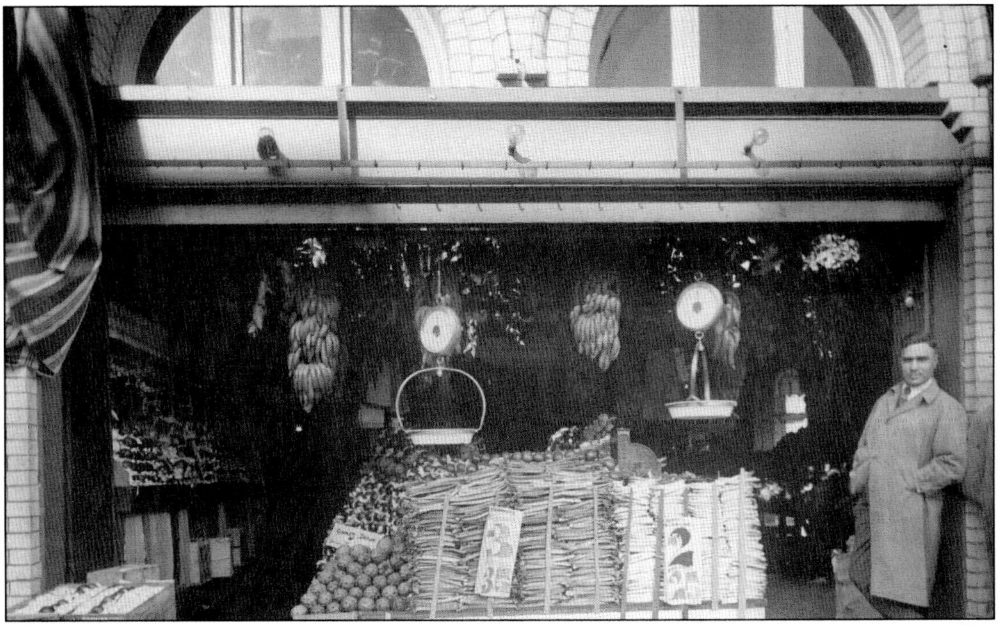

SF Fruit Market, After 1914. Michael Angelo stands before the San Francisco Fruit Market at 802 Tenth Street at the corner of H Street. The market is opening for the day's business. A wide variety of fruits and vegetables are on display. This market later moved to 801 Ninth Street and was named B & T Market. Renamed Angelo's Market in 1955, it remained in business until 1991 in various locations. (Faces of Stanislaus, Irene Angelo.)

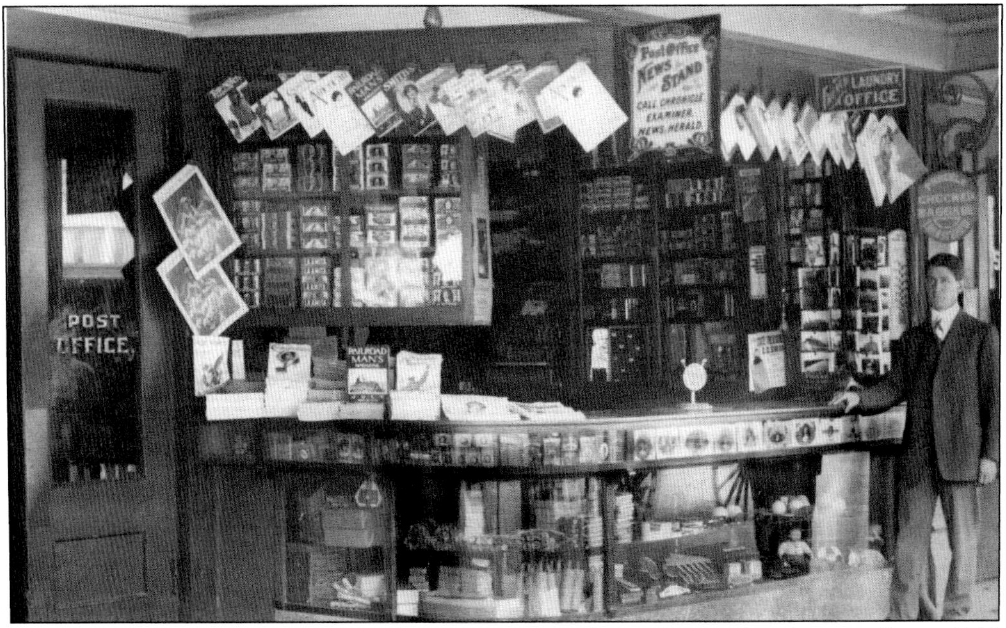

Post Office Newsstand, c. 1914. This newsstand was located in Modesto's post office at 110 I Street. A quick look at the variety of magazines, newspapers, goods, and sundries shows that the newsstand was well stocked for anyone venturing inside the post office. The local *Modesto News Herald* shares space with the *San Francisco Call*, *Chronicle*, and *Examiner*, plus a wide variety of cigars and magazines.

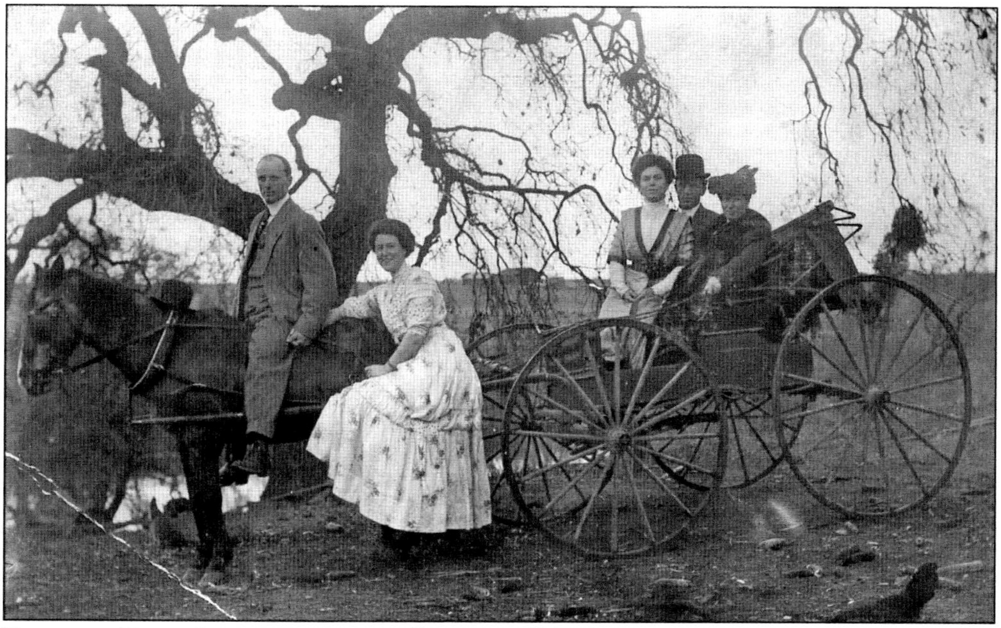

Tuolumne River Outing, c. 1911. Wallace Caswell (on horse), Jennie Whitmore Caswell, Helen Cross Caswell, Henry Caswell, and Minnie Caswell Colt are on holiday along the Tuolumne River south of Modesto. Jennie was the daughter of Daniel Whitmore, who founded Ceres, a neighboring community. Wallace and Henry were ranchers. Helen was a music teacher who rode the train from Ceres to Turlock to give music lessons. (Faces of Stanislaus, Mary Caswell Bucknam.)

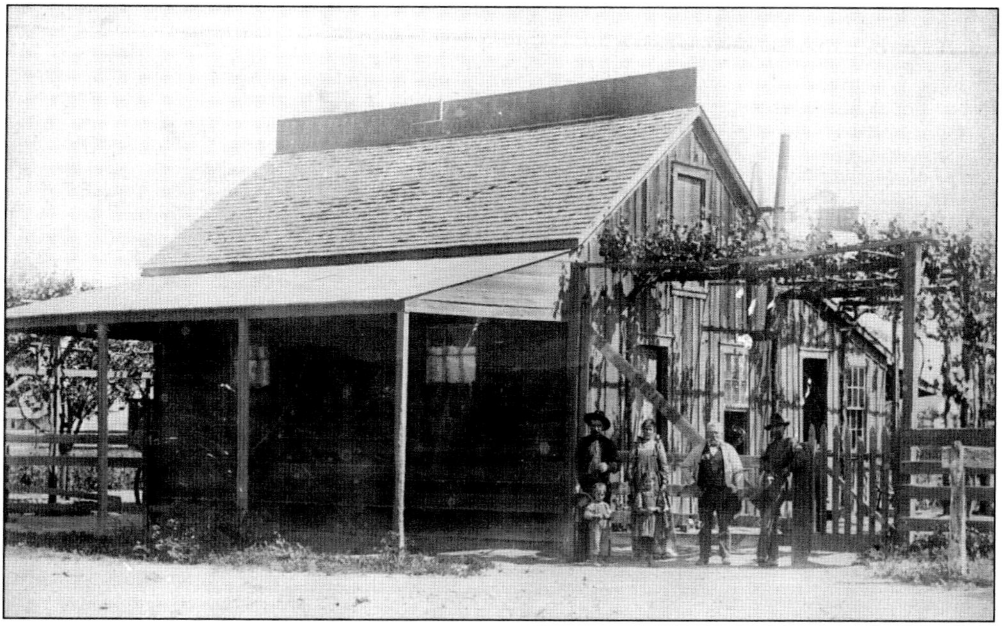

Foret French Gardens, c. 1901. The sign above the house says, "P. Foret French Gardens: Fruit, Wine, Vinegar, Vegetables." Philibert Foret came to California in 1850 in search of gold, eventually settling in Modesto in 1901. Shown are, from left to right, (first row) Charles Foret and Madeline Foret; (second row) Bernard Duplan, Rose Foret, unidentified, and Francois Foret. This photograph was taken at 416 Ninth Street. (Faces of Stanislaus, Jacqueline Foret.)

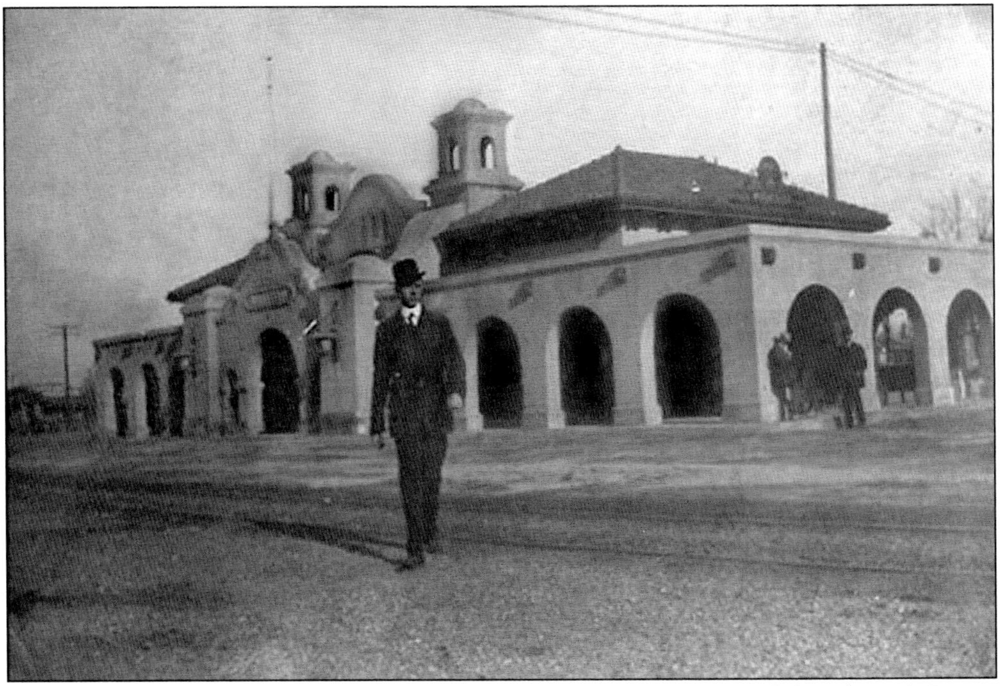

Southern Pacific Depot, c. 1915. The new station was built between Eighth and Ninth Streets and blocked J Street. It took a straw vote to approve blocking the street. Designed in a Spanish mission style, the building is now the hub of Modesto's transportation center, although no passenger trains stop at the station anymore. Pictured in front of the depot in this 1915 photograph is Clem Baker. (Clem Baker Collection.)

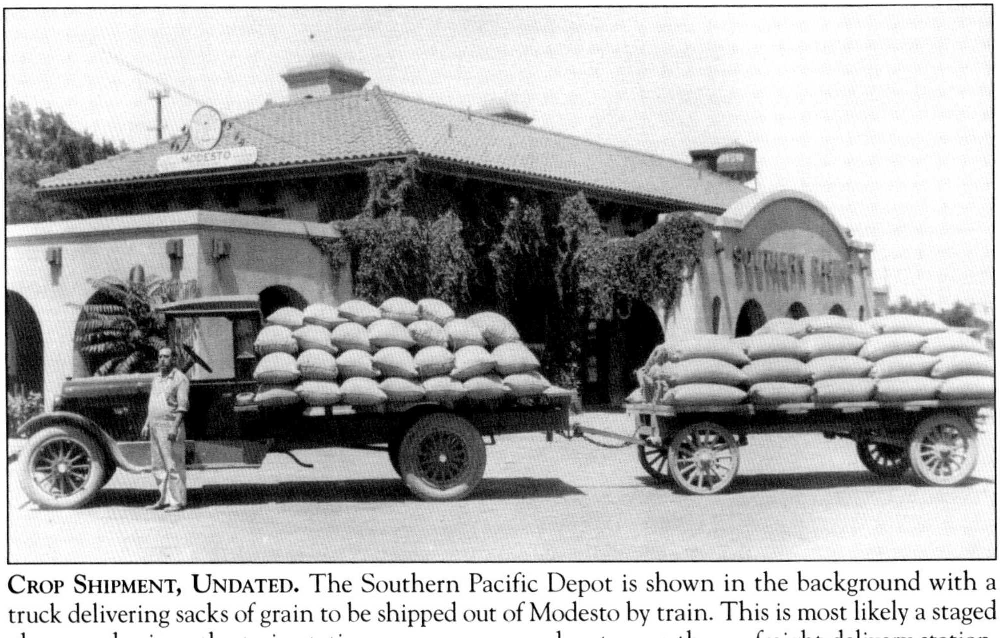

Crop Shipment, Undated. The Southern Pacific Depot is shown in the background with a truck delivering sacks of grain to be shipped out of Modesto by train. This is most likely a staged photograph, since the train station was a passenger depot more than a freight delivery station. The older SP depot built prior to this one was used primarily for freight.

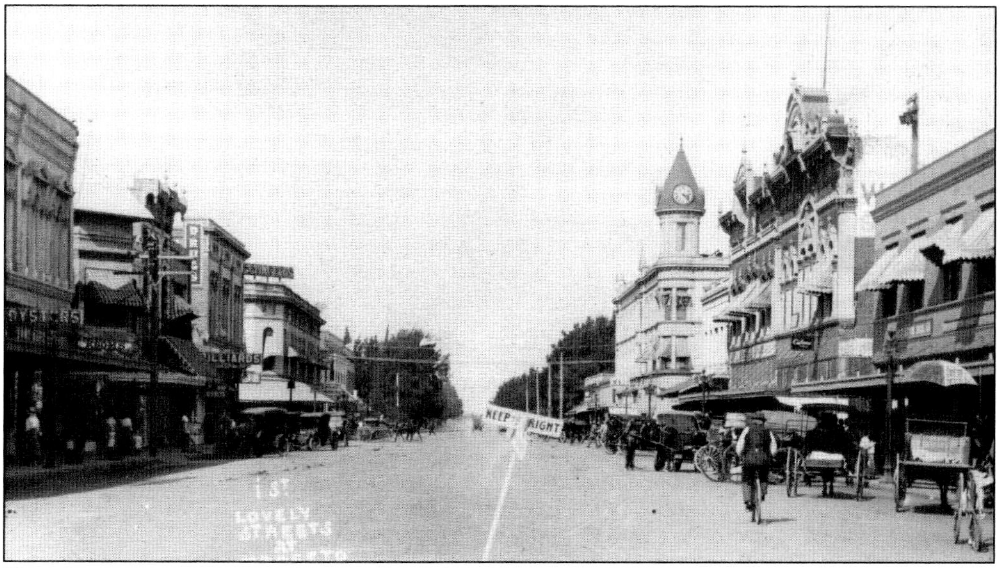

KEEP RIGHT, AFTER 1906. The sign says it all—whether driving a newfangled automobile, riding a bicycle, or using a horse and buggy, traffic had to "keep right." This is I Street facing east, with the Wood and Turner building on the right plus the Modesto Bank with clock tower. Schafer's is on the corner of Tenth and I Streets at left. Rogers Fountain is already gone from the intersection.

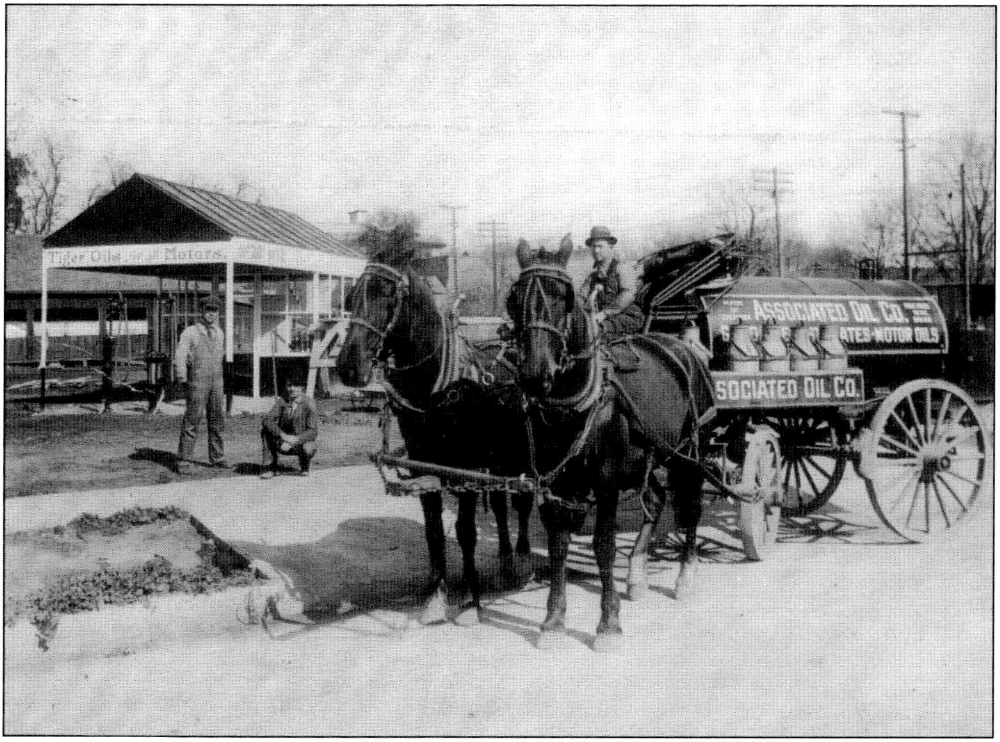

DELIVERING OIL PRODUCTS, C. 1918. Driver Emmett L. Haskell poses in this early advertising photograph for the Associated Oil Company in Modesto. While the automobile and first delivery trucks and vans were changing the way products made their way to the marketplace, even as late as 1918, the horse-drawn wagon was still in use. (Faces of Stanislaus, Beverly J. Hammon.)

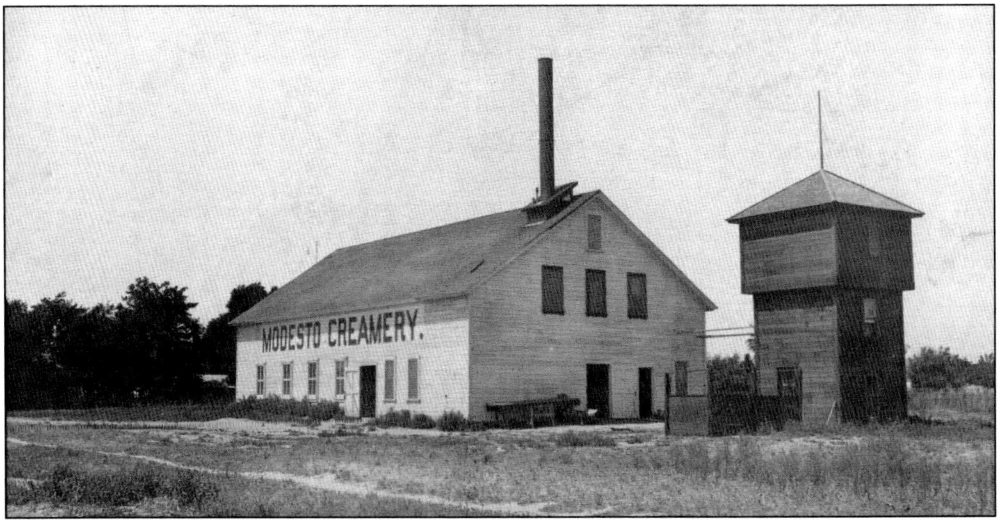

MODESTO CREAMERY, C. 1901. The creamery was built to encourage dairying in Stanislaus County. The creamery, a "gathered" cream factory, produced Modesto Butter and also manufactured ice. This building burned in 1912. The site on Ninth Street was purchased in 1918 by the Milk Producers Association of Central California, which became the largest dairy cooperative in the United States.

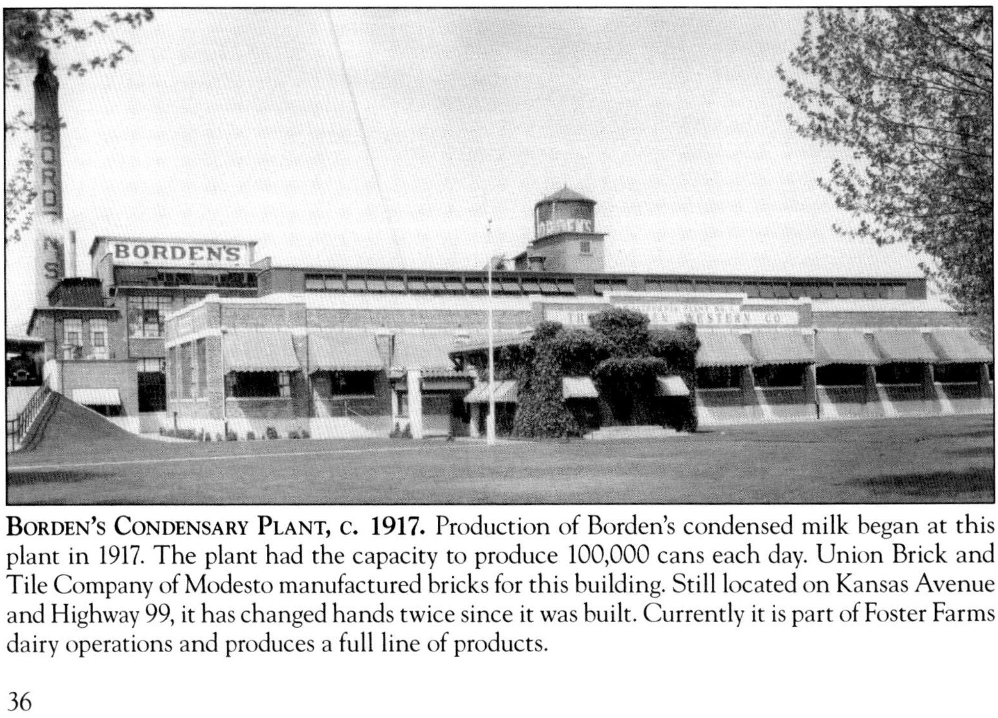

BORDEN'S CONDENSARY PLANT, C. 1917. Production of Borden's condensed milk began at this plant in 1917. The plant had the capacity to produce 100,000 cans each day. Union Brick and Tile Company of Modesto manufactured bricks for this building. Still located on Kansas Avenue and Highway 99, it has changed hands twice since it was built. Currently it is part of Foster Farms dairy operations and produces a full line of products.

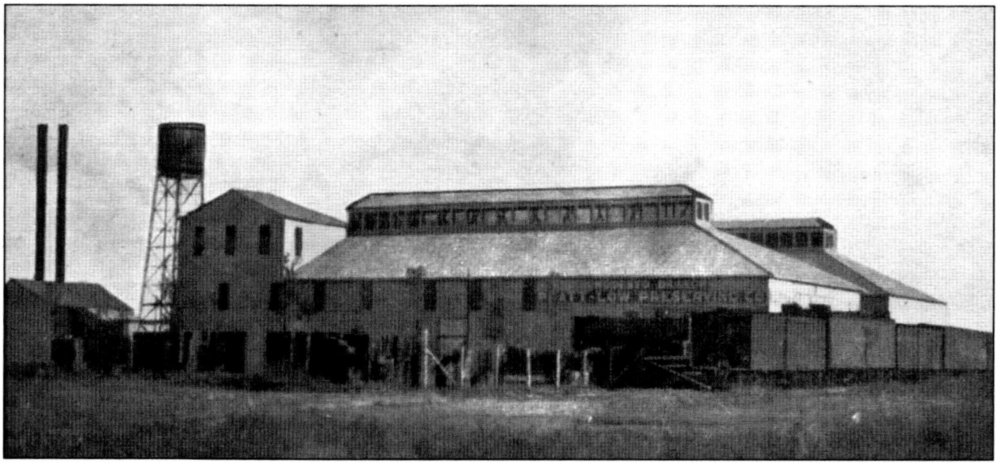

Pratt-Low Cannery, c. 1919. This cannery began as the Modesto Canning Company in 1908, located at Ninth Street near C Street. It employed up to 175 people during peak canning season. In 1919, it was sold to Pratt-Low and eventually became Flotill, which was owned by Tillie Lewis, a successful Stockton businesswoman. In later years, the cannery was known as Tillie Lewis Foods. (Author's collection.)

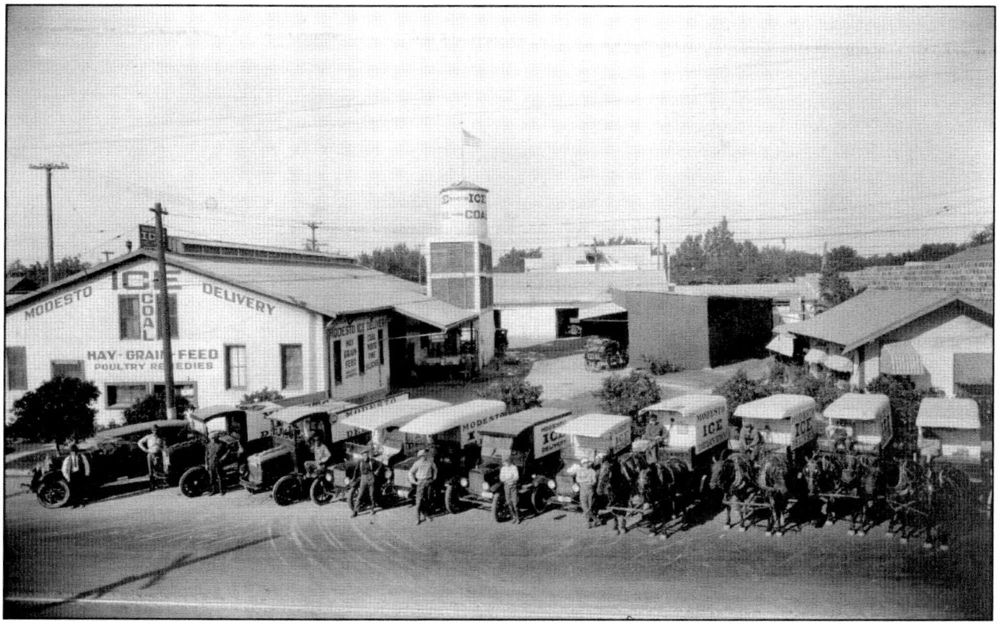

Modesto Ice Company, Undated. Delivery vehicles line the street in front of the Modesto Ice Company. The various modes of transportation include horse-drawn delivery trucks and powered vehicles—anything to get ice to the consumer on time. Also available were hay, grain, feed, coal, wood, and "poultry remedies!" Modesto Ice Company began business in 1893, organized by Admer Brown.

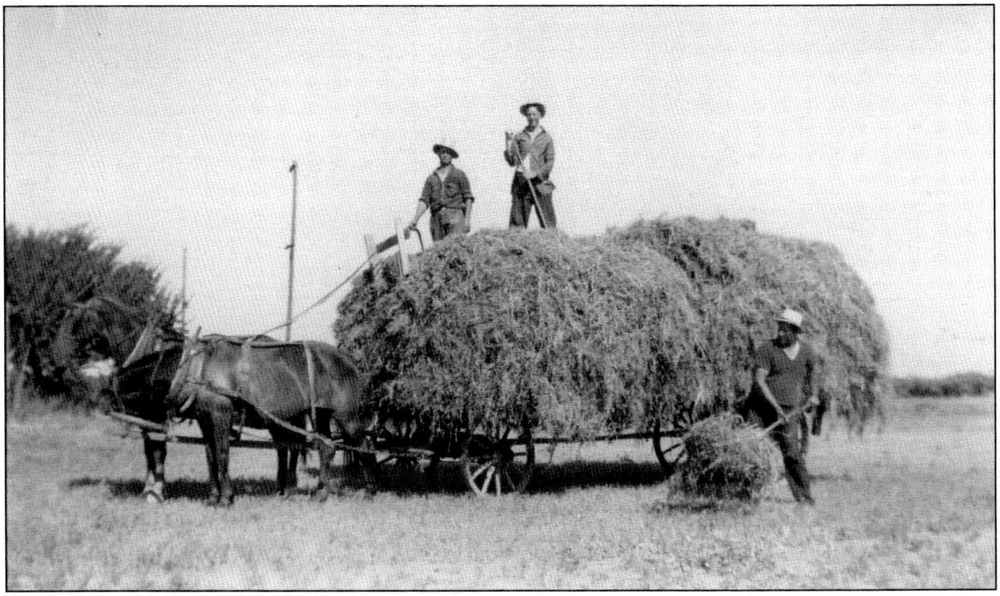

Hay and Apricots, Undated. These later photographs show the importance of agriculture to Modesto. Above, men are shown putting up hay on what is now Rose Avenue. The hay was cut, piled on a wagon, and taken to a barn for drying and storage or to feed the cattle. The photograph below shows W. F. "Bill" Orr with his three-year-old daughter, Eloise, riding on a sled load of apricots being taken to a cutting shed. While both of these photographs were taken around the late 1920s, both an increase in quantity and range of crops occurred as a direct result of irrigation. (Both, Faces of Stanislaus; above, Francis Landini; below, David Orth.)

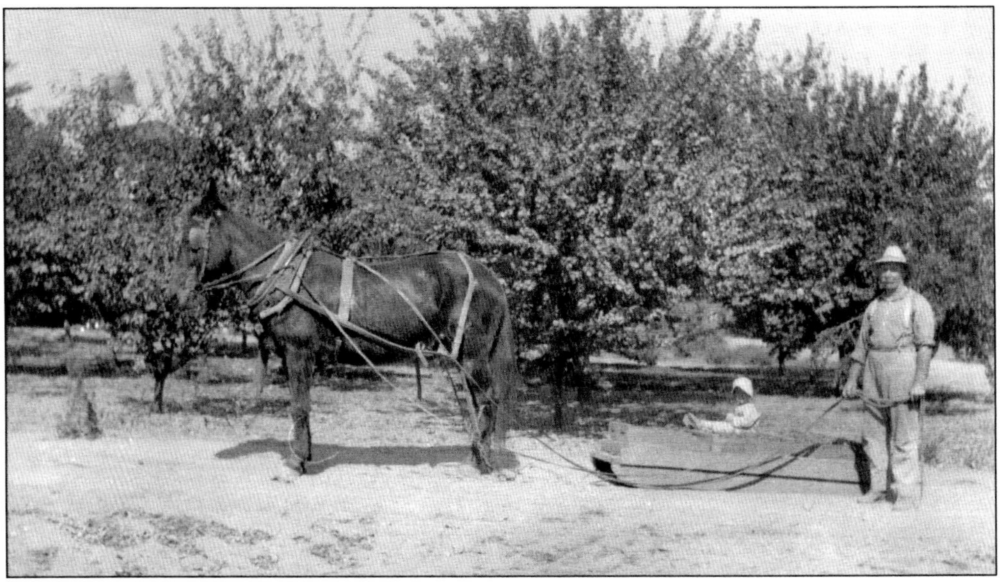

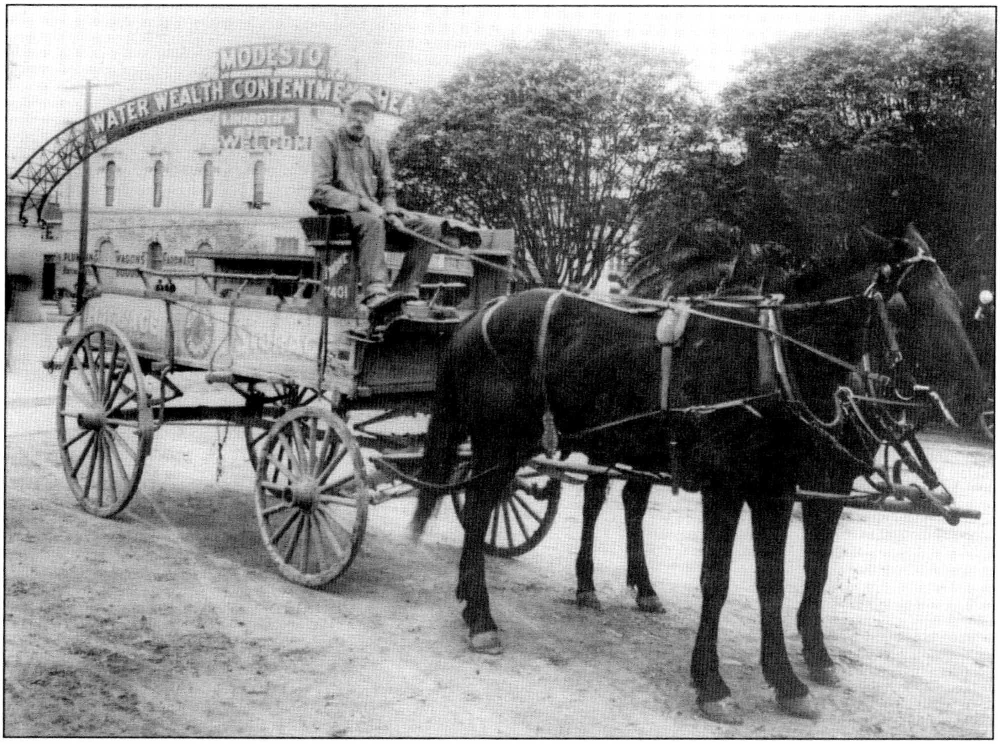

WESTSIDE TRANSFER, C. 1913. Robert Leonard Bright is pictured in 1913 with his wagon, drawn by Babe and Ouanita, stopped near the newly completed Modesto Arch, which still bears its "Welcome" sign. Bright ran the transfer service from 1913 to 1928. He was born in San Andreas in 1858; homesteaded near La Grange; married Marietta Elvira Ducot in 1880; and fathered eight children, five boys and three girls.

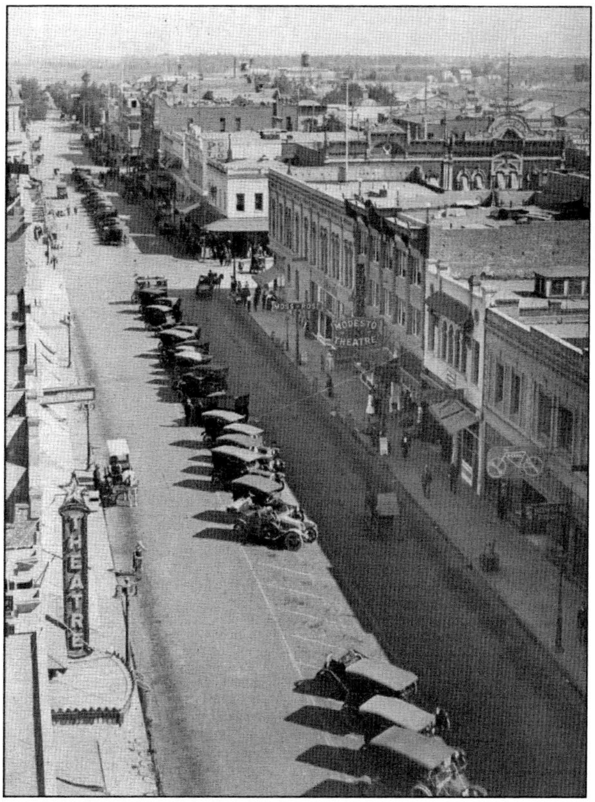

ABOVE TENTH STREET, C. 1914. The roadway is paved and automobiles are in the majority in this photograph of Tenth Street facing south. There are still a couple of horse-drawn vehicles, but their days are numbered. Mid-block on the right is the Modesto Theatre with Moss Rose Confectionary next door. The Star Theatre is in the left foreground. This photograph may have been taken from the recently completed Hotel Hughson.

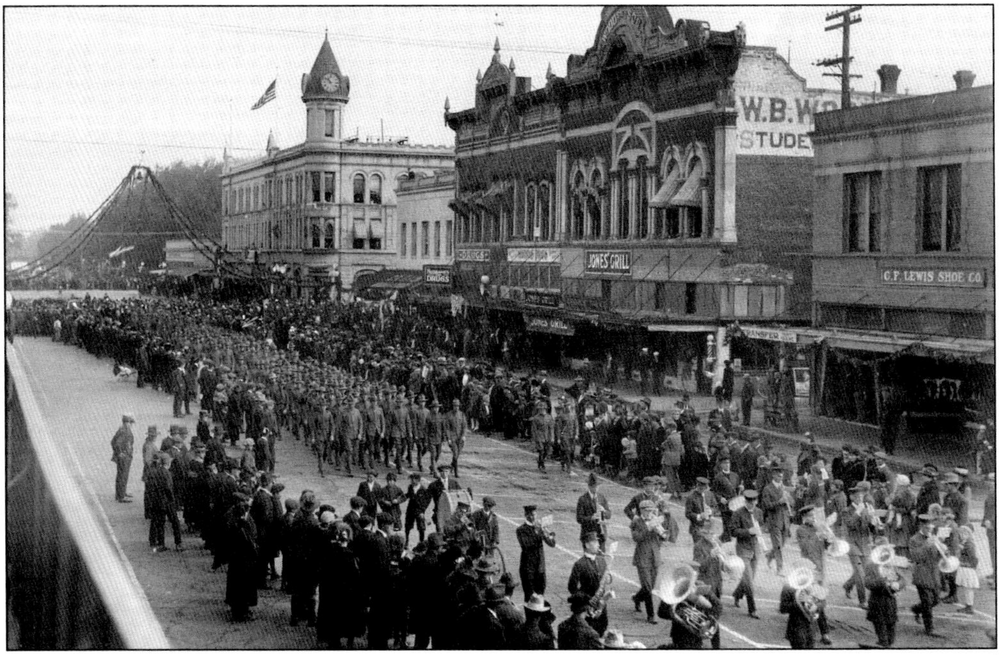

ARMISTICE DAY PARADE, 1920. November 11, 1920, was a historic day marking both the second anniversary of the end of World War I and the 50th anniversary of the founding of Modesto. Over 30,000 people attended (Modesto's population was 9,241). Eight of the 60 parade floats depicted the history of the city from 1870 to 1920; some 2,000 marchers took part. The Modesto Municipal Aviation Field was dedicated, and war ace Eddie Rickenbacher flew in to help celebrate. The *Evening News* called it "the greatest gathering of airplanes ever held in California." Historian Colleen Stanley Bare says that Casey Stengel's National League All-Stars played the Modesto Reds baseball team, with the first ball dropped from an airplane! There were vaudeville shows, band concerts, fireworks, street dancing, and a masquerade ball. Modesto had come a long way in its first 50 years.

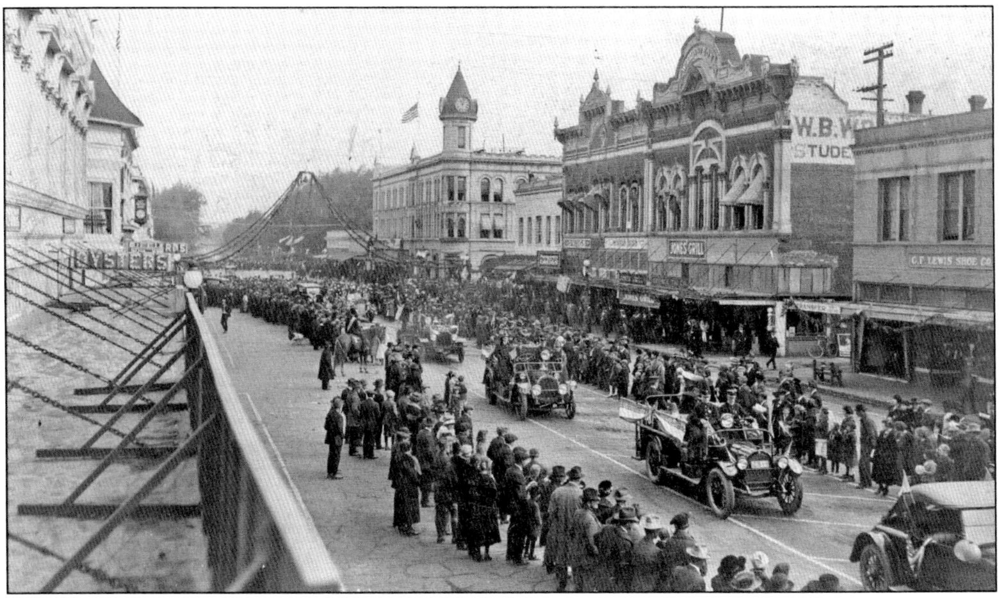

Three

The Streets of Modesto

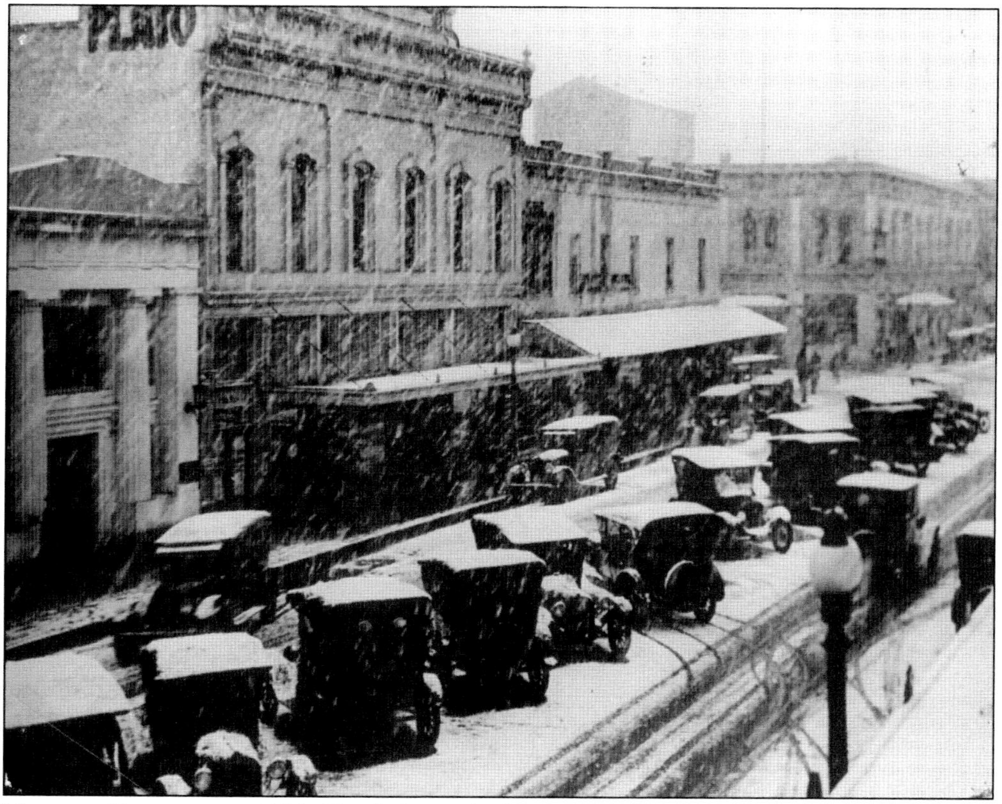

Modesto Blizzard, c. 1922. Tenth Street looks as if it belongs in the Midwest. The snow is falling and cars are covered in white. This view is between H and I Streets, with cars parked diagonally along the street. Plato's Opera House dominates the photograph toward the center left. Snow occasionally falls in the Central Valley of California but does not often end up "sticking." This may have been March 1922.

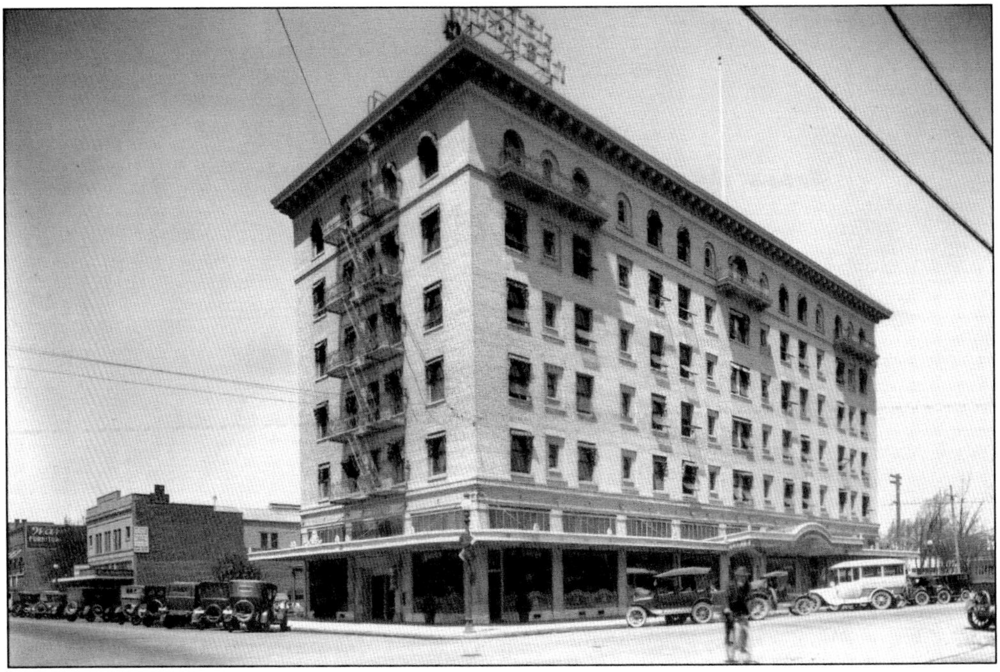

HOTEL HUGHSON, 1914. This was the year of hotel expansion in Modesto. The Hughson opened to great fanfare on March 6 and featured a "blue-tiled swimming pool" in the basement. Located at the corner of J and Tenth Streets, it had 98 rooms, a restaurant, and a ballroom. Bernard J. Joseph, the architect who designed the Modesto Arch, also designed the Hotel Hughson. The hotel was owned by Louella Hughson.

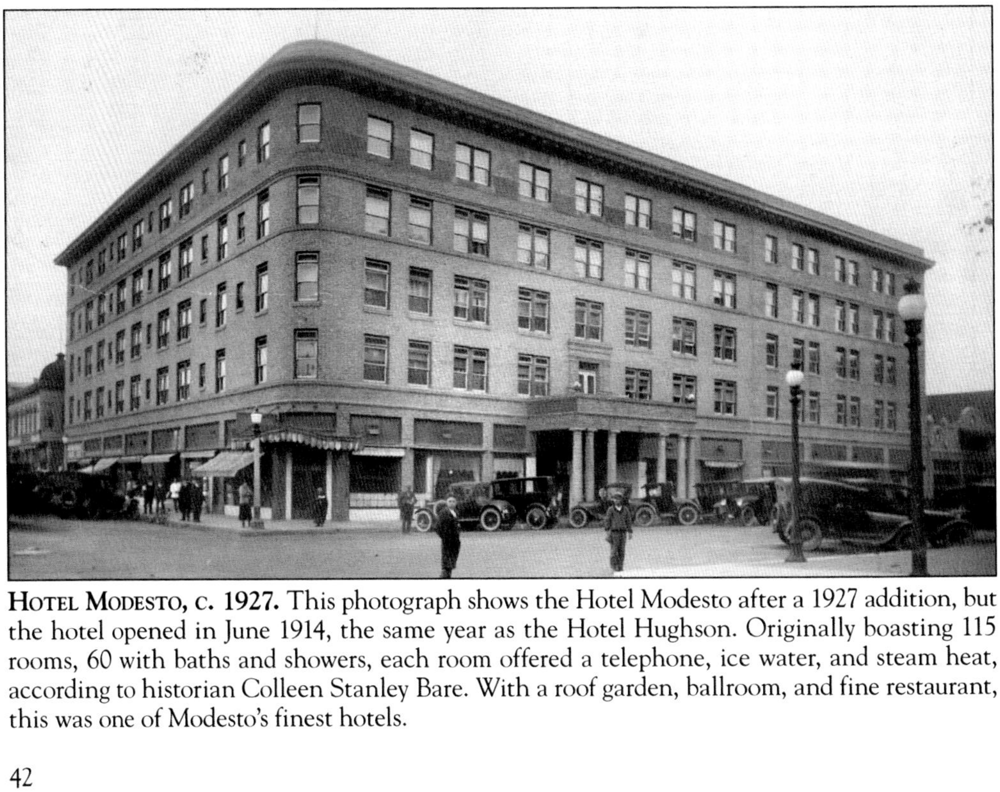

HOTEL MODESTO, C. 1927. This photograph shows the Hotel Modesto after a 1927 addition, but the hotel opened in June 1914, the same year as the Hotel Hughson. Originally boasting 115 rooms, 60 with baths and showers, each room offered a telephone, ice water, and steam heat, according to historian Colleen Stanley Bare. With a roof garden, ballroom, and fine restaurant, this was one of Modesto's finest hotels.

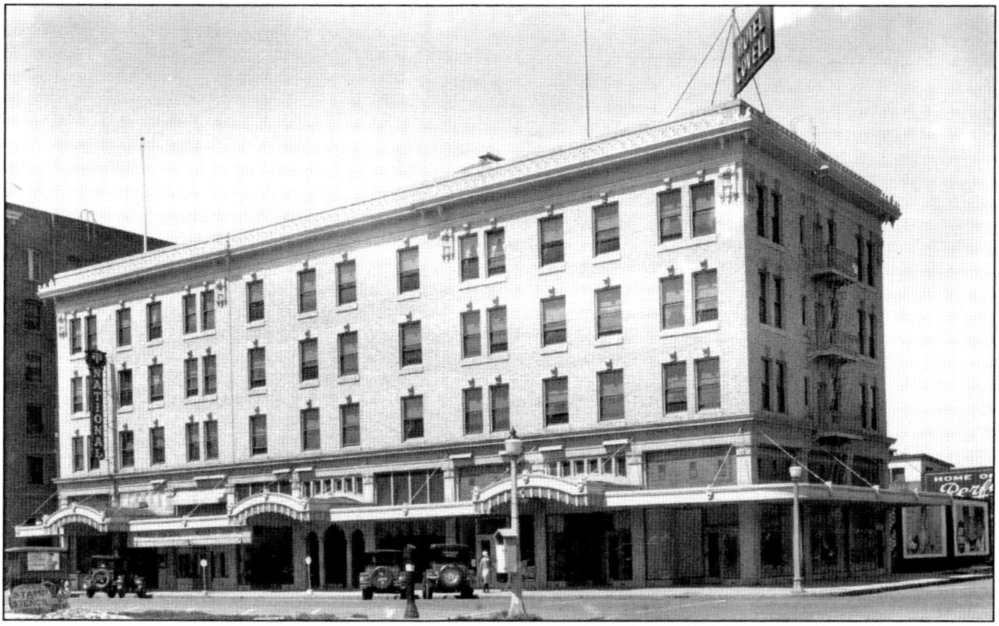

HOTEL COVELL, C. 1924. Another hotel was added to the roster on May 1, 1924, when rancher George Covell and his wife, Grace, opened their 70-room edifice. This hotel also featured a movie theater as part of the building (National, later Princess and Covell). The hotel lobby was ornate with marble floors. Rooms were decorated in imported English wallpaper, mahogany furnishings, and dark-red carpets. The hotel was expanded in 1929.

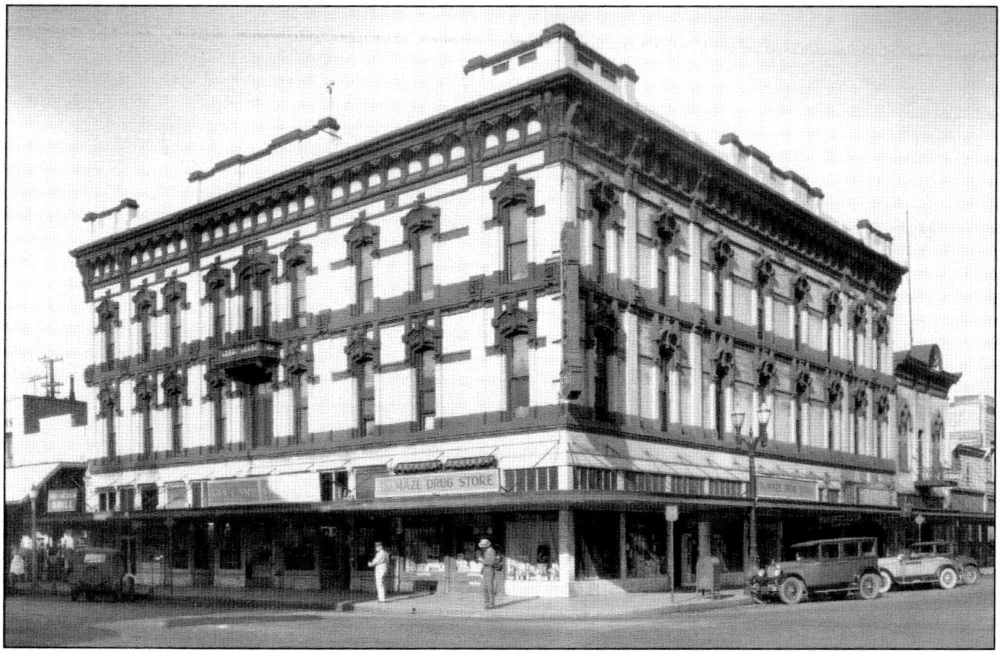

STATE HOTEL, C. 1931. The State Hotel is actually the refurbished Tynan Hotel. With new hotels being built in Modesto, it was time to give the grand old lady a new paint job and name. The empty clock tower was removed in 1916. On the ground floor are the Maze Drug Store, Pan American Grill, and a Velvet Ice Cream sign. The hotel's Victorian trim was also eventually removed.

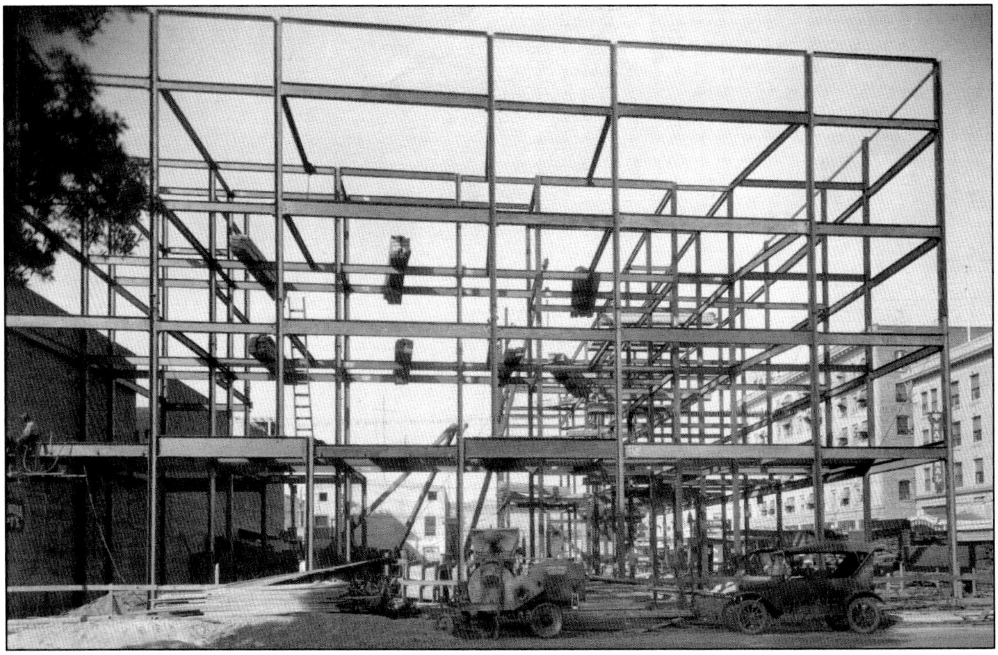

BEATY BUILDING FRAME, C. 1925. Construction began on the four-story, $250,000 Beaty Building in February 1925. The owner was Jack Beaty, manager of the Hotel Hughson. Located at J and Eleventh Streets, the building contained 90 offices and 12 ground-floor stores. The office floors were of flint tile from Luxembourg, Germany. It was the first Modesto office building with an elevator. In March 1926, tenants, mostly doctors, began moving in.

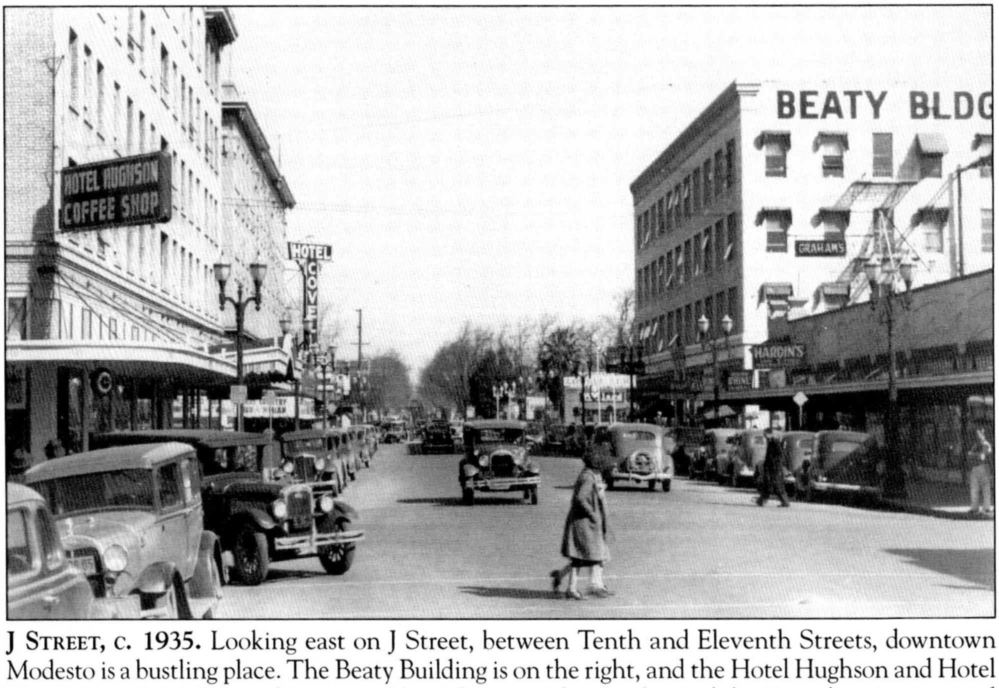

J STREET, C. 1935. Looking east on J Street, between Tenth and Eleventh Streets, downtown Modesto is a bustling place. The Beaty Building is on the right, and the Hotel Hughson and Hotel Covell are at left. Trees and a more residential area can be seen beyond the immediate commercial development in the foreground. This too would soon give way to growing commerce.

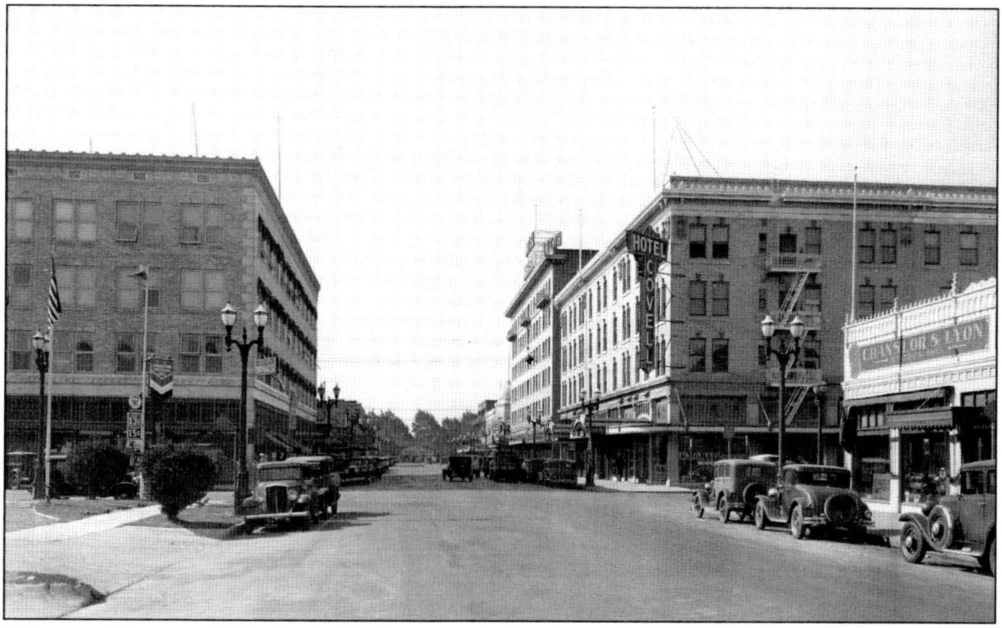

J Street West, c. 1934. Probably photographed earlier than the picture on the opposite page, there is still a filling station on the southeast corner of Eleventh and J Streets. Gasoline is 15¢ and 13¢ a gallon. The 1929 addition to the Hotel Covell is complete, as is the new Beaty Building. An auto parts store is across Eleventh Street from the Hotel Covell.

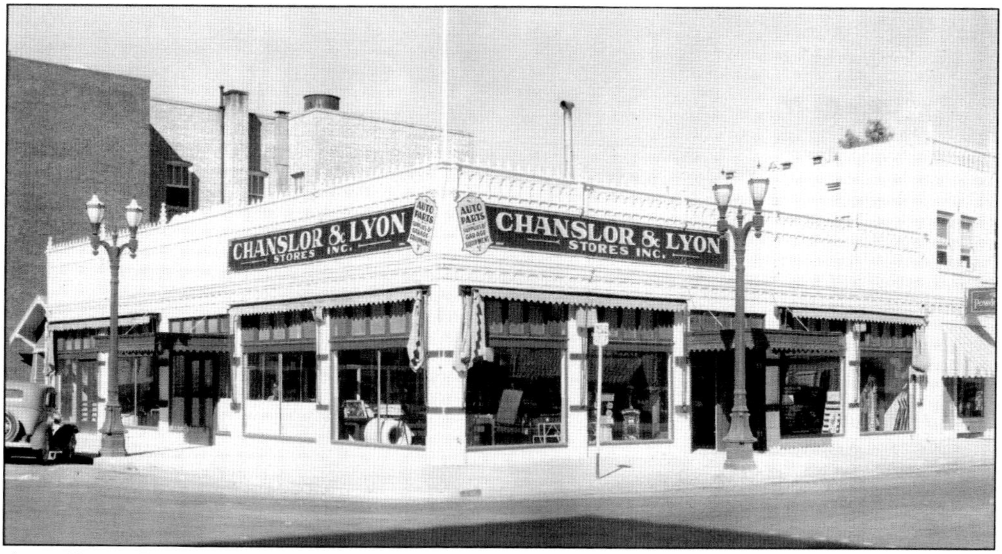

Auto Parts Store, c. 1930. Chanslor and Lyon Stores, Inc., is located on the corner of Eleventh and J Streets. This was an auto parts store that also handled supplies of "garage equipment," as the sign indicates. This structure would be replaced by a solidly constructed bank building later remodeled into an upscale restaurant.

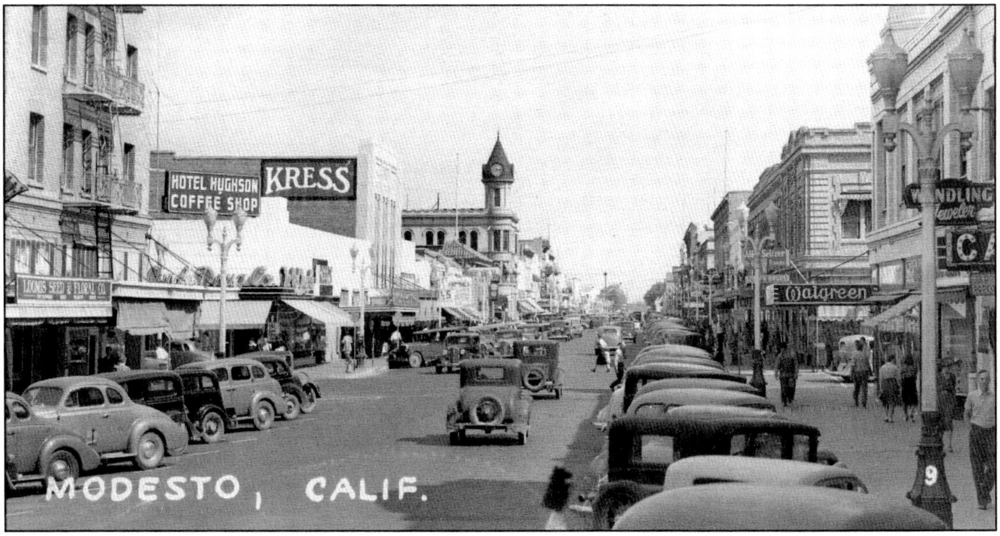

TENTH STREET SHOPPING DISTRICT, 1930S. This scene shows Tenth Street from the Hotel Hughson at J Street south. The photograph gives an idea of how busy downtown often was. Cars are parked diagonally on both sides of the street (no more middle-of-the-road parking). The Modesto Bank clock tower rises above the buildings near the center of the street.

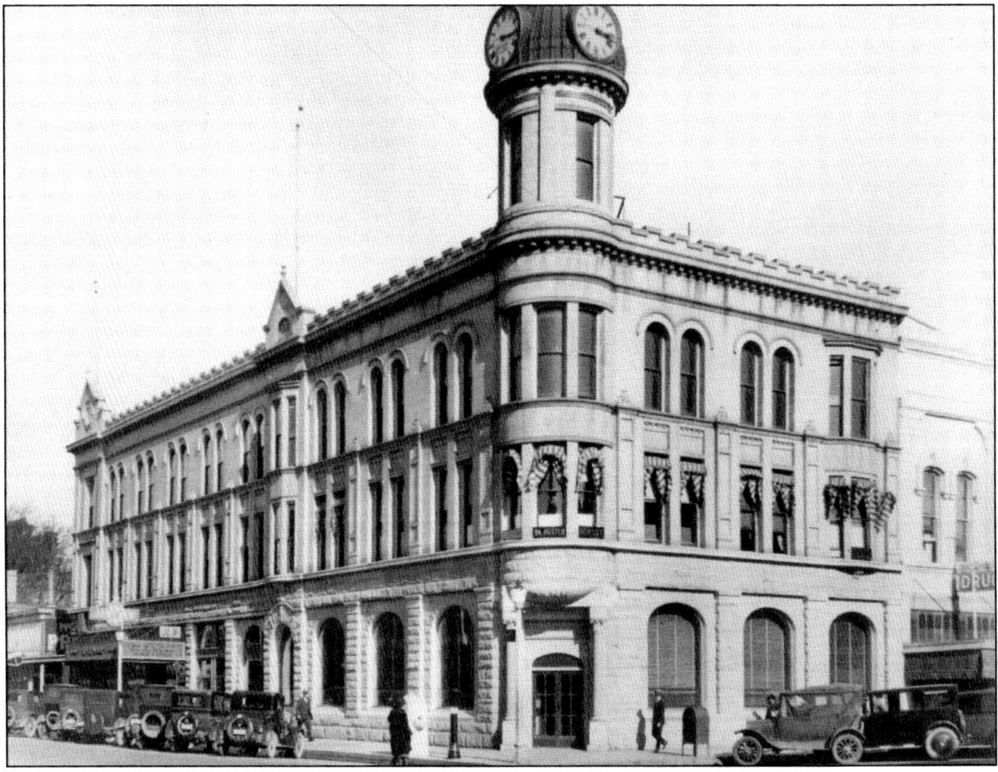

MODESTO BANK BUILDING, C. 1926. This building was constructed in 1893 and remodeled in 1922. It housed the bank that moved from Front Street and later became the Modesto Trust and Savings Bank. In 1936, the bank was sold to Anglo California National Bank, which razed the building and replaced it with a new one in 1941. It later became Crocker-Anglo Bank.

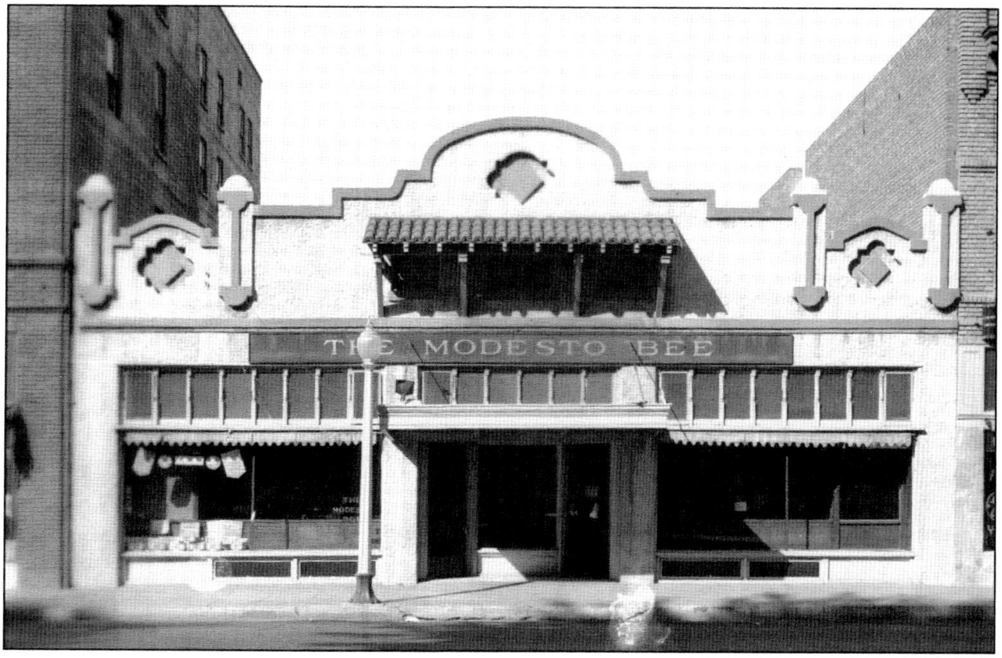

MODESTO *BEE* BUILDING, C. 1937. This building was located on Eleventh Street next to the Hotel Modesto. Once the *Modesto News-Herald* building, it proved particularly useful in May 1944 when the Hotel Modesto burned. Many of the guests who were unable to escape the smoke from the fire exited windows onto the roof of the *Bee* building.

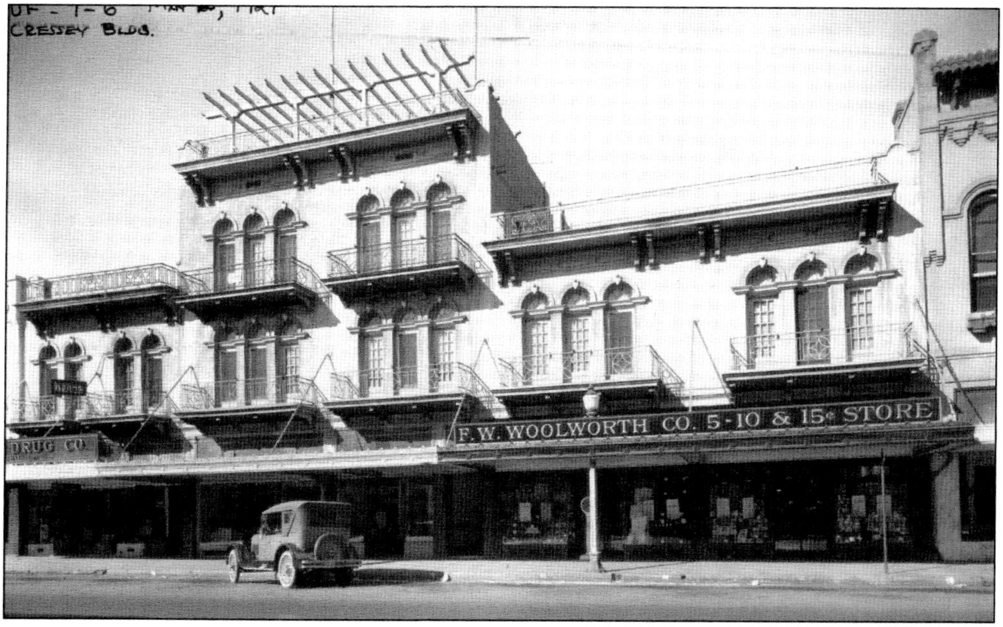

CRESSEY BUILDING, C. 1927. The center of the Cressey Building, constructed in 1911, was uniquely designed with two ground-floor stores and four three-room apartments. The pergola on top was part of a rooftop garden, new at the time in Modesto. The lower extensions including F. W. Woolworth Company were added later. Each of the apartments featured a front balcony, rear porch with laundry equipment, and built-in beds that disappeared into the walls.

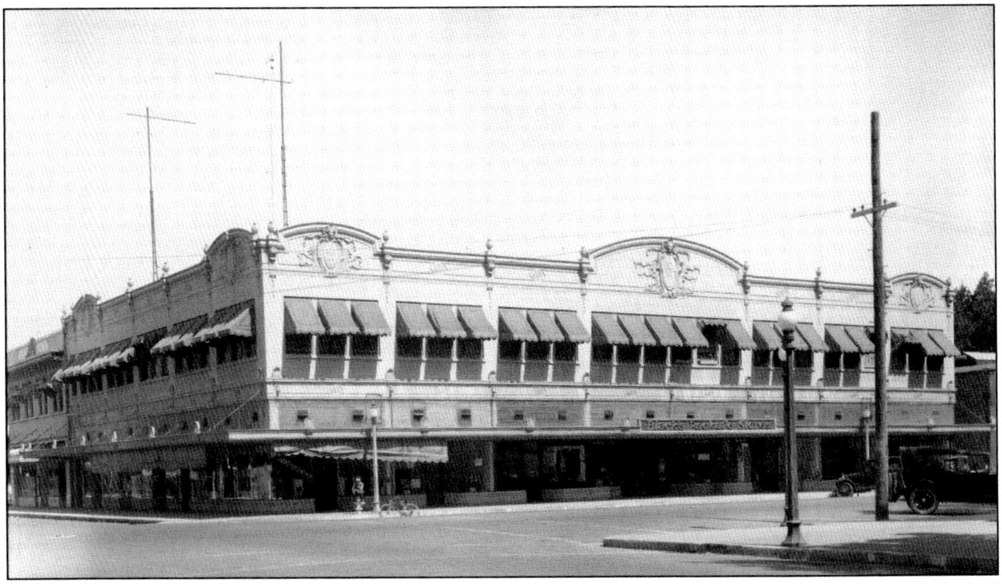

Black Building, c. 1924. Constructed in 1922 for $100,000, this office building included storefronts on Eleventh and I Streets. It was built during a flurry of activity in downtown Modesto. The Hotel Covell site had just been excavated, the Richards Theatre (also National, Princess, and Covell) was under construction, and Jack Beaty had just purchased the Elks site at Eleventh and J Streets for his office building, constructed in 1925.

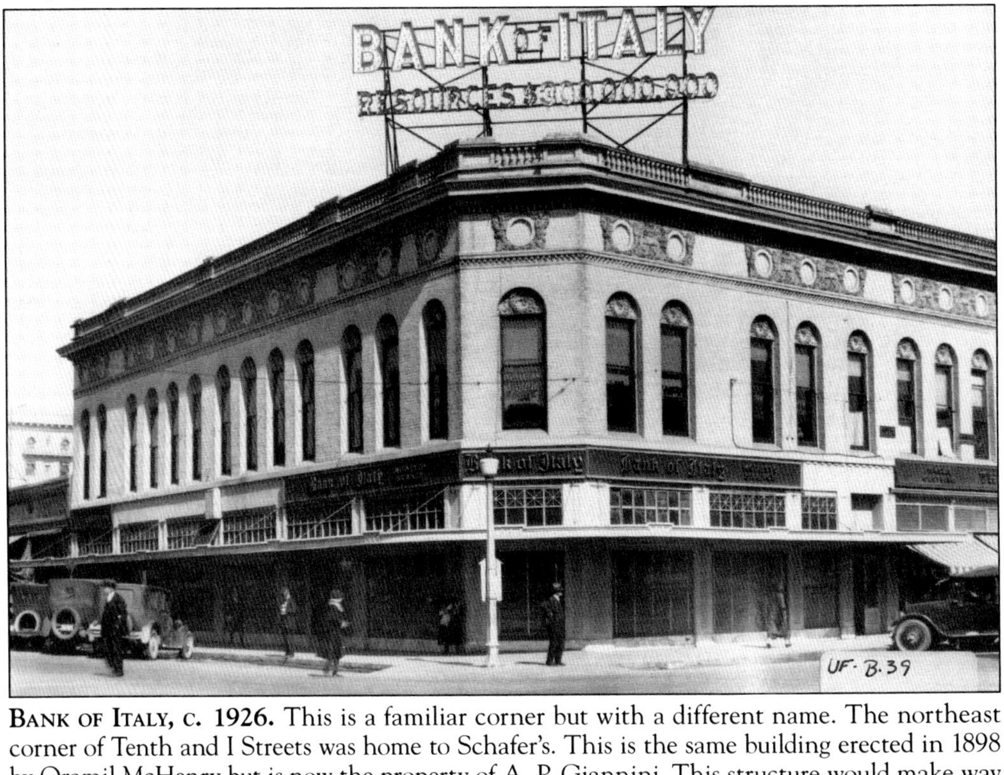

Bank of Italy, c. 1926. This is a familiar corner but with a different name. The northeast corner of Tenth and I Streets was home to Schafer's. This is the same building erected in 1898 by Oramil McHenry but is now the property of A. P. Giannini. This structure would make way for a new bank building in 1928 and eventually a new name, Bank of America.

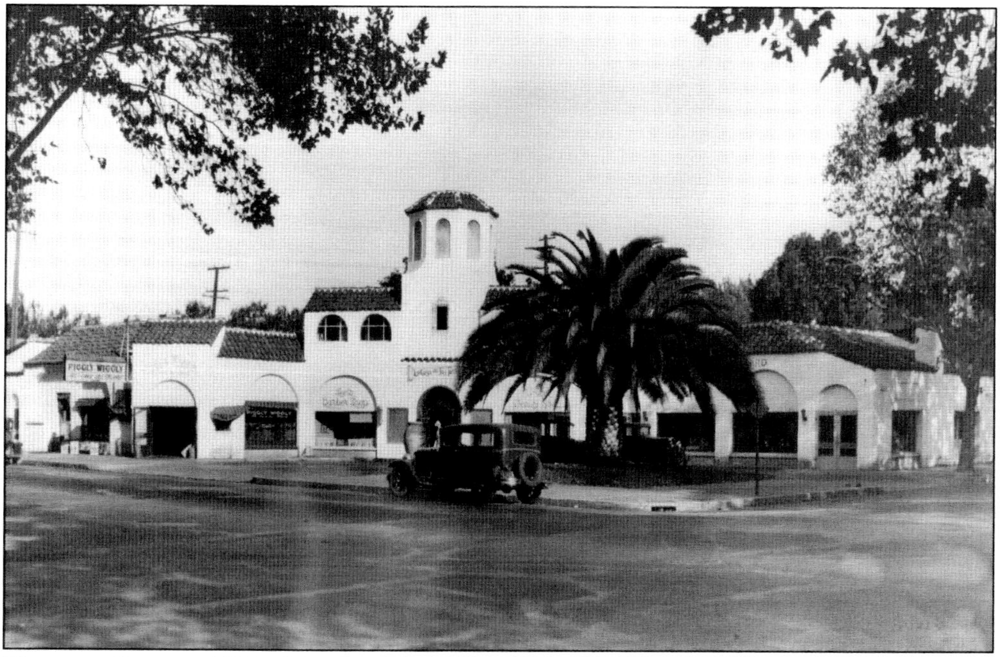

House of Stores, 1930s. This large Spanish-style building was located at the corner of J and Sixteenth Streets. The name on the building is La Casa de las Tiendas, loosely translated as "house of stores." Original tenants included Piggly Wiggly Market, Lem's Barber Shop, and Unique Beauty Shop. Before the building was torn down, it also housed a restaurant and banquet hall, as well as Louis Hammer Flowers. (J. Broome, Camera Center Collection.)

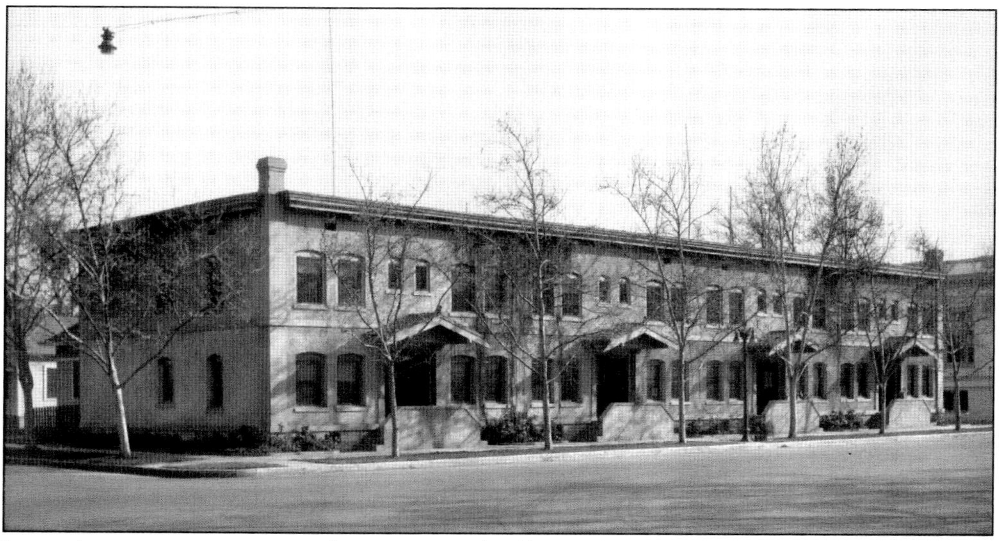

James Apartments, c. 1931. This apartment building is located at I and Fifteenth Streets, near the McHenry house. Advertised as strictly new in 1914, with three-bedroom apartments suitable for two to four people and with hot and cold running water, the building has changed little over the years. It is one of the few buildings remaining in town from its era. To the right is the McHenry Library (now museum).

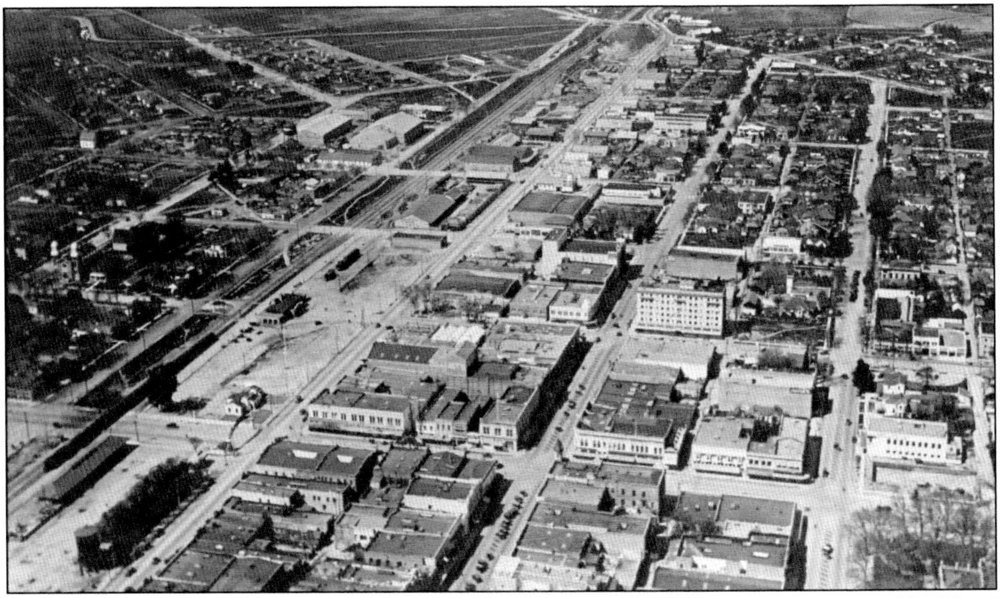

Modesto by Air, c. 1921. This aerial view of Modesto was taken prior to construction of the Hotel Covell and the Beaty Building. Center right is the six-story Hotel Hughson, and slightly up to the left is the Strand Theatre. Following Tenth Street down toward the bottom, the Modesto Theatre is also visible. The arch stands by itself to the left. Homes still dot the downtown district.

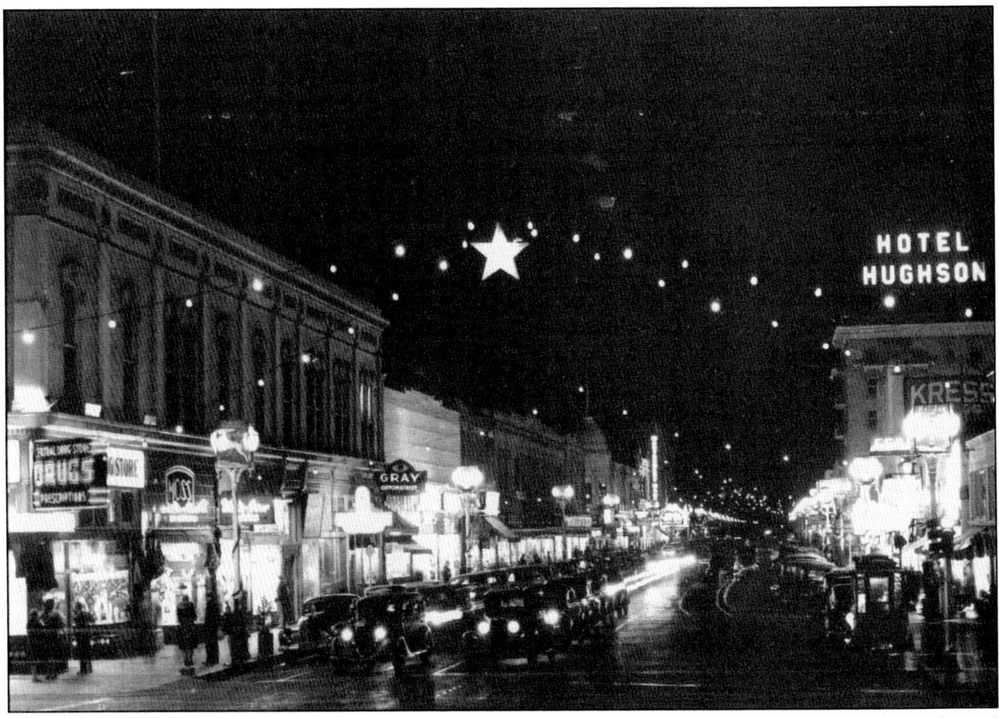

Tenth Street at Night, c. 1933. Holiday decorations hang over the intersection of Tenth and I Streets in this nighttime photograph. The Hotel Hughson sign dominates the scene, but a close look reveals several landmarks, including the Strand, Montgomery Ward, Gray Optometrist, Moss Rose Confectionary, a drugstore, and, on the right, Kress.

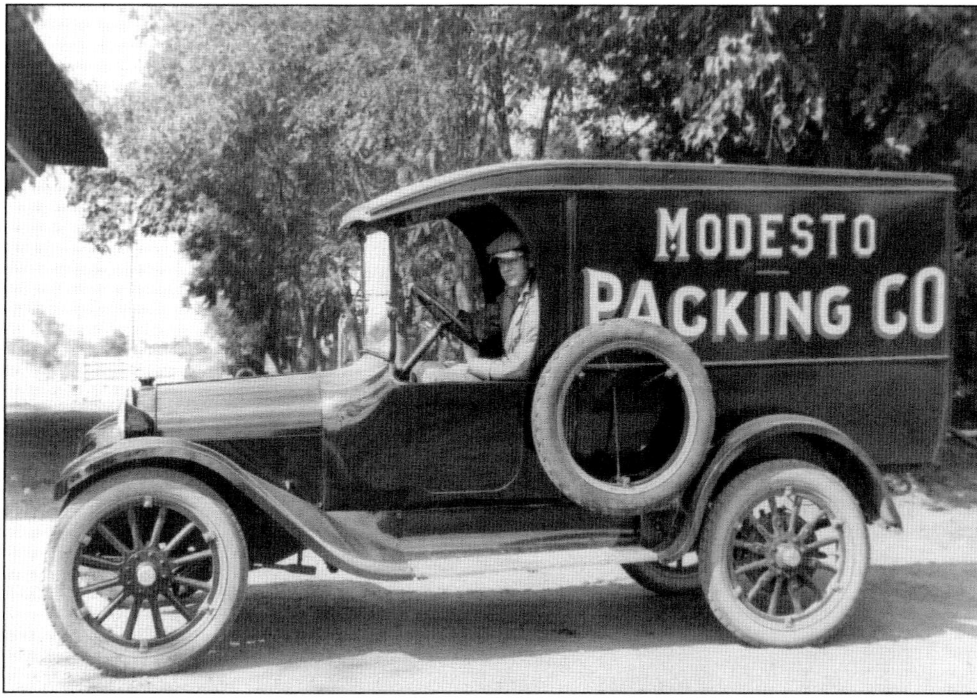

Delivery Vans, Undated. It seems that most companies in Modesto providing sales to the public also delivered the goods. In these two photographs, Ford delivery vans are in use for two different companies. Modesto Packing Company was a meat packer located on Crows Landing Road. In 1922, the company advertised that it had an inspector on-site who could inspect meat brought to the plant. A new city ordinance required that all meat sold in the city had to be inspected. The bottom photograph shows a van in use for the Sun Maid Market, delivering groceries through town. It is easy to imagine how simple it would have been to phone in an order and have it delivered right to the front door.

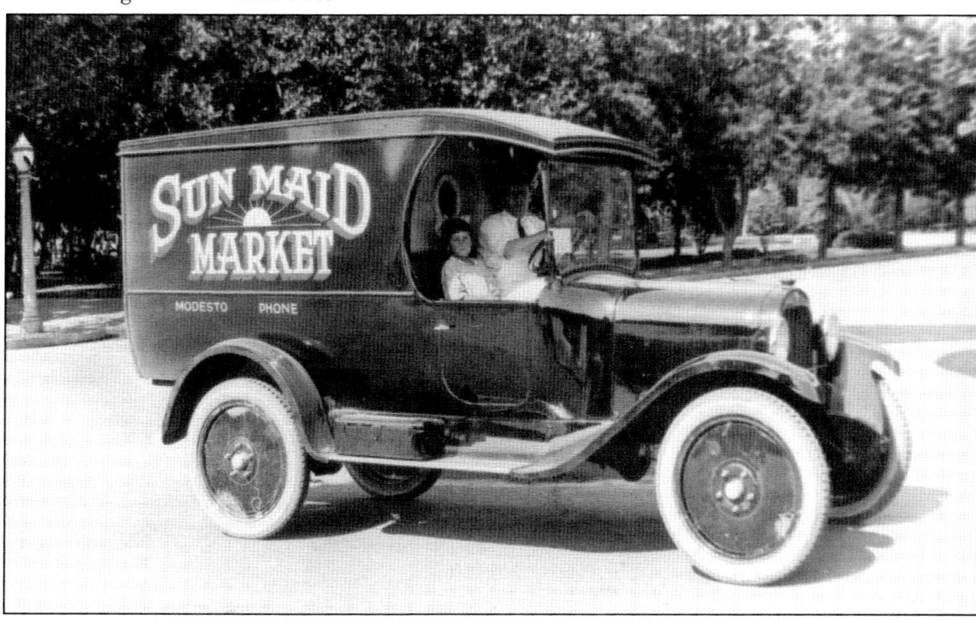

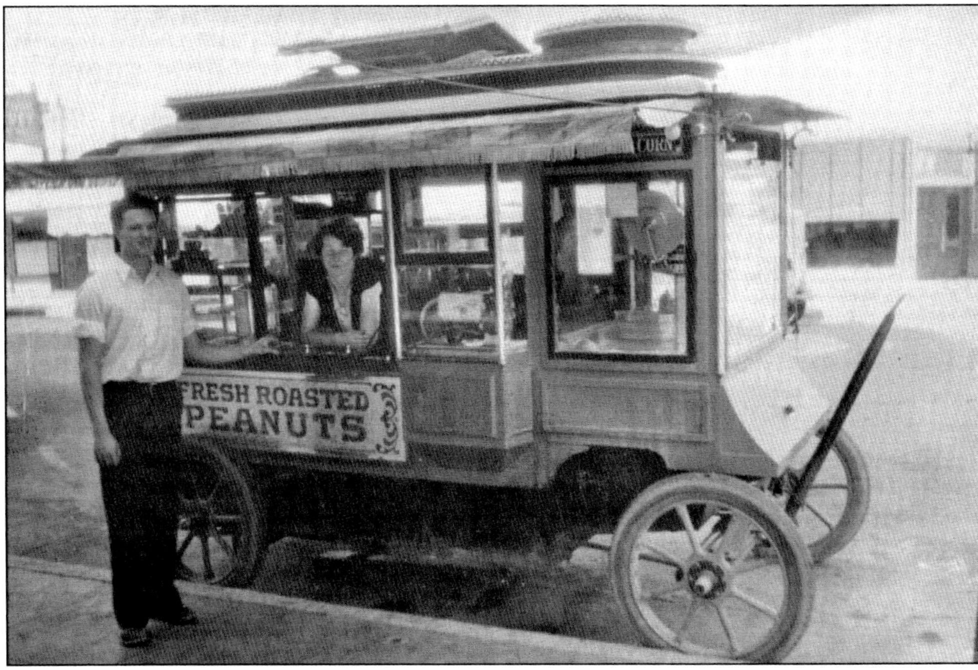

PEANUT AND POPCORN WAGON, UNDATED. This wagon owned by Ernest and Evalyn Huls was a familiar sight on Tenth Street through the 1940s. Peanuts sold for a nickel, with larger bags going for 10, 15, and 25¢. The steam gauge was kept at 25 pounds to heat the peanut bin and the freshly popped corn. Patrons of the train station and area theaters frequently stopped to grab a bag.

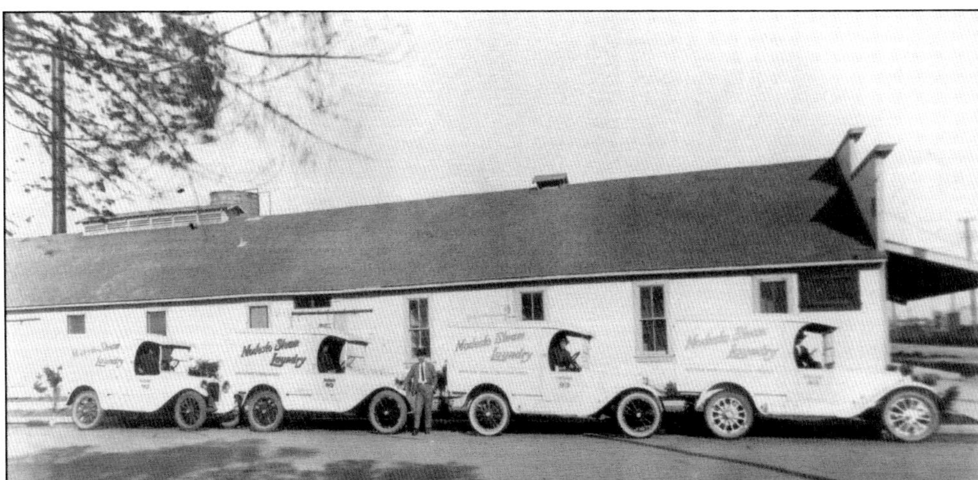

LAUNDRY DELIVERY, 1920S. Modesto Steam Laundry began operation in 1895. With the name of the company and its motto, "Particular Work for Particular People," on the side of the trucks, this group of vans delivered cleaned and washed clothes throughout the city. Modesto Steam Laundry was in business for 114 years, closing in 2009.

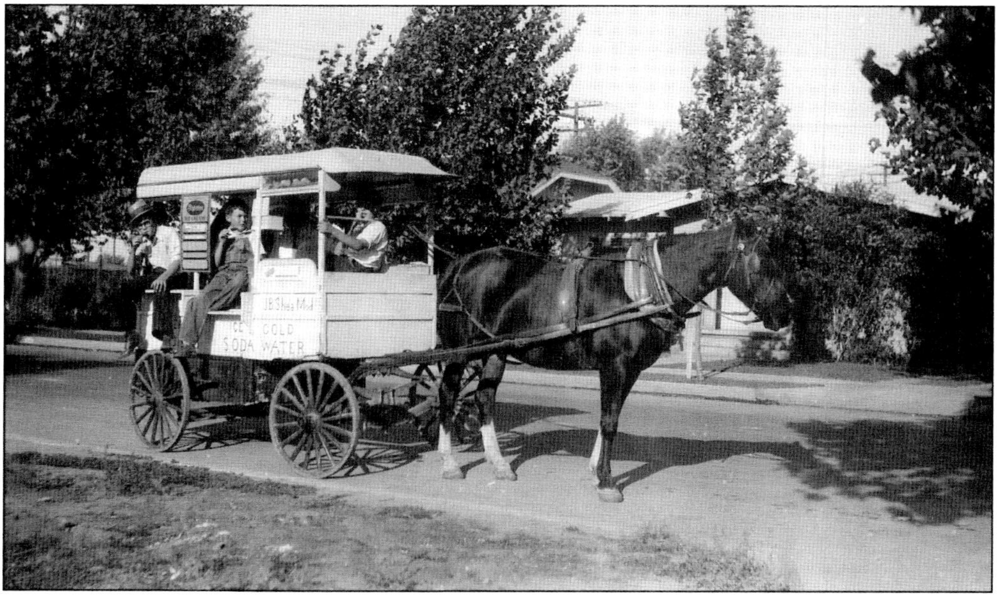

ICE CREAM WAGON, C. 1924. A nickel bought an ice cream cone and "an afternoon of happiness for a little kid," says Robert Smith, at the far right. The price included petting Nellie. Mr. Shea rang the bell on his cart with a big railroad spike as he made his rounds. Robert's mother, Helen, took the photograph in the 400 block of Hackberry Avenue. Also shown are Cecil Jessen (left) and Billy Jones (center). (Faces of Stanislaus, Robert Smith.)

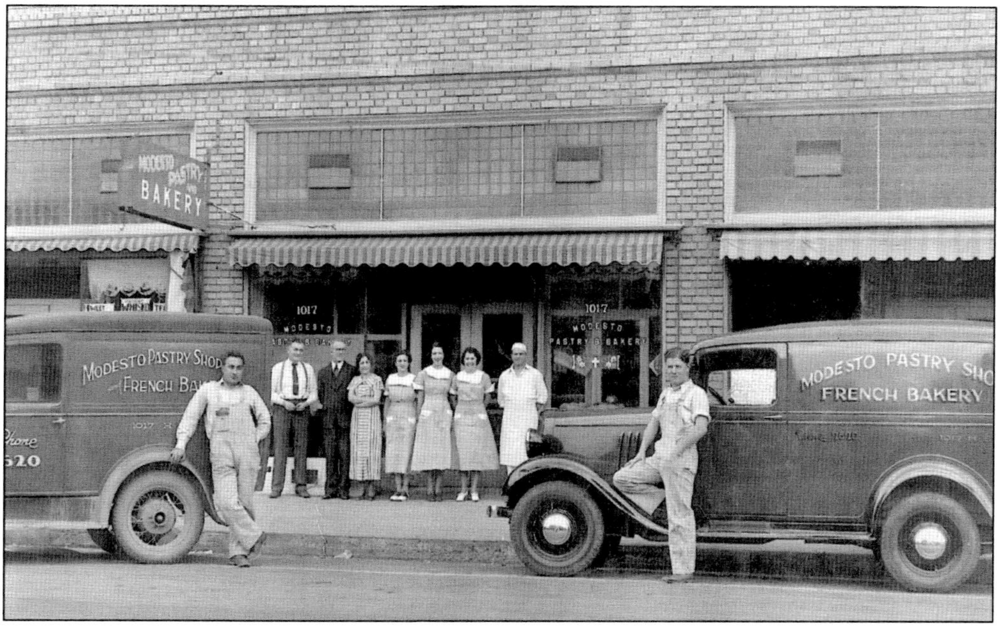

MODESTO PASTRY AND BAKERY, 1930S. Leo Ciccarelli stands with his van from which he sold Modesto Bakery's products. John Scaglione owned the bakery. Charles Madonna Sr. owned the liquor store to the left. Taken by Shoob Photography, this photograph represents the hard work and dedication of Italian immigrants who gave their families the benefits of American citizenship. Both businesses were located in the Hotel Modesto building. (Faces of Stanislaus, Joyce Scaglione Turner.)

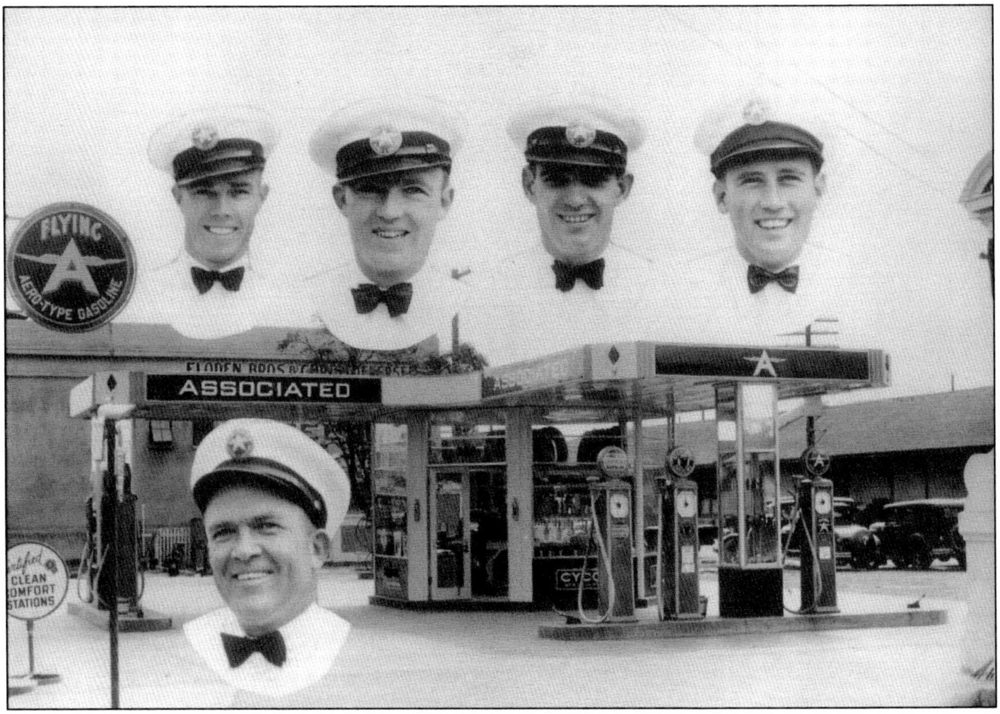

FLYING-A FULL SERVICE, C. 1935. Harry Ivy owned the Associated Station at Ninth and I Streets in the shadow of the arch. Pictured are, from left to right, (top) Roy Coffee, Louie Witt, Bill Stivers, and Gilbert Wendell. Harry Ivy is at bottom left. Ivy owned the station until December 1937, when he died at the age of 40. Bill Stivers and Roy Coffee then took ownership. (Faces of Stanislaus, Nancy Lee.)

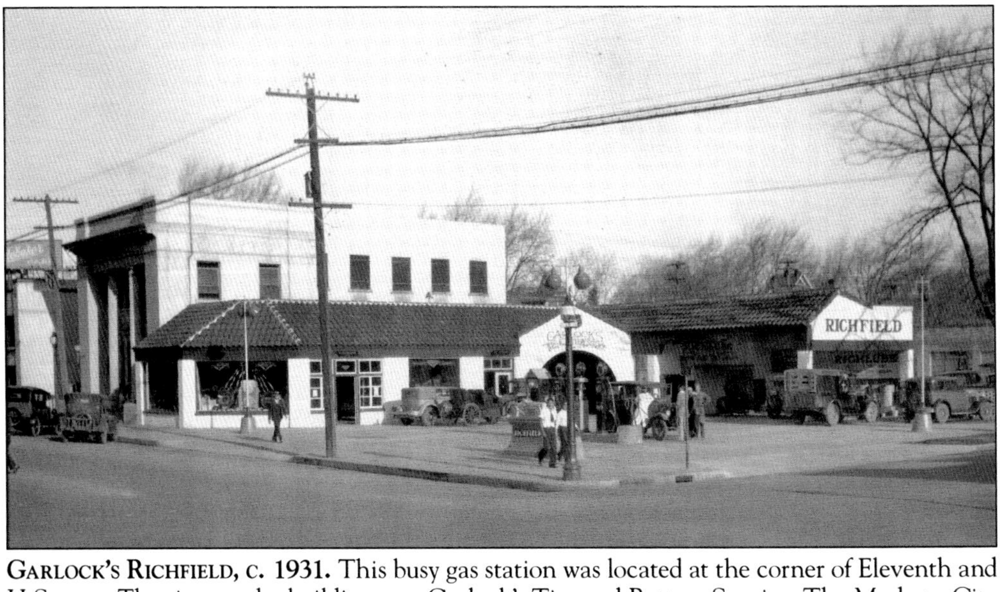

GARLOCK'S RICHFIELD, C. 1931. This busy gas station was located at the corner of Eleventh and H Streets. The sign on the building says Garlock's Tire and Battery Service. The Modesto City Jail is located behind the station.

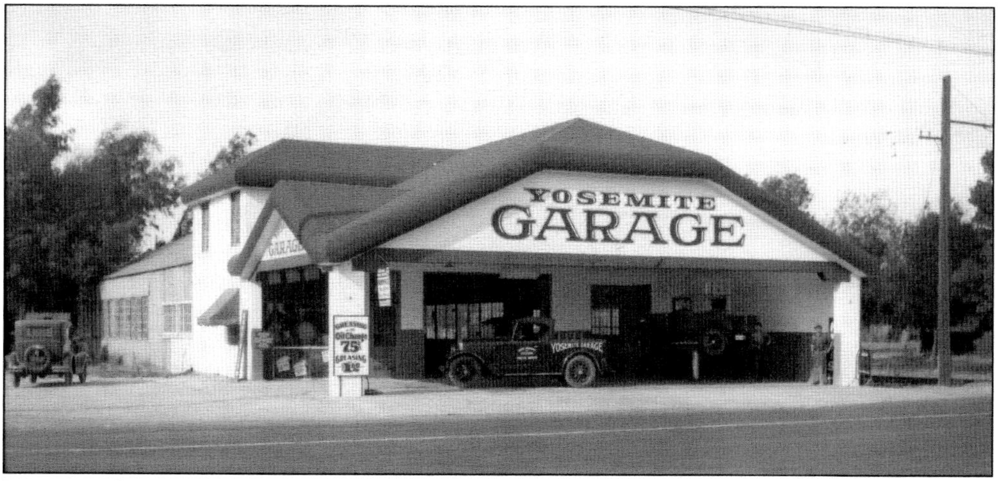

Yosemite Garage, c. 1931. This garage was far from its namesake, being located at Needham and Ninth Streets (Highway 99) in Modesto. Note that an oil change at this time was only 75¢. (J. Broome, Camera Center Collection.)

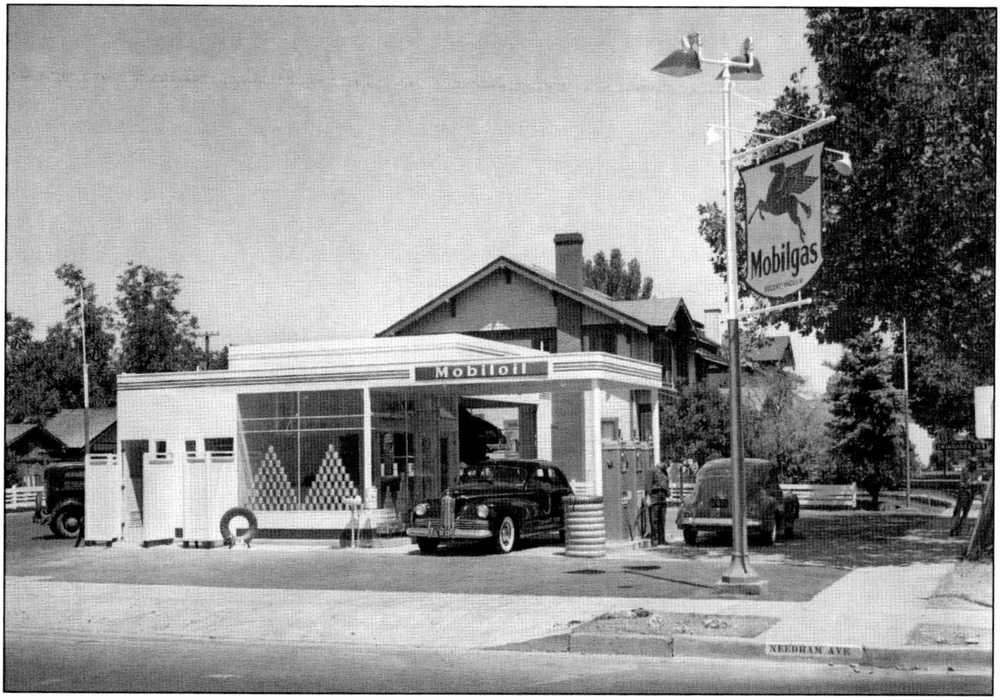

Mobil Oil Station, 1940s. Again on Needham, this filling station is near the McHenry Avenue intersection and not very far from residential areas. An observation by the author's mother, Antoinette Baggese, who had arrived from Chicago in 1944, was that Modesto had "more banks and gas stations than anything else."

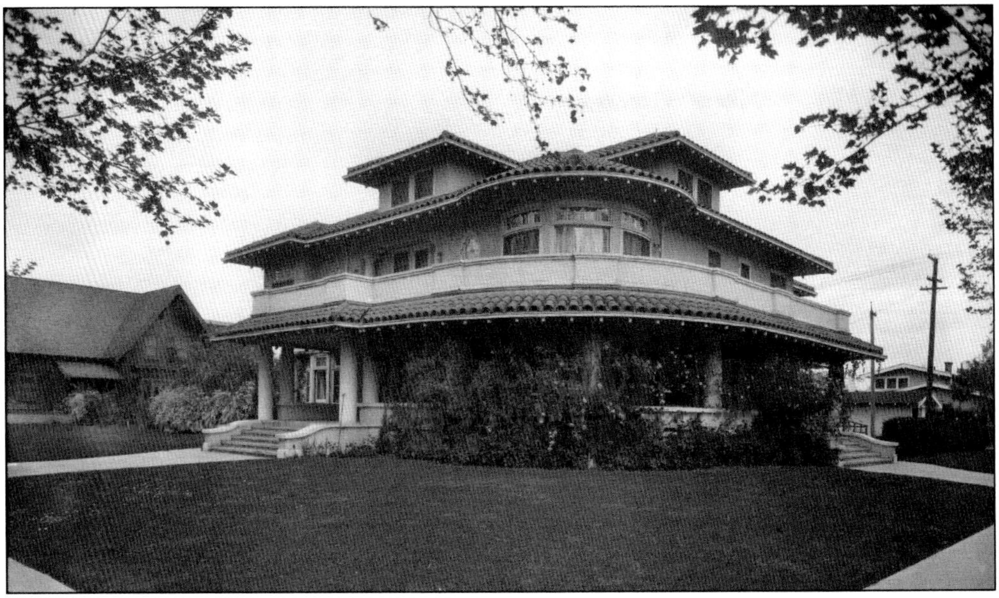

T. K. Beard Home, Undated. The Thomas K. Beard home was built in 1914 and located at 102 Sycamore Avenue. Beard was the founder of the Modesto and Empire Traction Company and an MID director from 1901 to 1907. Considered one of Modesto's most beautiful homes, it was razed in the 1960s by its owner in a zoning conflict with the city.

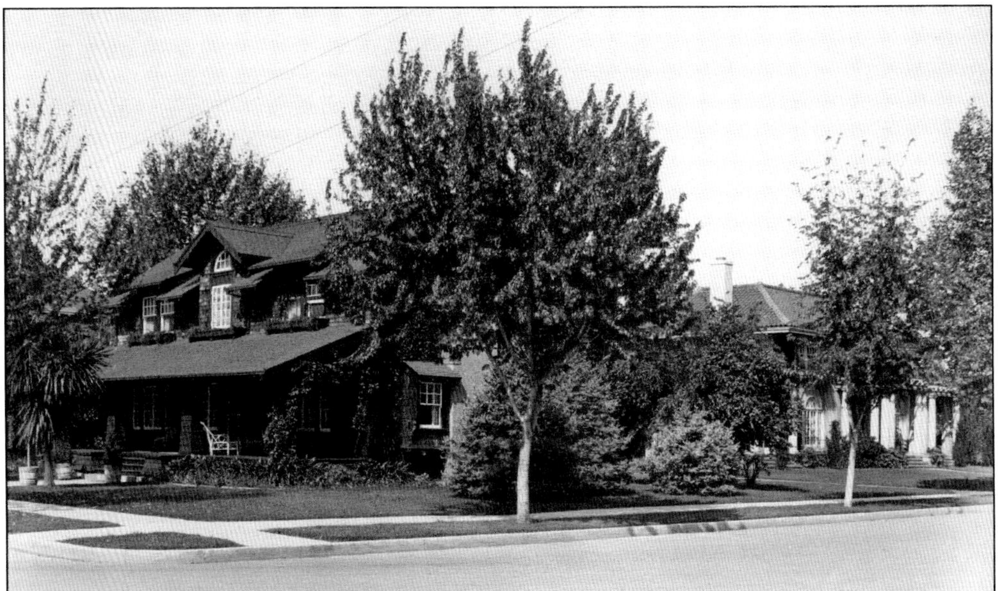

Carl Shannon Home, Undated. This home was located on the northwest corner of Seventeenth and I Streets, next to Shannon Funeral Home that was built in 1936. Shannon was mayor of Modesto from 1939 to 1950. To the right of the Shannon house is the Cressey house (shown on the next page). The Shannon house was eventually moved out to a rural site, but the art deco mortuary was demolished.

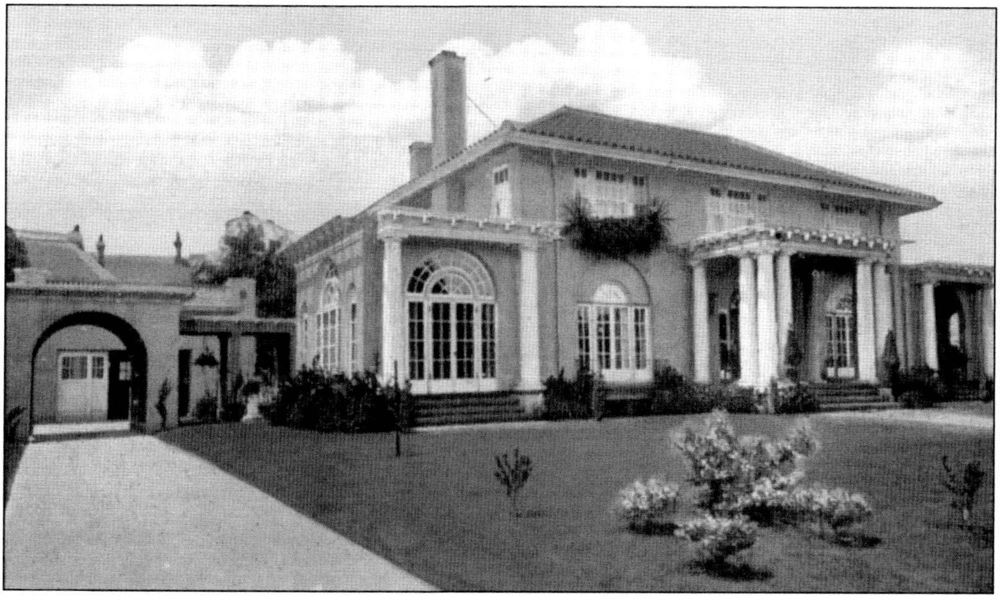

George Cressey House, c. 1900. This elegant home belonged to banker George Cressey. Cressey had been vice president of the Modesto Bank in the early 1900s. Located at 915 Seventeenth Street, the home later was owned by well-known physician and surgeon Dr. Richard Husband. The home is still standing and is currently in use as an office building. (Author's collection.)

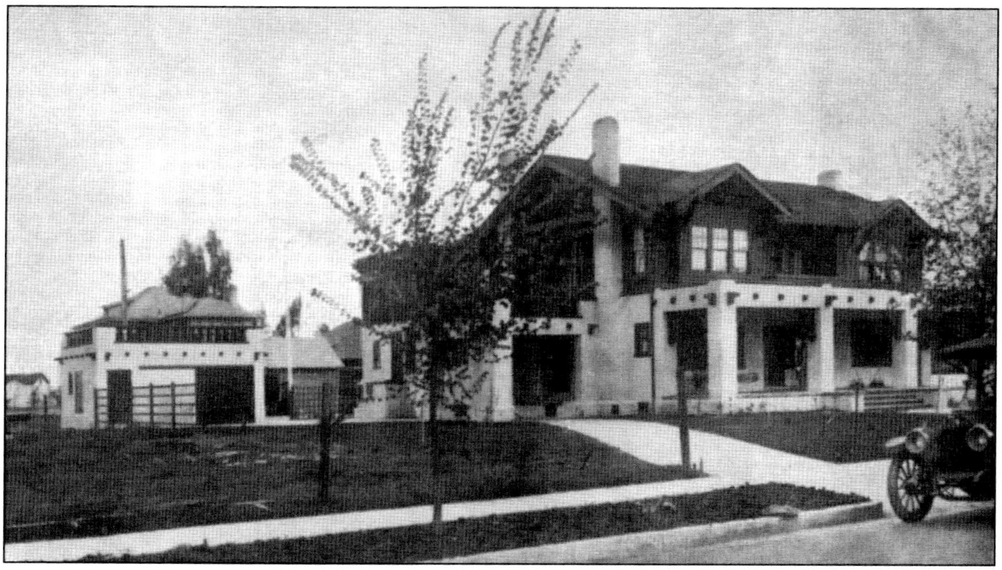

Maze Home, Undated. This is the William C. and Helene Maze residence at 1020 Fifteenth Street built about 1912. Maze and his partner, George J. Wren, developed real estate and sold insurance. They donated the property for the Maze-Wren Park where Bud Coffee's plane crashed in 1921. The house was sold to Dr. J. C. Robertson, then to Dr. James A. Porter. It was later moved to property on Ladd Road. (Author's collection.)

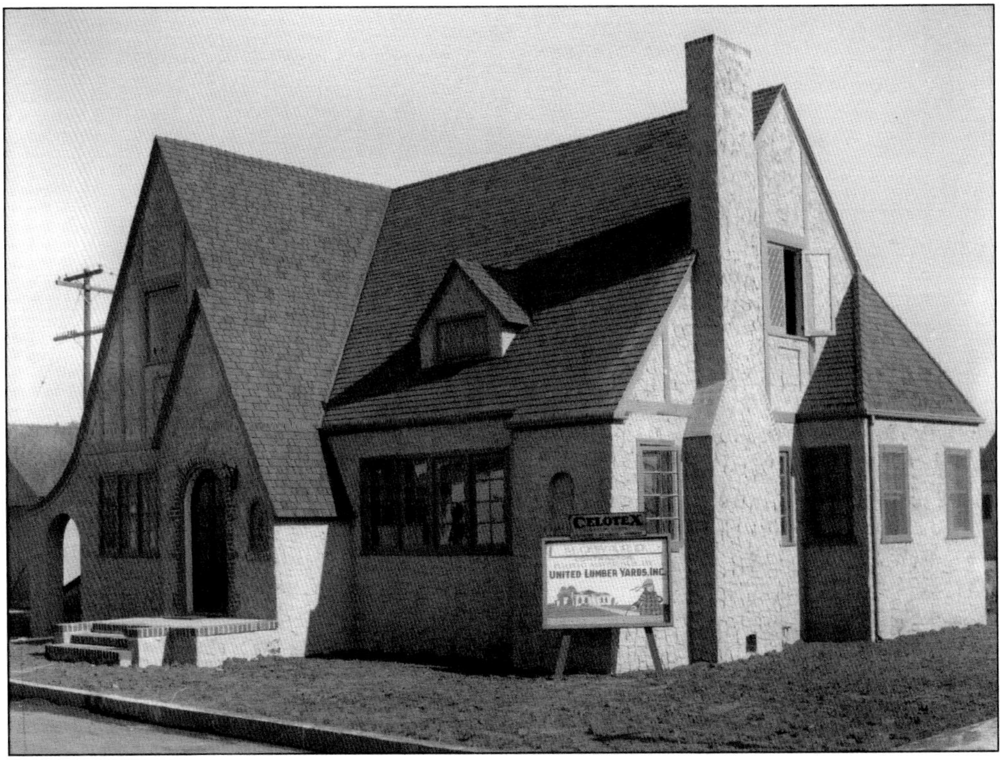

Model Home, c. 1927. This home was located at the corner of Achor Court and Lottie Street and became part of National Better House Week in April 1927. The house featured "English architecture and a high green gabled roof," according to newspaper reports. The model had seven rooms furnished for $1,005.25. It also featured Celotex lumber, highlighted as "insulating lumber" to help keep out heat and cold.

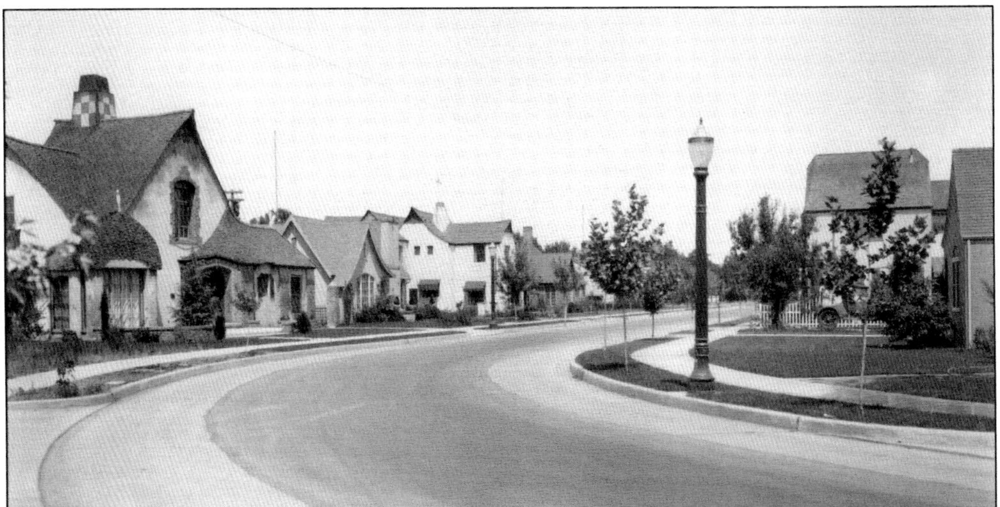

A Storybook Street, c. 1927. This quaint street is in the same area as the photograph above. The homes still exist today off of McHenry Avenue. Many of the homes have what appear to be television antennas on the roof, but they are actually radio antennas. New subdivisions in east Modesto Village One have emulated this architectural style.

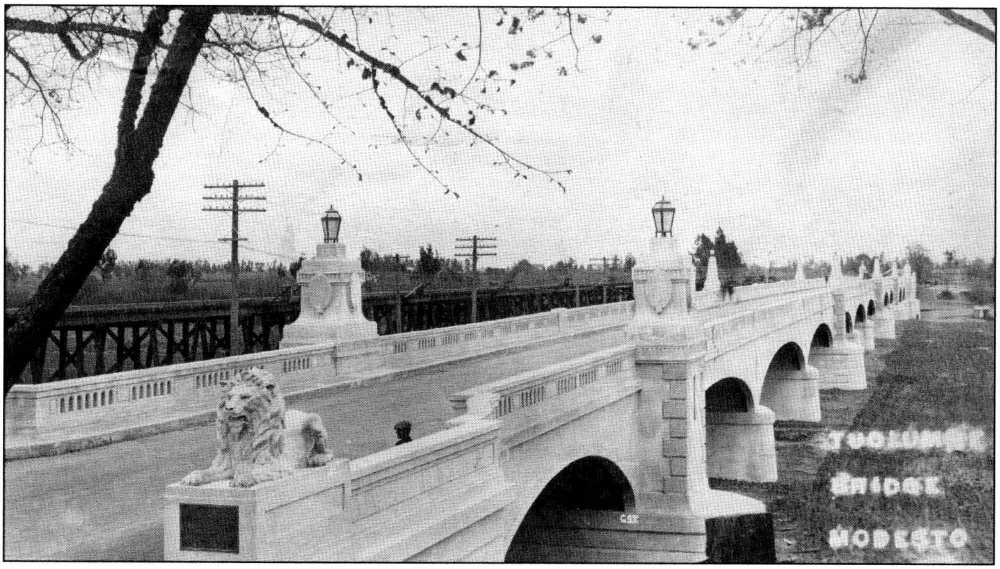

SEVENTH STREET BRIDGE, C. 1917. This $110,000 bridge over the Tuolumne River is affectionately known as "The Lion Bridge." The bridge is a "Canticrete" type of bridge, according to historian Colleen Stanley Bare, which entails pouring concrete over cantilevered steel trusses. Highway 99 once crossed here, and this was Modesto's only bridge over the Tuolumne until 1933. The photograph below shows the celebration that took place at the dedication of the 1,250-foot span on March 22, 1917. The celebration included two parades, one for each side of the bridge; speeches, band music, singing, and christening of the bridge with a milk bottle; plus a grand finale with everyone singing "America." The bridge, still standing, has even been used as a movie backdrop.

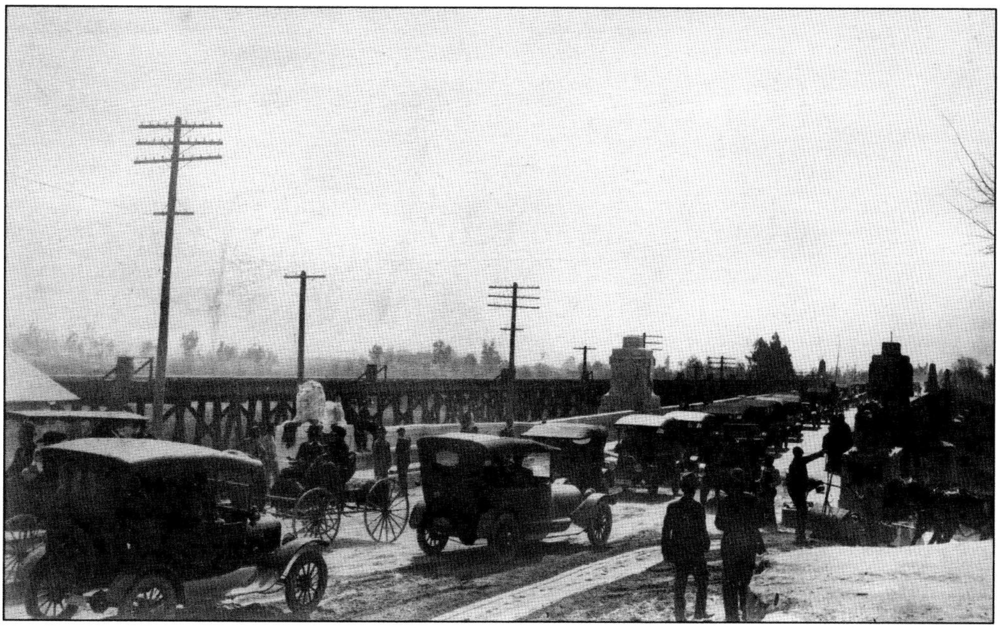

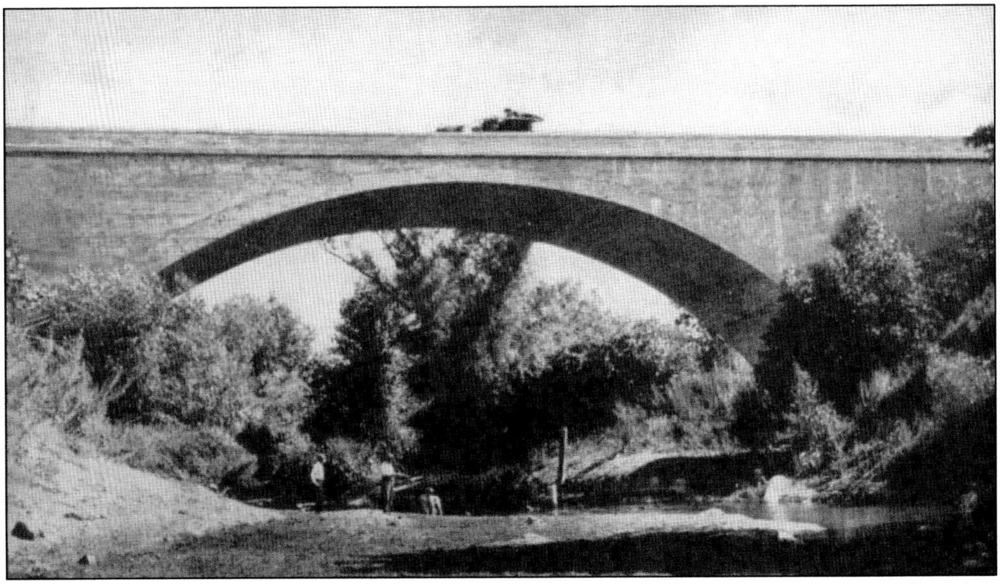

Dry Creek Bridge, c. 1906. This was also known as the Jennie-Grand or the Grand Bridge, referring to the streets that led up to it. It is a reinforced concrete bridge with a graceful, oval-shaped arch. This look was a trademark of pioneer designer John B. Leonard, according to Colleen Stanley Bare. The Dry Creek Bridge was one of his firsts, and he later designed the Seventh Street Lion Bridge, as well. (Author's collection.)

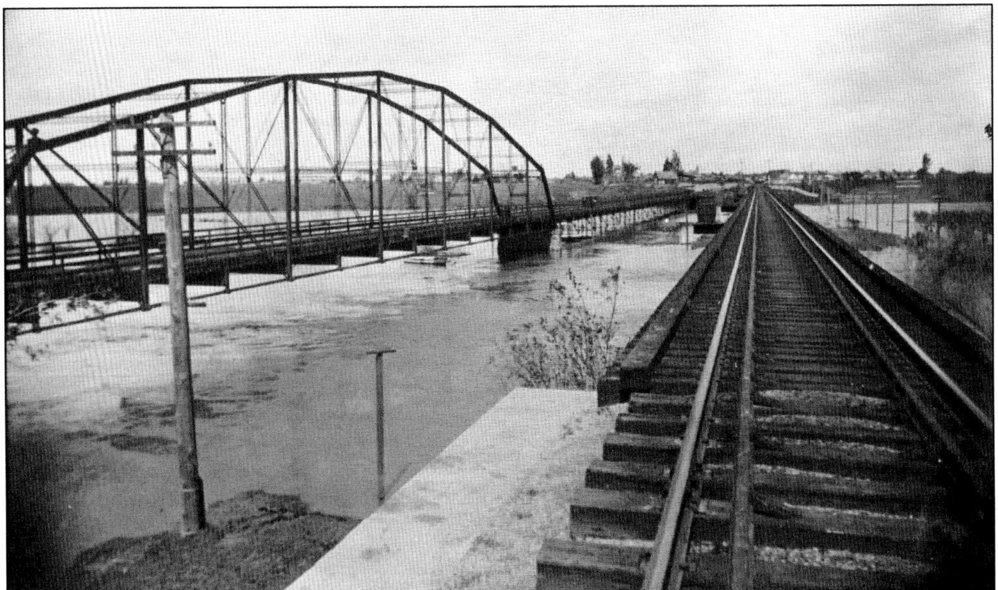

Early Tuolumne Bridges, Undated. The railroad crossed the Tuolumne River on this trestle in the early part of the 20th century. A wagon bridge across the river is on the left. The new Tuolumne River Bridge to accommodate up-to-date automobile traffic was built in 1917 and is shown on the previous page.

Four

A Sense of Community

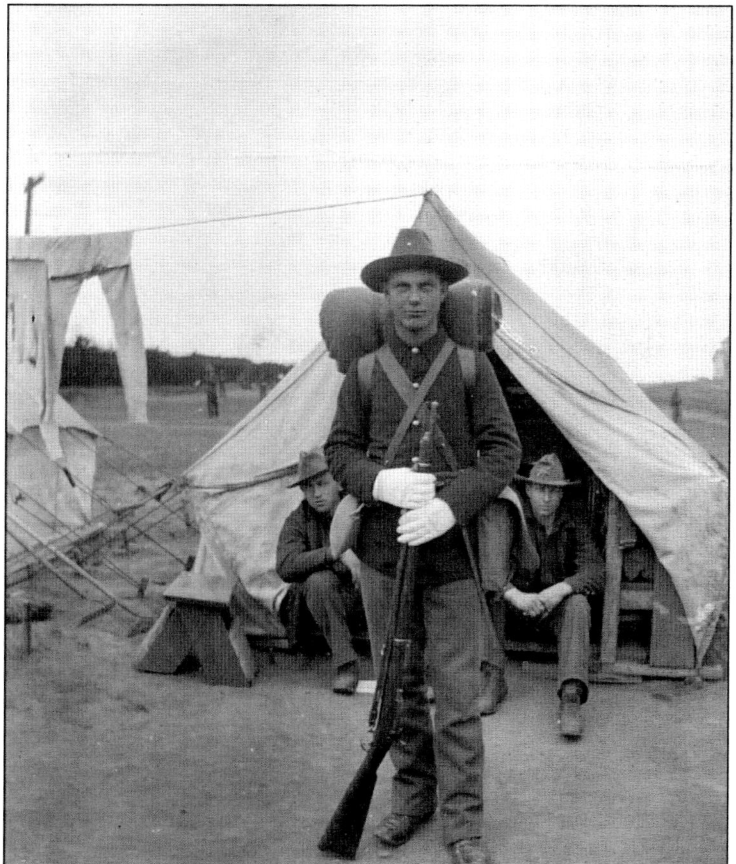

Spanish-American War, c. 1898. Training took place in the San Francisco Bay Area for troops whose destinations were to be the battles in Cuba, Puerto Rico, and the Philippines during the April–August 1898 conflict. The war was basically about independence for Cuba and American expansion. Pictured at right is Modestan Ed Turpin. Standing is Alabama Smith. Neither of them saw action in the war.

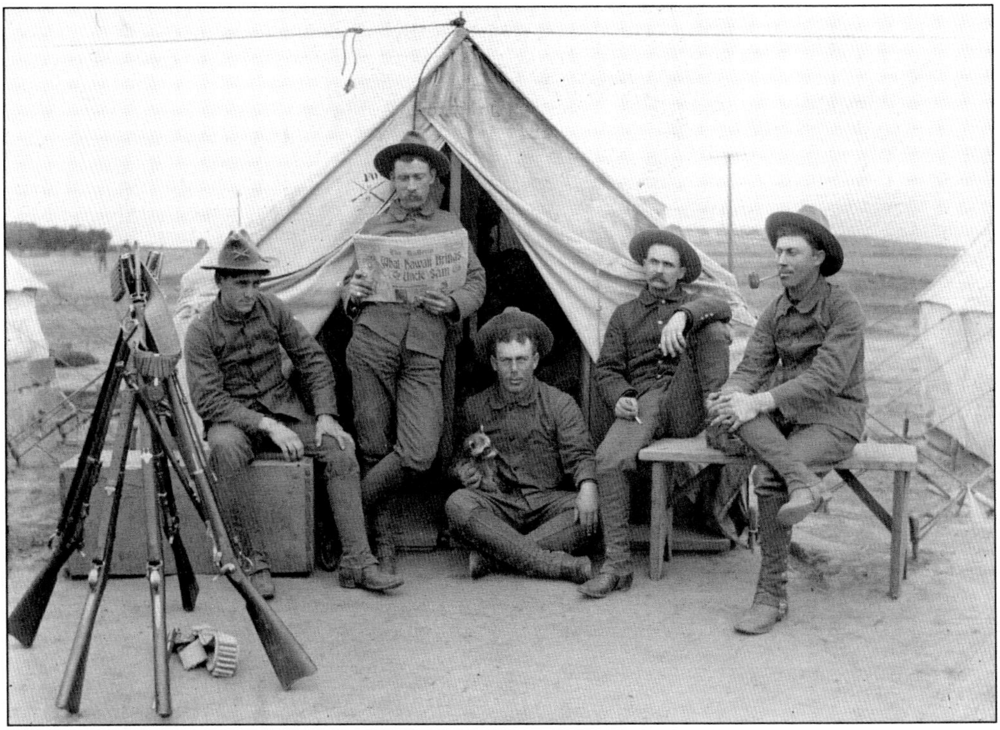

Local Soldiers, c. 1898. Members of Company D mustered into the army were disappointed when they did not see action. They are, far left, Will Arnold; Jim Rhea, center with raccoon; and Forrest Wilson, on Rhea's immediate right. The Spanish-American War occurred from April to August 1898. This may be in July since the newspaper headline says, "What Hawaii Brings Uncle Sam." Hawaii was annexed as a territory July 6, 1898.

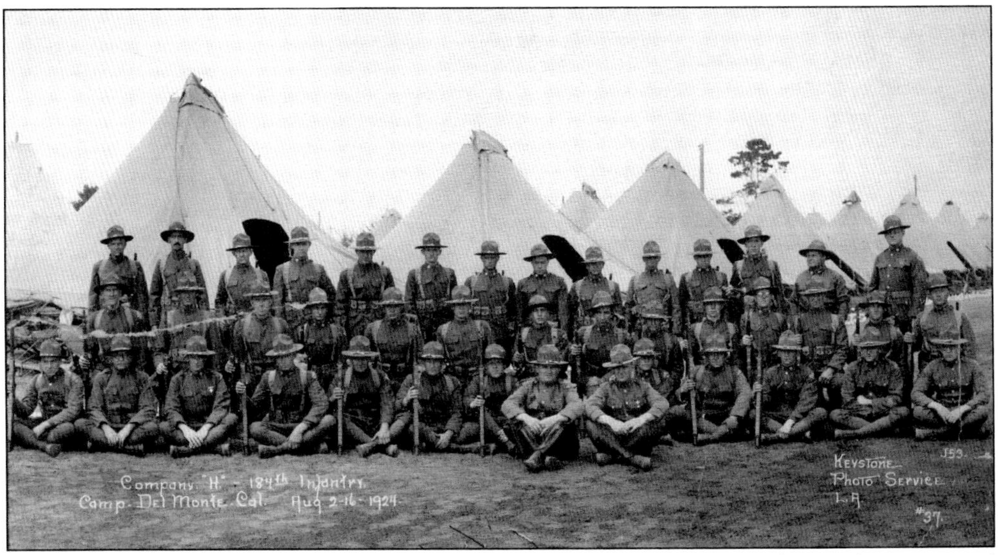

Modesto National Guard, c. 1924. Members of the Modesto National Guard are pictured with their unit. They are part of Company H of the 124th Infantry. Training took place at Camp Del Monte near Monterey from August 2 to 16 in 1924. The camp was considered a "citizens' military training camp." (Faces of Stanislaus, Samuel E. Courtney.)

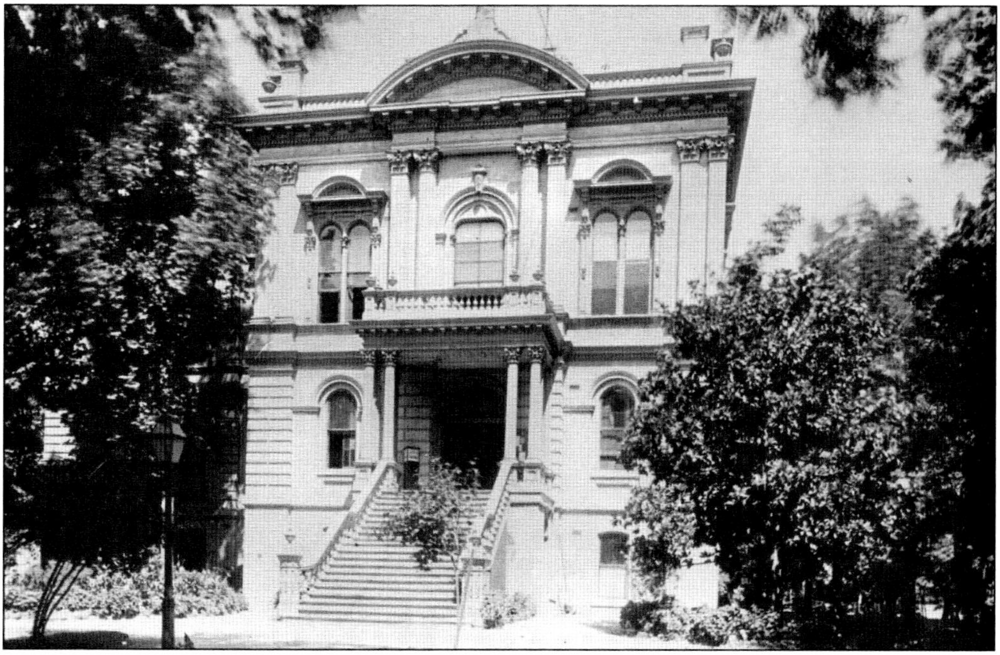

County Courthouse, c. 1910. Pictured is a front view of the Stanislaus County Courthouse, long after Courthouse Park was developed on the grounds. The building was completed in 1873, with a Hall of Records added in 1901. The courthouse was demolished in 1958 to make room for new buildings. All that remains of the original courthouse is the Goddess of Justice statue.

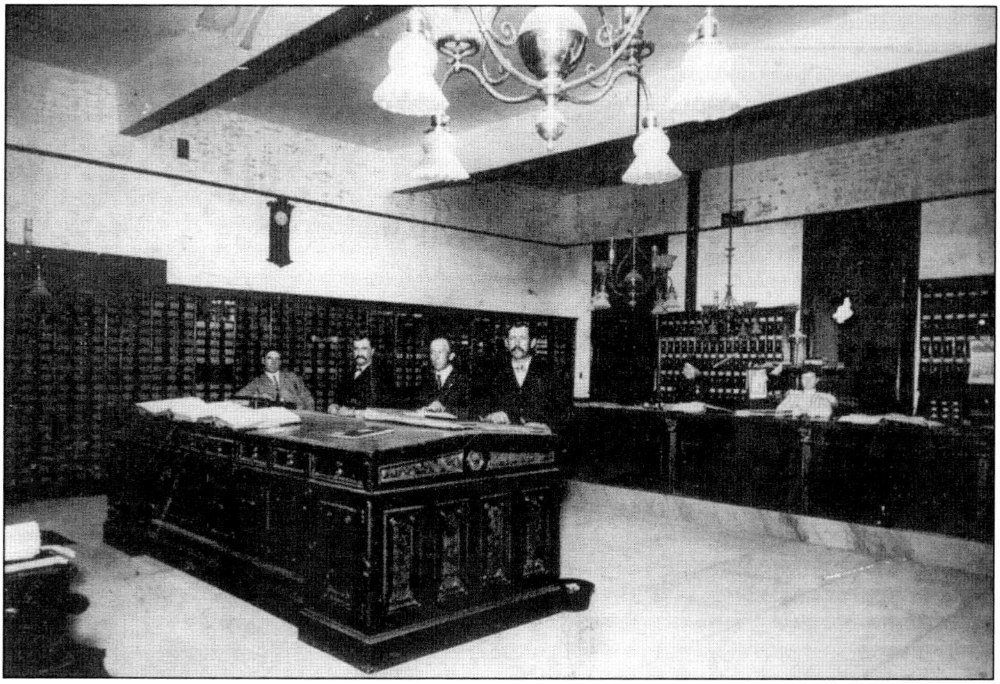

County Assessor's Office, c. 1900. Employees are shown working on property tax rolls in the County Assessor's Office around 1900. The present office has 69 full-time employees to deal with 134,000 property parcels. (Faces of Stanislaus, Mike DeFerrari.)

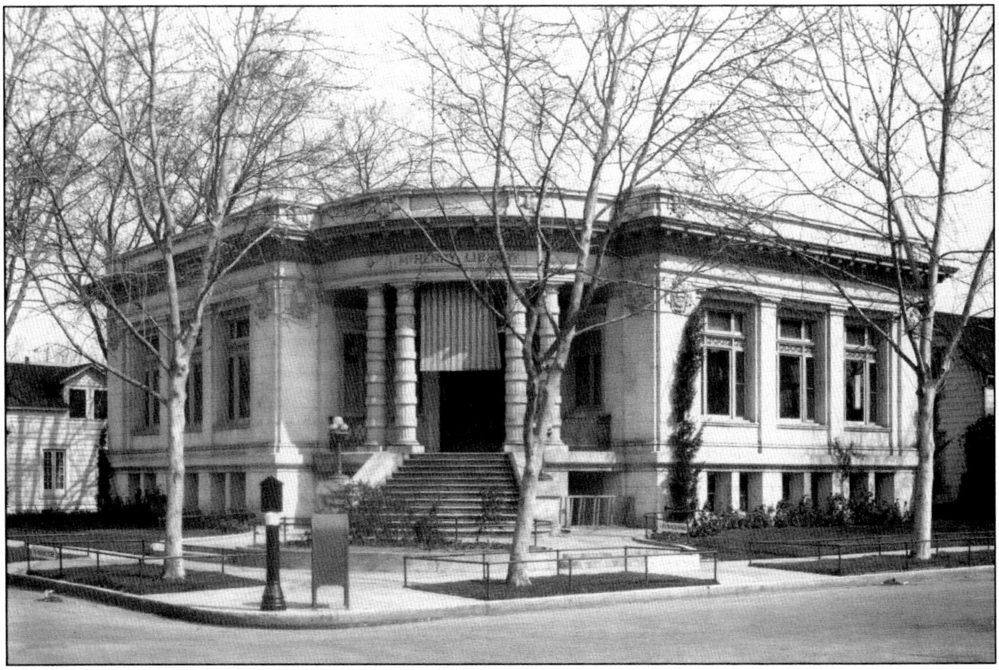

McHenry Library, c. 1912 (Above) and c. 1928 (Below). Oramil McHenry's bequest at his death in 1906 included three lots on Tenth Street and $20,000 to build a public library for Modesto. When Tenth Street was found to be too noisy and busy for a library, the lots were sold and property was purchased at Fourteenth and I Streets. W. H. Weeks was hired as architect for the new building and Robert Trost as contractor. Both were from San Francisco. The neoclassical-styled building was constructed for $22,500 with an additional $3,000 for furnishings. The library was dedicated on April 29, 1912. In 1927–1928, an addition to the library doubled its size, as seen below. When a new Modesto-Stanislaus Library was built down the street from the McHenry Library in 1971, the old library became the McHenry Museum.

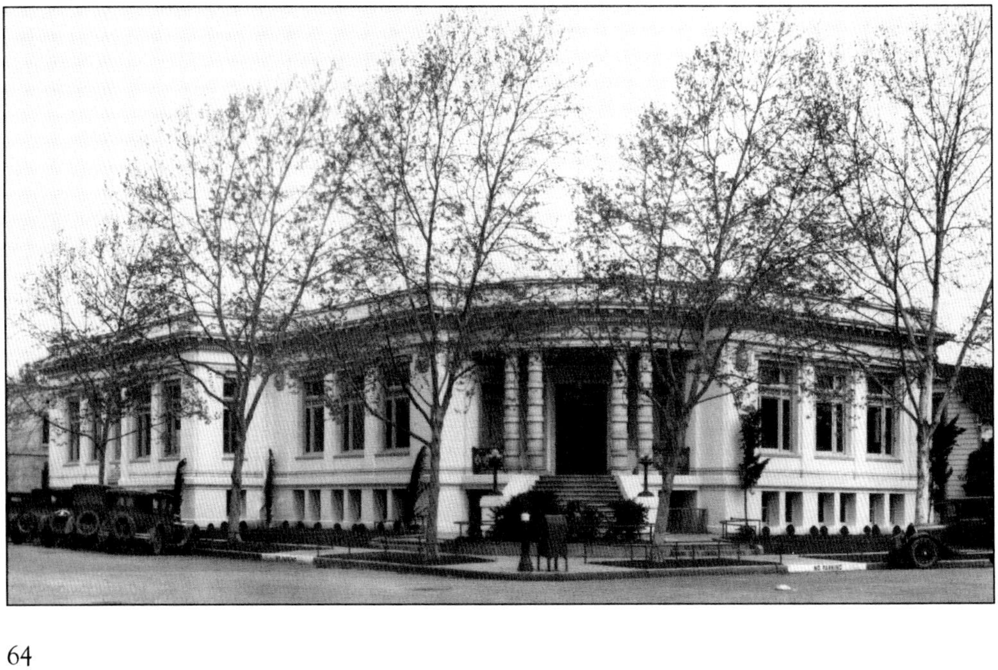

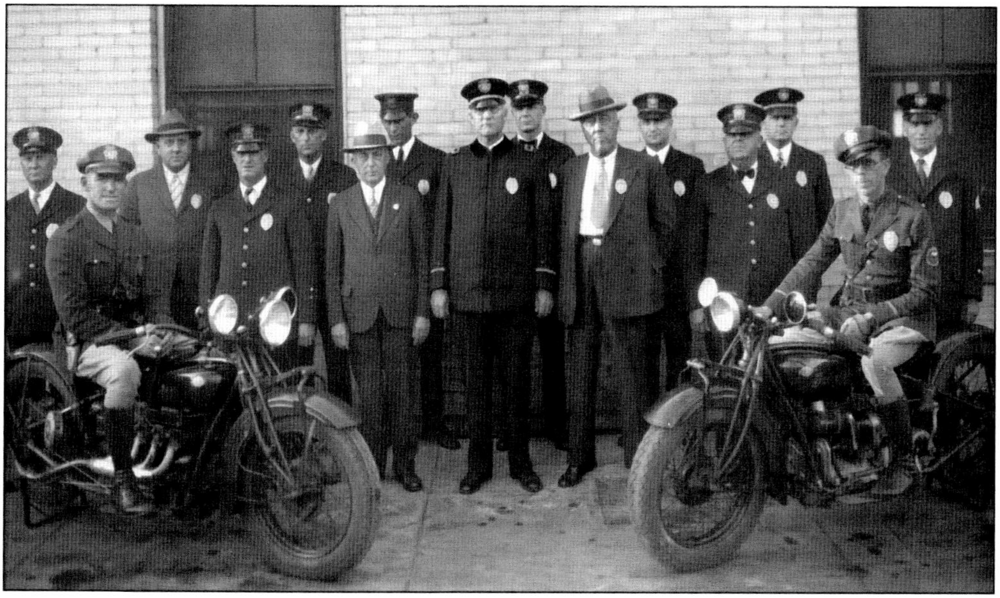

MODESTO POLICE, C. 1930 (ABOVE) AND C. 1938 (BELOW). Looking very much as they should for this time period, members of the Modesto Police Department are shown with Mayor Sol P. Elias (at left with light hat). This photograph was taken in front of City Water Pumping Station No. 4. The photograph below shows the entire motor pool of the police department at 614 Tenth Street in 1938. According to Robert Gauvreau, the 1937 Plymouth (left) and the 1934 DeSoto (center) were patrol cars; the 1935 Studebaker on the right was the chief's car. Seated on the brand-new Harley-Davidsons are, from left to right, Ed Russell, Oscar Orvis, and Clayton Green. The top floor of this building housed the City Engineer's Office.

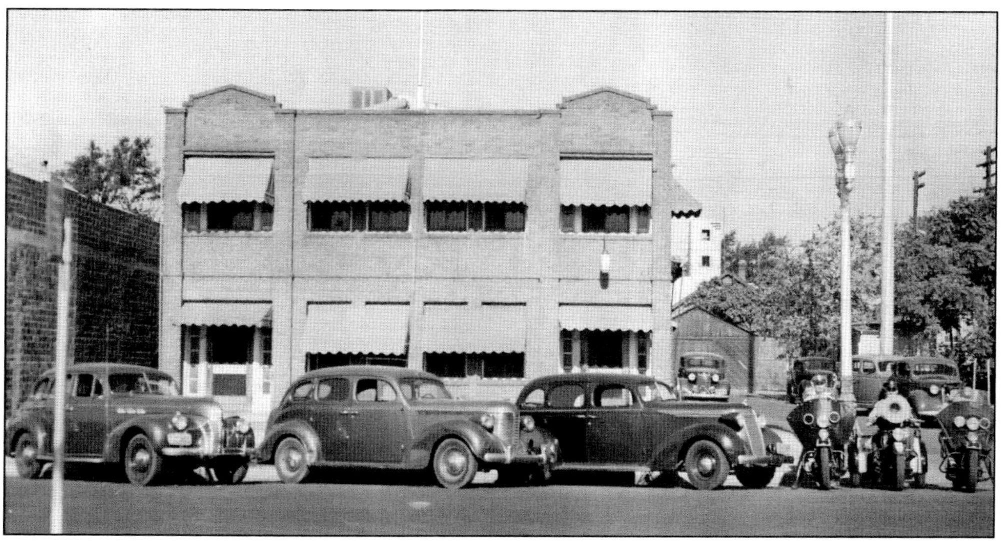

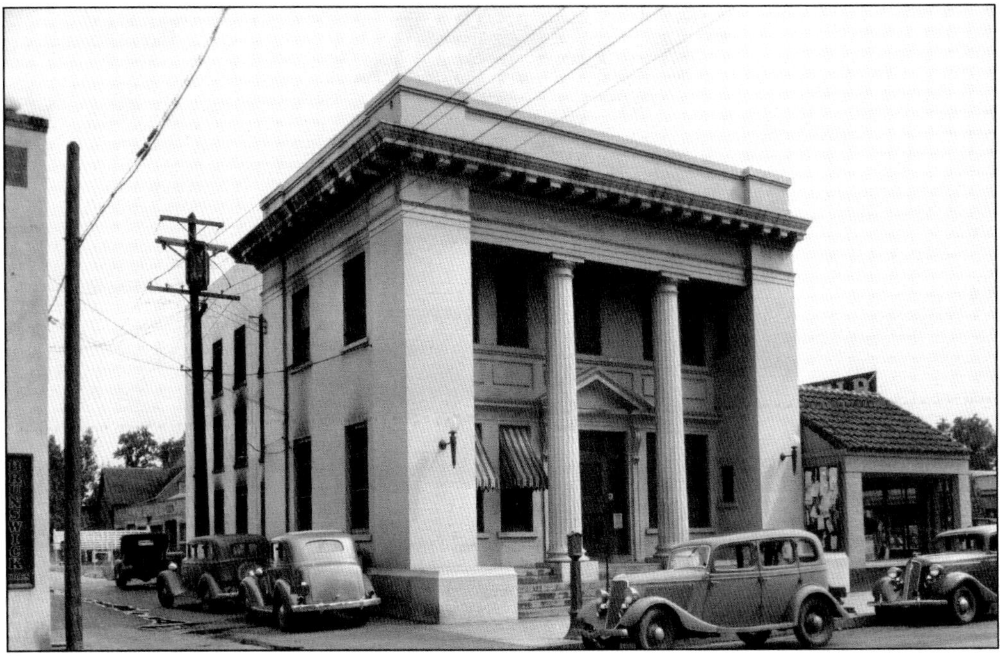

City Jail, c. 1930. This building housed the city jail and was across the street from the Stanislaus County Courthouse. The building was next to Garlock's Richfield Service Station on H Street. It was eventually demolished to make room for the Stanislaus County Administration Building, now the home of the county schools office.

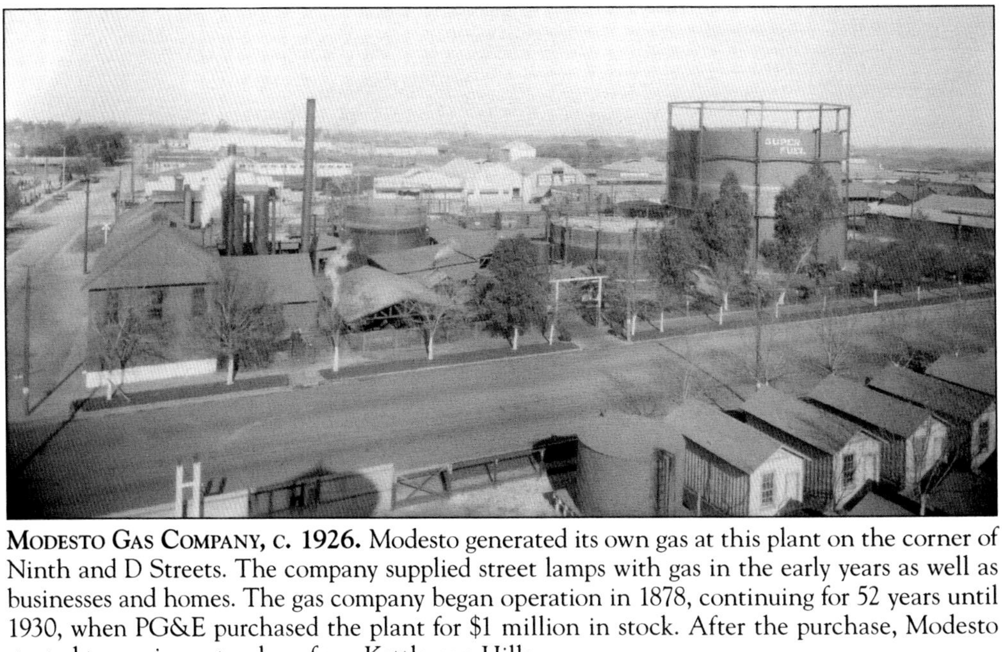

Modesto Gas Company, c. 1926. Modesto generated its own gas at this plant on the corner of Ninth and D Streets. The company supplied street lamps with gas in the early years as well as businesses and homes. The gas company began operation in 1878, continuing for 52 years until 1930, when PG&E purchased the plant for $1 million in stock. After the purchase, Modesto started to receive natural gas from Kettleman Hills.

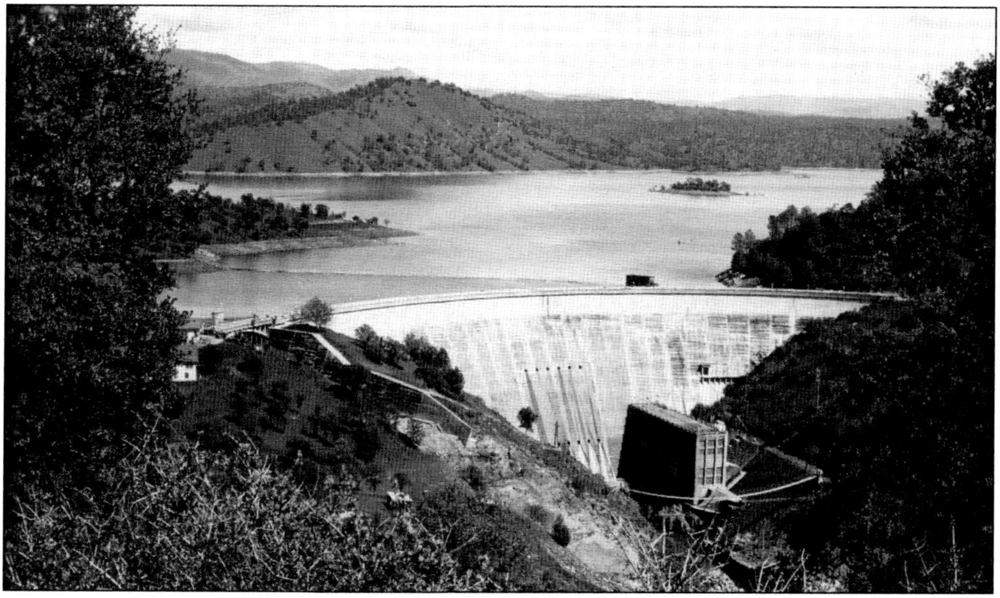

DON PEDRO DAM, C. 1923. Built jointly by the Modesto and Turlock Irrigation Districts at a cost of $3,724,000, Don Pedro Dam was dedicated on June 25, 1923. The powerhouse at the dam cost an additional $1,140,340. The dam was as tall as an 18-story building. With the generation of electricity, the first MID electric meter went into service in October 1923, according to historian Colleen Stanley Bare.

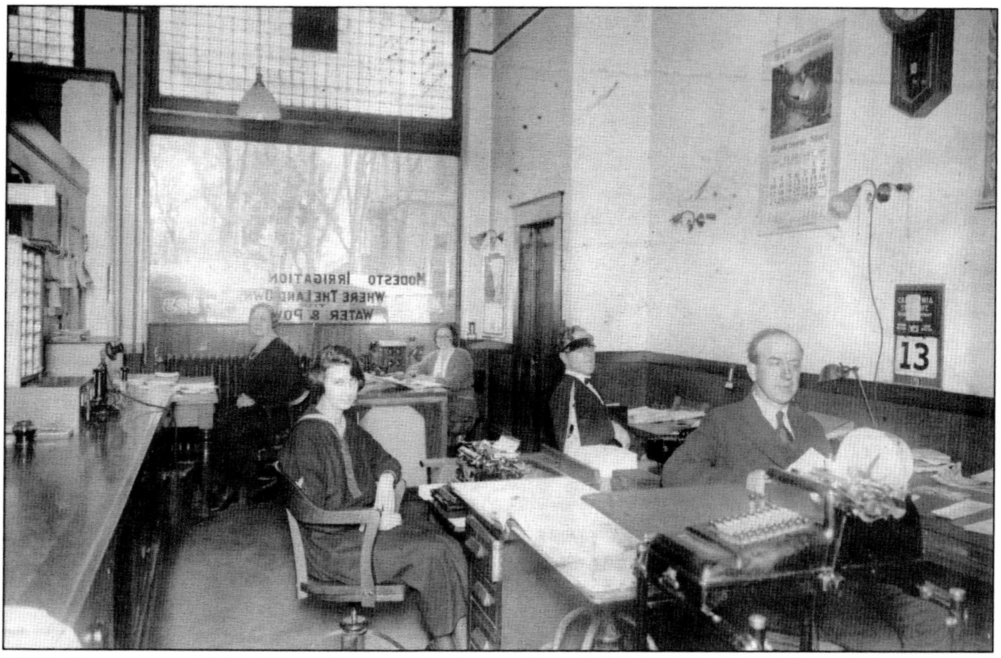

MID OFFICES, C. 1923. This photograph shows the Modesto Irrigation office staff when Don Pedro Dam was completed. Written on the window is MID's slogan, "Where the Land Owns the Water and Power." Early career woman Mary Rasmussen (center), a 1923 Modesto High School graduate, is shown at work. She attended Culpepper's Business College on I Street and worked for the irrigation district until 1928. (Faces of Stanislaus, Robert Courtney.)

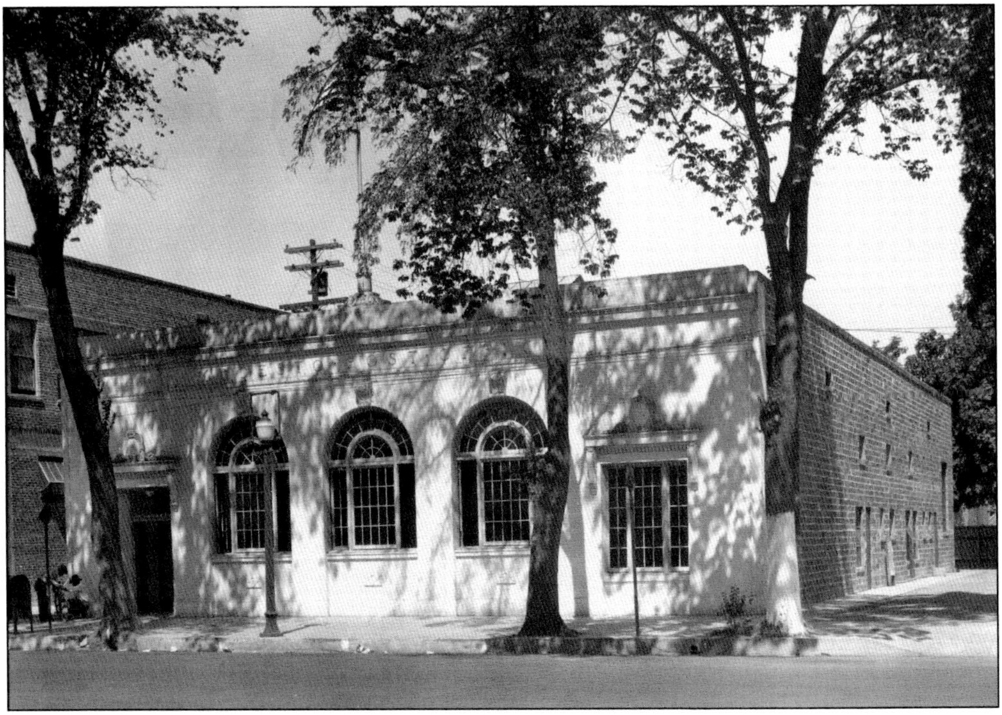

Modesto Post Office, c. 1926 (Above) and c. 1933 (Below). The post office in the above photograph was built at Twelfth and I Streets as the result of funding by the Modesto Post Office Improvement Association. Federal funding was not available. This building took 72 days to build and cost $26,000. The building was leased back to the Treasury Department and used for 10 years until a new post office was constructed on the same site. The new post office, pictured below, was a Works Progress Administration (WPA) project, designed in the Renaissance Revival style used by the government. It opened in October 1933. Cost of the new building was $195,000. This was Modesto's main post office until 1962, when the Kearny Post Office was built and this one renamed the El Viejo ("old one") Station.

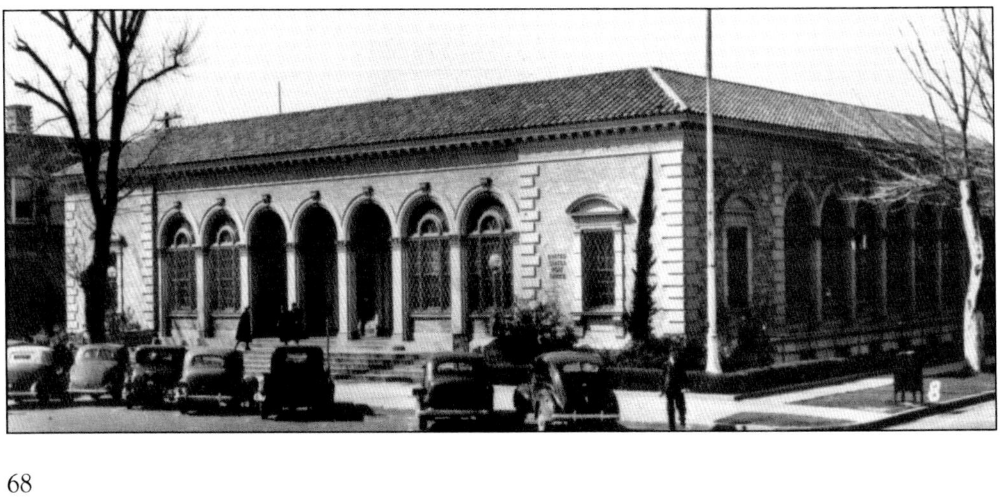

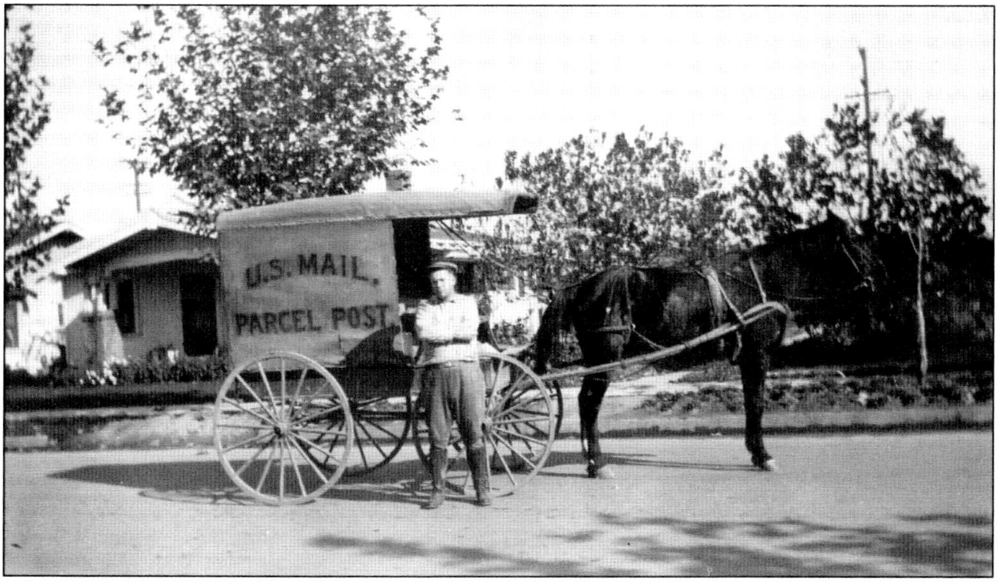

Postal Delivery Methods, 1920s. Both of these photographs were taken on the same street, but in different seasons. The above photograph offers an idea of the type of delivery vehicle used in the early years of Modesto's history. This is a horse-drawn U.S. Mail Parcel Post wagon. The photograph below shows an up-to-date motorized panel truck, Parcel Post No. 1. The photographs probably date from the 1920s by the look of the two vehicles. The person in the photographs is unidentified but postmaster during this period was Maj. D. W. Morris. Major Morris had served in the early part of the century as postmaster and then was reappointed in 1920 by Pres. Woodrow Wilson. He had also served as mayor of Modesto and was on the MID board of directors.

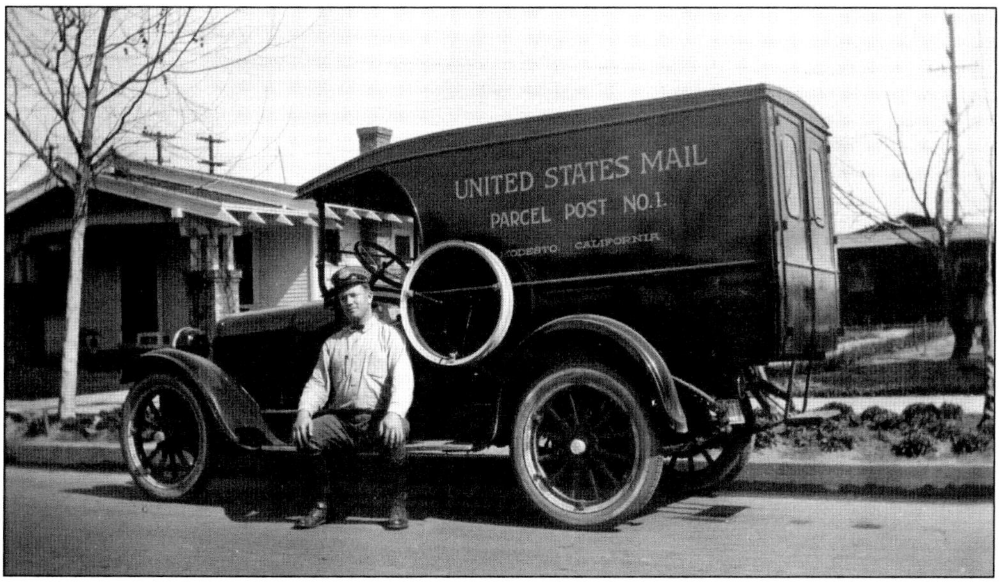

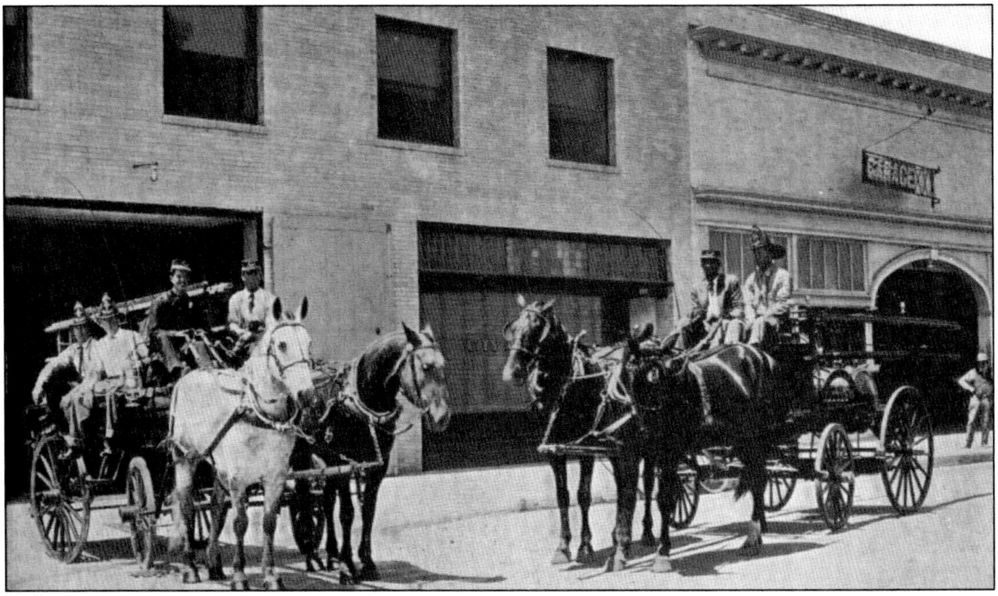

LAST FIRE HORSES, C. 1919. It was a sad story in the *Modesto Evening News* July 24, 1919: the last two Modesto Fire Department horses were being sold, replaced by a motorized fire truck. This photograph in front of the Tenth Street fire station shows four horses used by the department: Prince, Charley, Bud, and Queen. As late as 1923, a benefit dance was held to earn money to buy Prince and Charley so they could be gracefully retired.

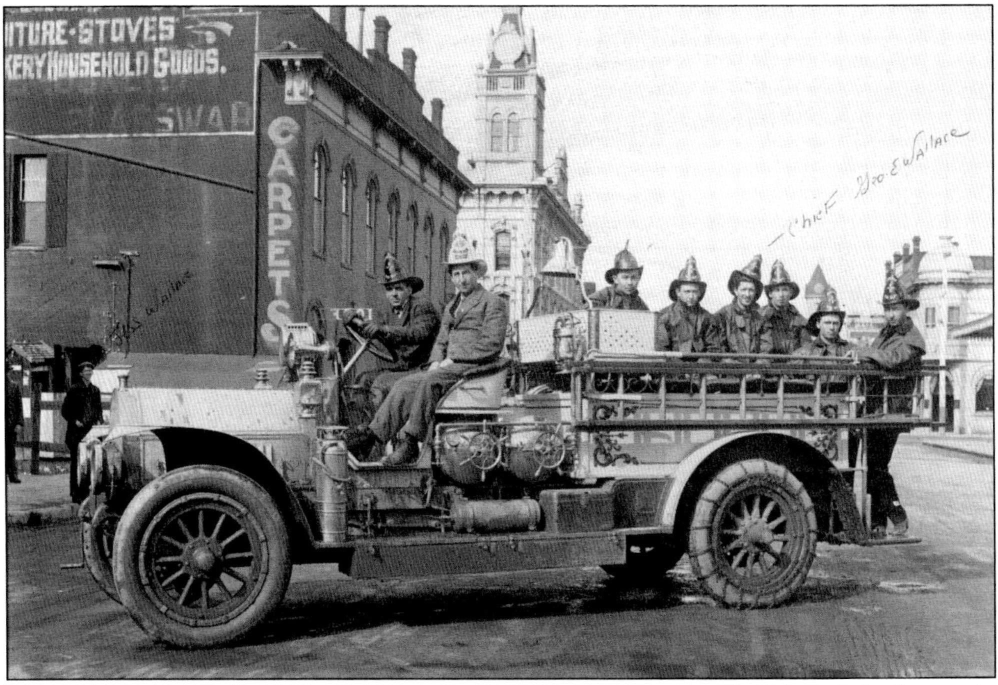

EARLY FIRE TRUCK, C. 1912. A salesman for the Seagrave Company, builders of the fire truck, is in the driver's seat. The rest of the men are part of the volunteer fire department, including future chief George E. Wallace, third from the left. At this point, there were two paid firemen and 12 volunteers.

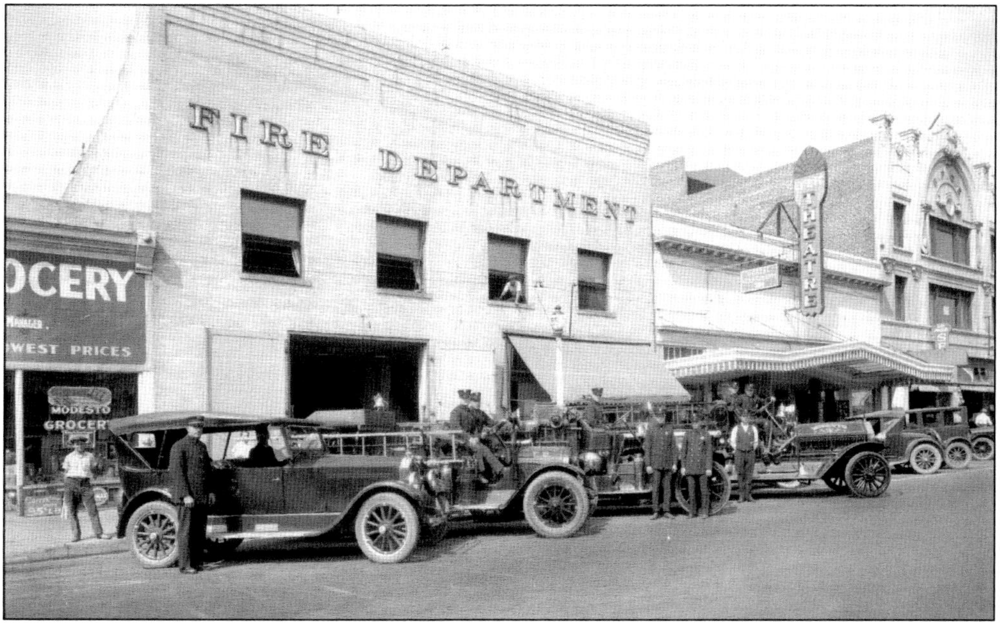

FIRE DEPARTMENT, C. 1925. The Modesto Fire Department's automobiles and fire trucks are lined up in front of the 715 Tenth Street firehouse. City offices were housed upstairs in this building, and when the fire department moved to Eleventh and F Streets, this building became city hall. Next to the firehouse is the Lyric Theatre (later known as the Esquire), which featured movies and vaudeville.

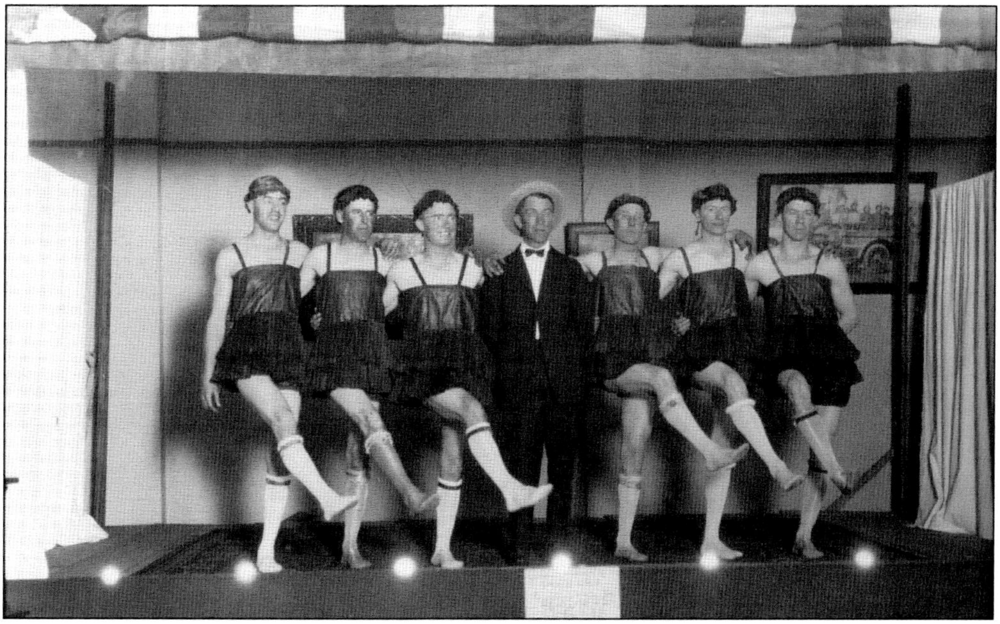

FIRE DEPARTMENT BANQUET, C. 1926. It was all in fun. Every year, the Modesto Fire Department scheduled its annual banquet and provided entertainment. This particular year's show was a little bit different. Here are members of the fire department dressed as flappers (except for the guy in the middle), performing a song-and-dance routine. This may have been at Plato's Opera House, with a makeshift stage.

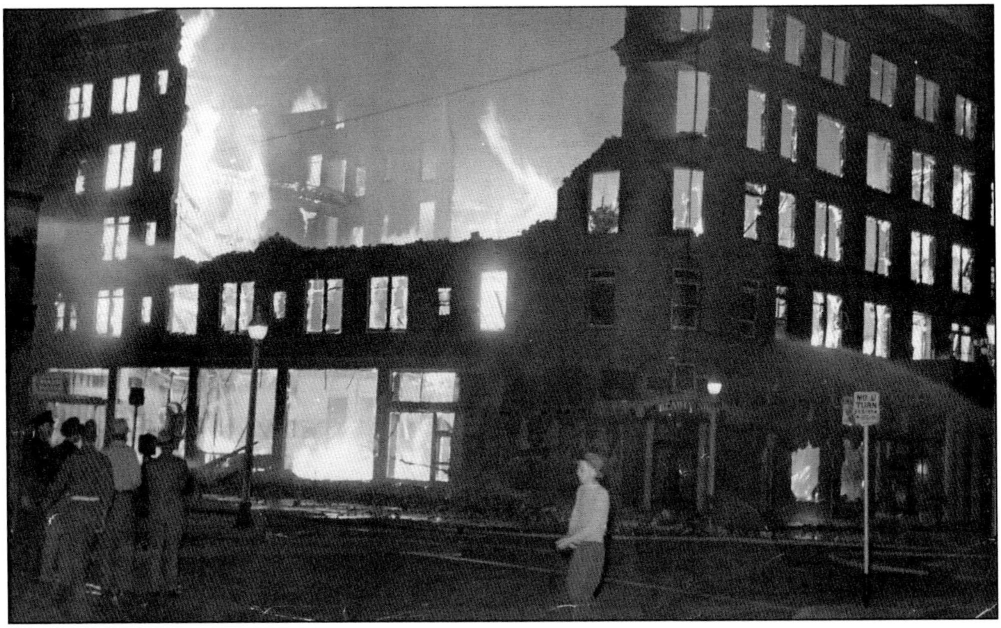

HOTEL FIRE, C. 1944. One of the biggest fires in Modesto history occurred on May 3, 1944, when the Hotel Modesto went up in flames. The building at H and Eleventh Streets had been expanded over the years and was considered one of Modesto's finest hotels. The fire started at 10:30 p.m. in the basement of the Dutch Boy paint store. Exploding paint cans, acrid smoke, and flames blocked stairways and elevators for those on the top floors. The hotel had 16 permanent residents and about 100 guests. Surprisingly there were only two fatalities as a result of the fire. One was a sailor from the Crows Landing Naval Air Station who fell five stories when he tried to grasp the top rung of a ladder. A businessman from Los Angeles died of smoke inhalation.

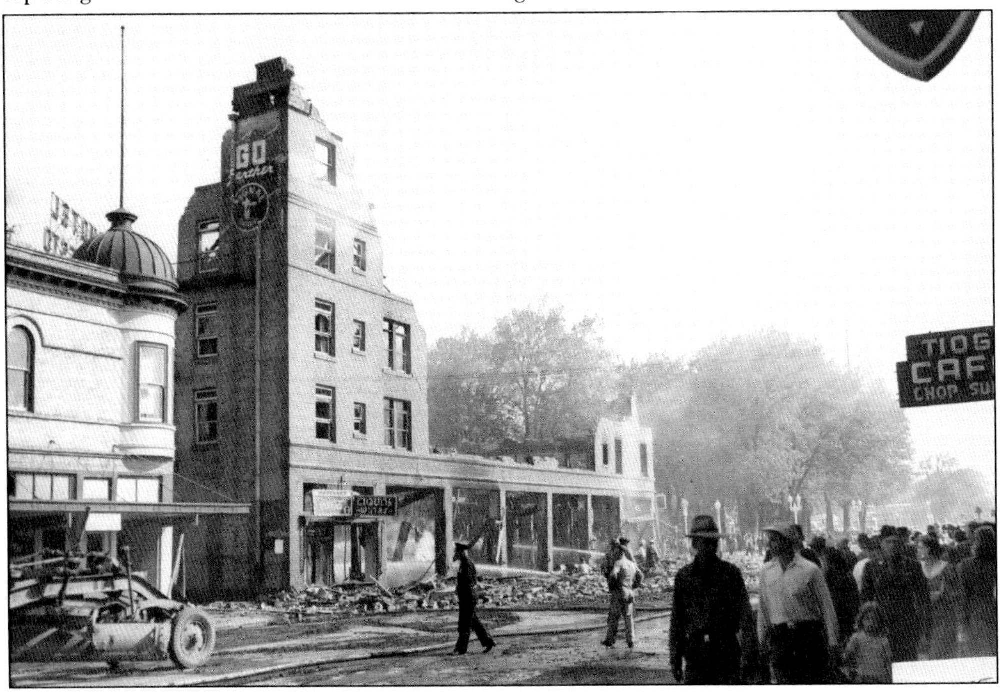

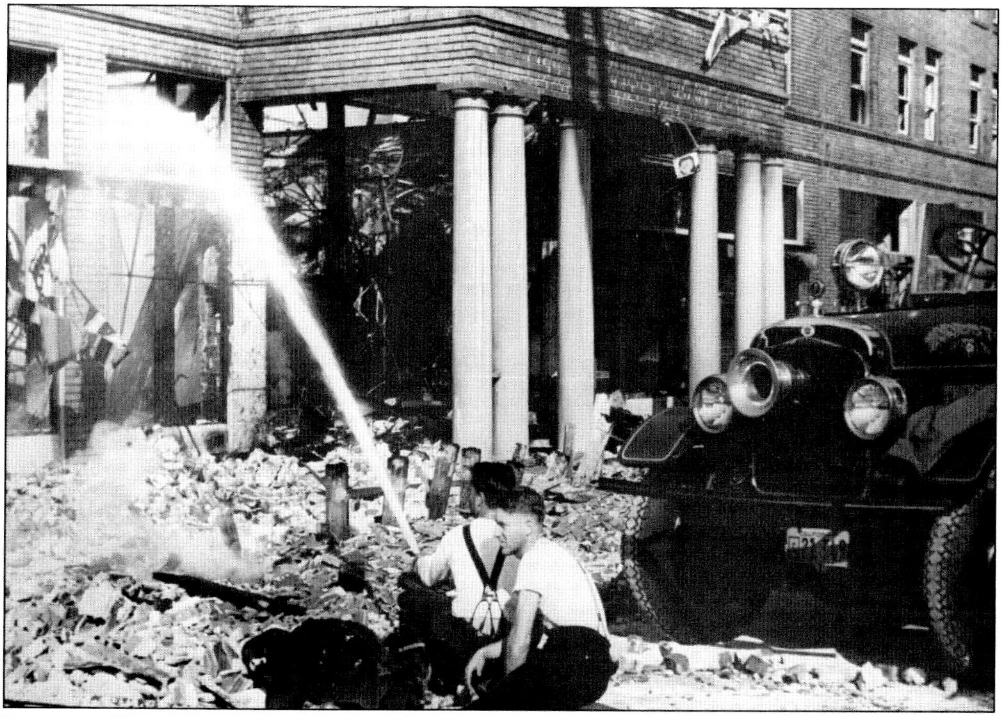

DOUSING HOT SPOTS, C. 1944. The $500,000 loss to the building and its contents included Madonna's Wine and Liquor Store with a stock valued at thousands of dollars, according to historian Colleen Stanley Bare. The next day, firemen were kept busy spraying water on the ruins of the hotel so that the fire could not restart. During the fire, sparks showered down on several nearby buildings, causing some damage. A Tenth Street meat market roof caught fire and collapsed. Some of the hotel guests had climbed out of their windows onto the roof of the *Modesto Bee* building next door on Eleventh Street. The Hotel Modesto was never rebuilt and remained a fenced-in eyesore until 1959, when the city bought the property and built a new city hall.

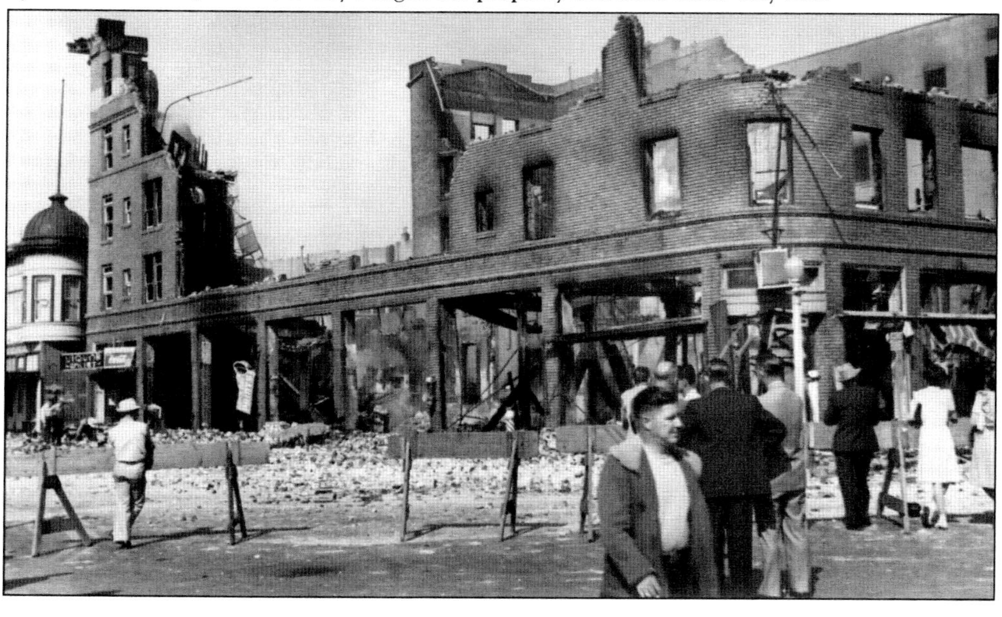

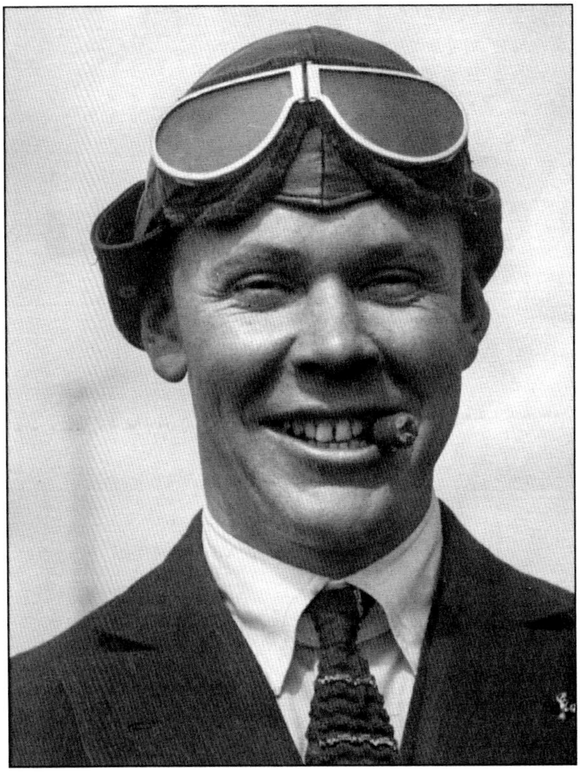

Harold L. "Bud" Coffee, c. 1921. Known as a flying "ace," Bud Coffee was an expert with airplanes, even at the young age of 19. He passed the examination for a first lieutenant commission in the aviation corps in San Francisco in 1917 and was one of the youngest commissioned officers in the corps. After the war, he was an instructor at Rockwell Field near San Diego. Coffee was a member of one of Modesto's pioneer families.

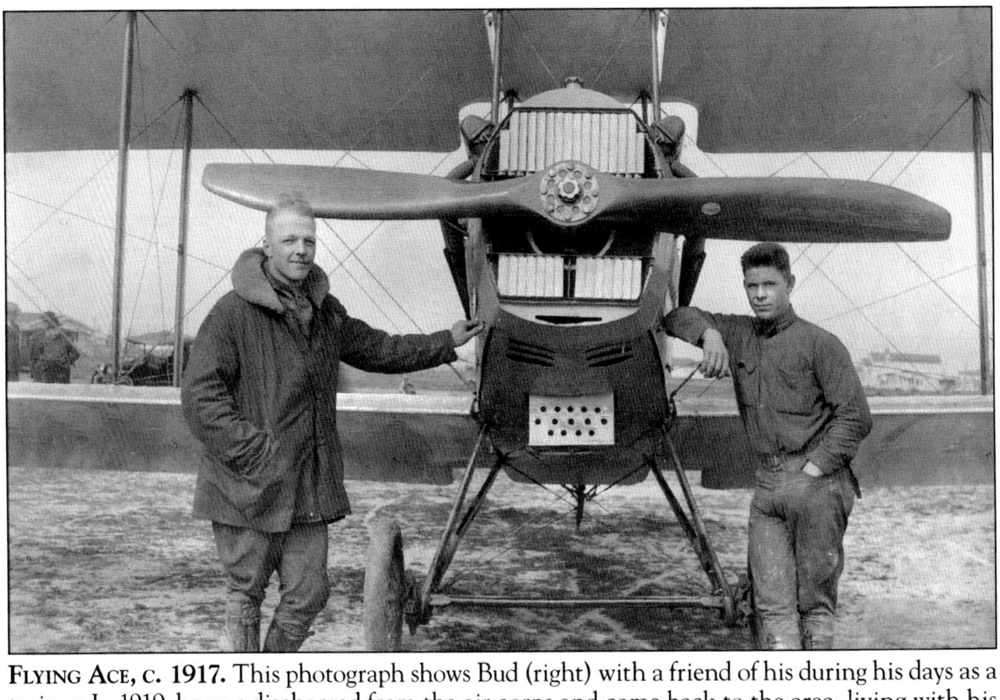

Flying Ace, c. 1917. This photograph shows Bud (right) with a friend of his during his days as a trainer. In 1919, he was discharged from the air corps and came back to the area, living with his parents, Mr. and Mrs. Lou Coffee of Oakland. He continued his flying exploits in and around Modesto, offering lessons, flights, and passenger service for anyone who wanted to fly.

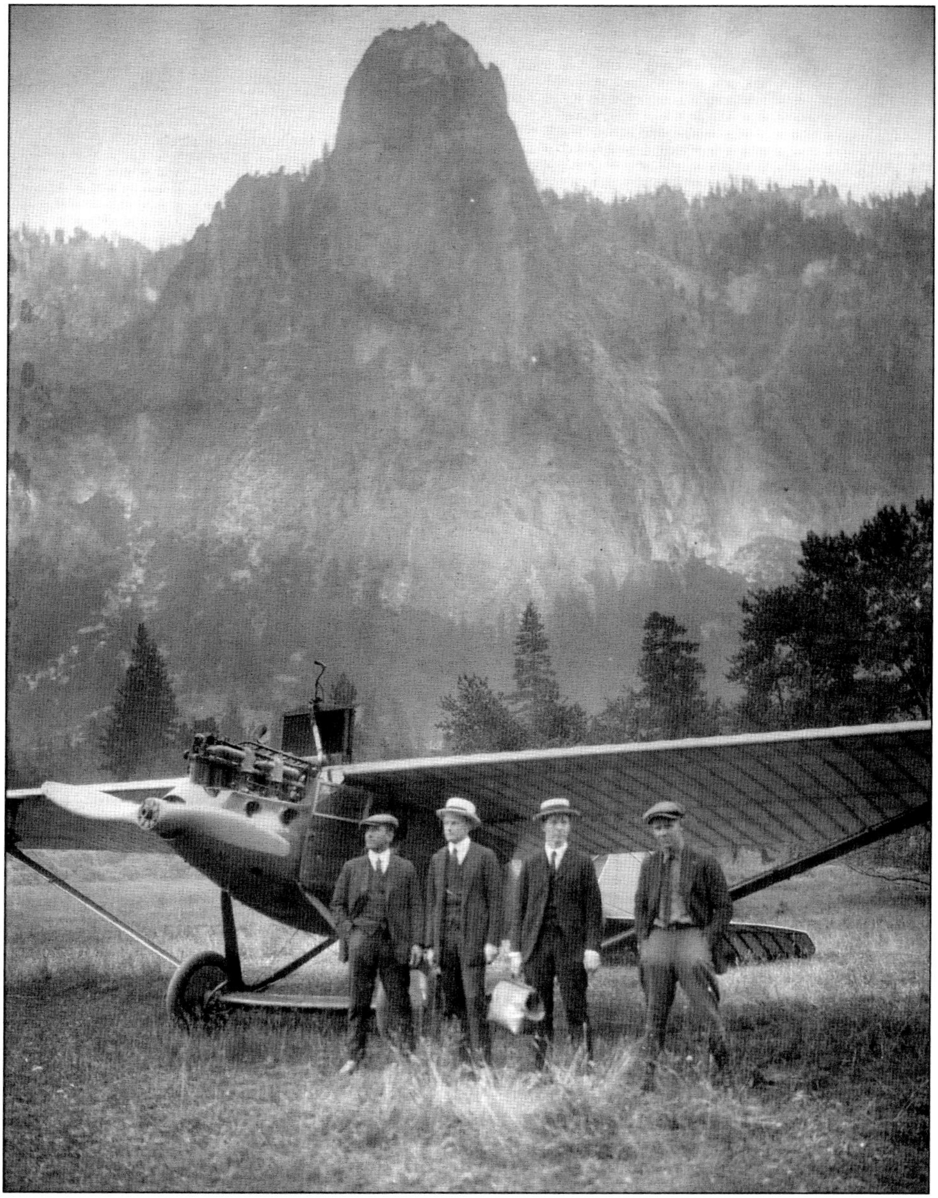

TRAGIC FLIGHT, C. 1921. The idea was to establish an air route from Oakland to Yosemite Valley. The flight to Yosemite took only two hours and was a tremendous success, with regular trips "probably beginning in the spring," according to the *Oakland Tribune*. There were four men on the Jacuzzi J-7 monoplane for the return trip: Giocondo Jacuzzi, plane builder; John H. Kauke and A. Duncan McLeish, Jacuzzi employees; and Harold "Bud" Coffee, 23, pilot. A stop for lunch was planned in Modesto on the return trip. Something happened near Maze Wren Park: the plane lost its wing and fell 600 feet through electrical wires, bursting into flame and killing the four men. Later L. J. Coffee would tell the *Tribune* his son had not wanted to pilot the plane because he had just flown 4,000 miles in 10 days, including "carrying the Dempsey-Carpenter fight pictures. However he was urged to go, and considered it a duty. 'Bud' would do anything to help aviation and this was a pioneer undertaking." The camera containing this photograph was found in the wreckage.

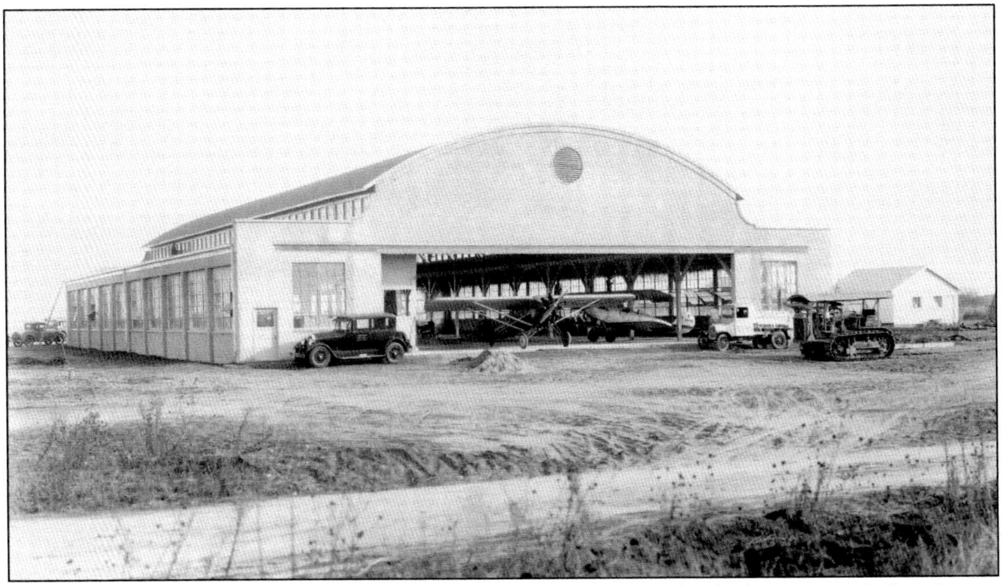

Modesto Municipal Field, c. 1930. This is an early photograph of a hanger at Modesto's new airport, which replaced "Bud" Coffee Field. Coffee Field was near Modesto High School, where the Municipal Golf Course is now located on Tuolumne Boulevard. Modesto was obsessed with flying. The first city-owned airport in the country was established on paper in 1910 when Modesto adopted a resolution to acquire land for an airport.

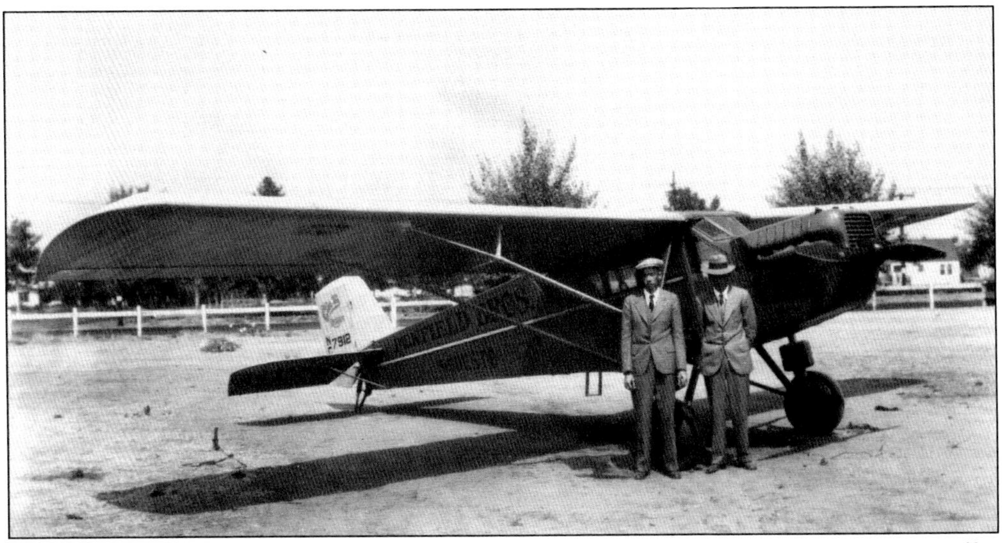

Penfield Brothers, c. 1929. John and Tom Penfield started an aviation business at Coffee Field. They built the first permanent hanger at the airport and taught Modesto's early pilots how to fly. In 1932, John was instructing Willie Porter in spin recovery when the plane had problems. Porter escaped by parachute, but Penfield, waiting until Porter cleared the cockpit, did not have time for his chute to open and was killed.

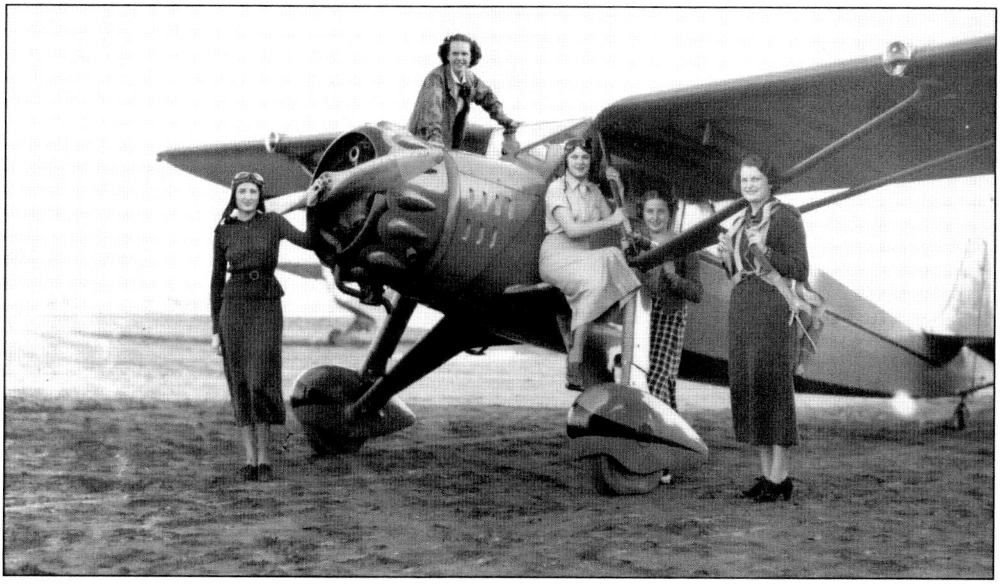

Female Fliers, Late 1930s. Flying was not just for men, as this photograph proves. There were many women who took to the air, especially trying to emulate the success of such fliers as Amelia Earhart. Pictured above are, from left to right, unidentified, Bettie Lewis, Geraldine Beach, Elaine Crow, and unidentified. This photograph was taken at Modesto Municipal Airport, now Harry Sham Field on Mitchell Road in South Modesto.

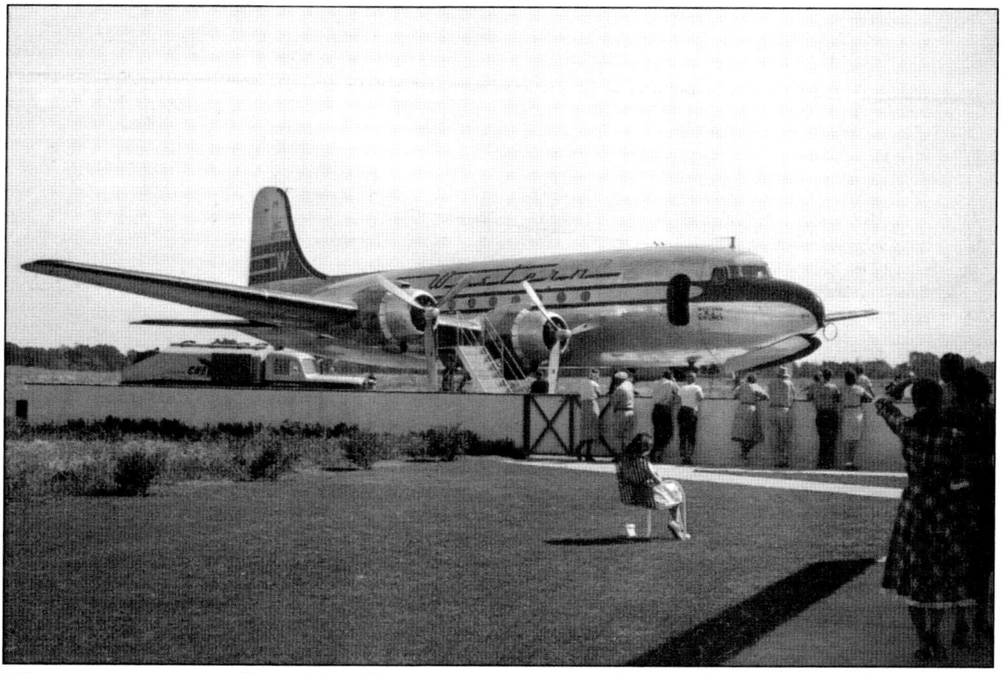

Western Airlines, 1950s. This Western Airlines DC-6B prop plane has landed at Modesto Municipal Airport. The airline served Modesto for a number of years. Western considered the DC-6B, which carried 60 passengers, to be a symbol of air service in the west—it was called "Queen of the Western Airlines Fleet." United Airlines eventually replaced Western at the airport. (J. Broome, Camera Center Collection.)

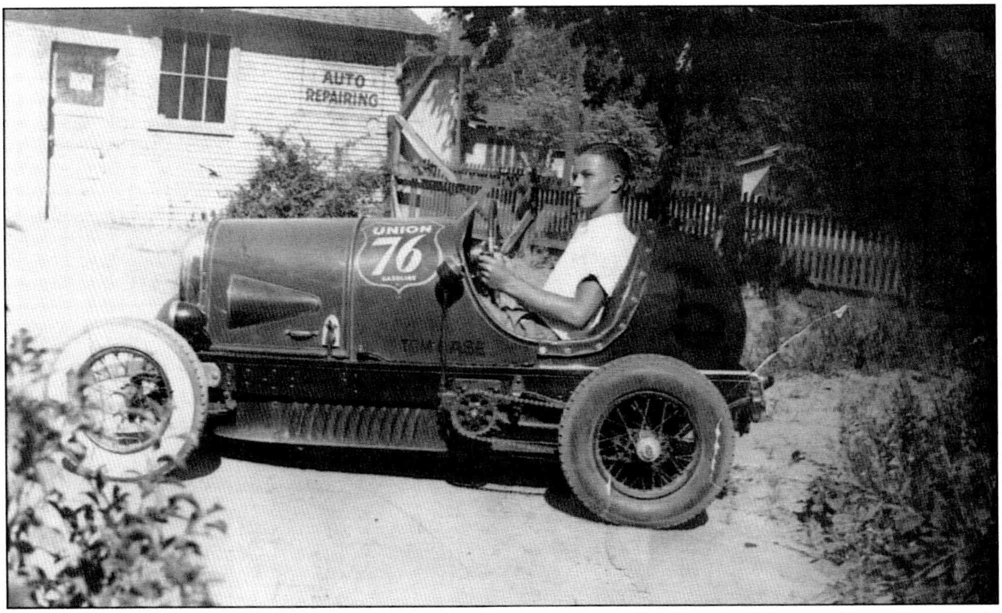

FIRST MIDGET RACER, C. 1934. This is the first midget racer built in California. Tom Case built the "midget" race car his son Larnard sits in at his auto repair shop located at Eleventh and M Streets in downtown Modesto. The car became so well known that Tom's grandson, Loren, still hears stories about it from people outside his family. (Faces of Stanislaus, Loren Case.)

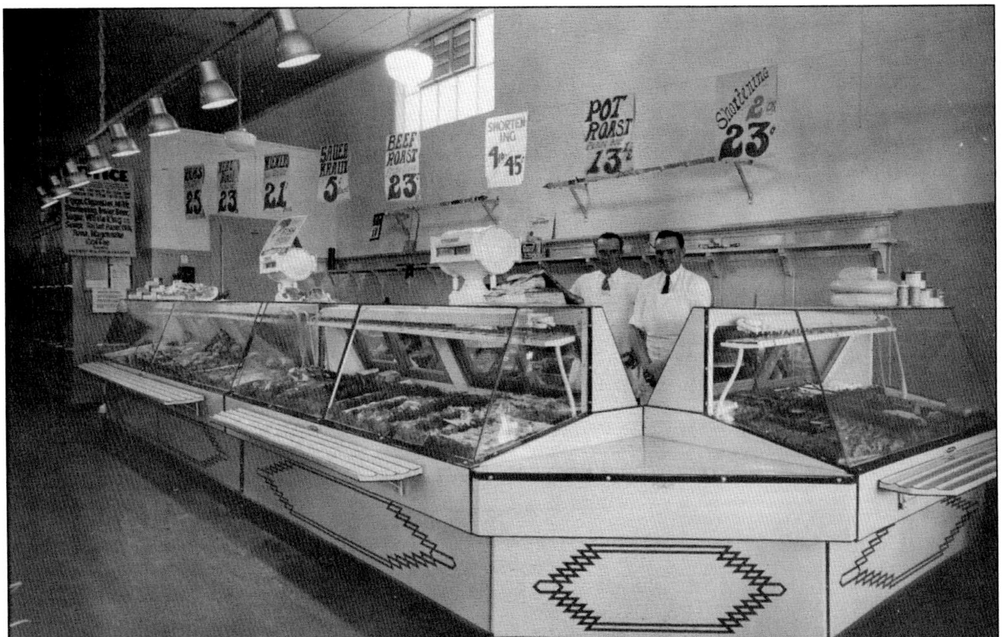

NEW SAFEWAY, C. 1937. The new Safeway grocery store opened in 1937 on H Street. This photograph shows the meat department, where the men in charge of the butcher shop are waiting for the doors to open. The man on the left is unidentified, but Clarence M. Skelly is on the right. The first customers arrived after the ribbon-cutting ceremonies. (Faces of Stanislaus, Karen Skelly.)

Five

Enriching Life in the Central Valley

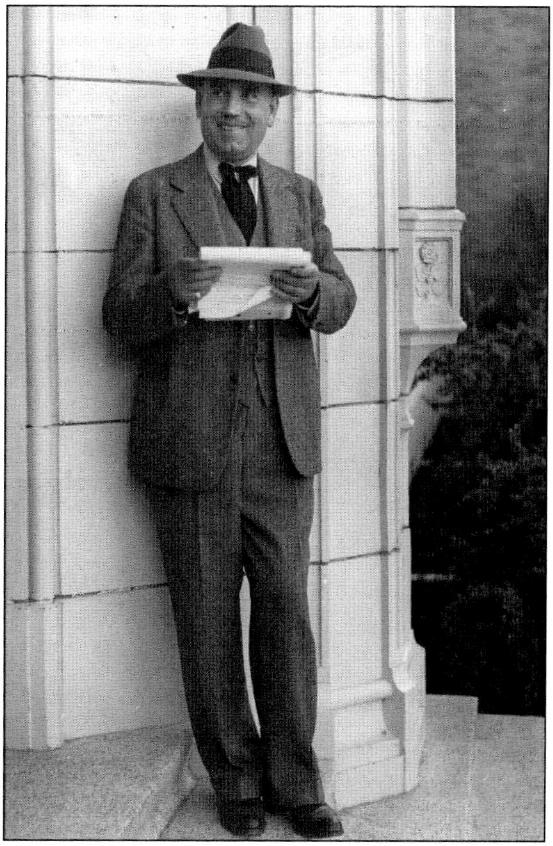

"Proof" Mancini, 1930s. Francesco Nicolo ("Frank") Mancini arrived in Modesto to perform at the grand opening of the Strand Theatre in 1921 and stayed the rest of his life. His impact on the community was profound. He taught music at Modesto High School, consistently producing award-winning bands. He took over the Stanislaus County Band for summer concerts and helped establish the Modesto Symphony. He was truly Modesto's music man.

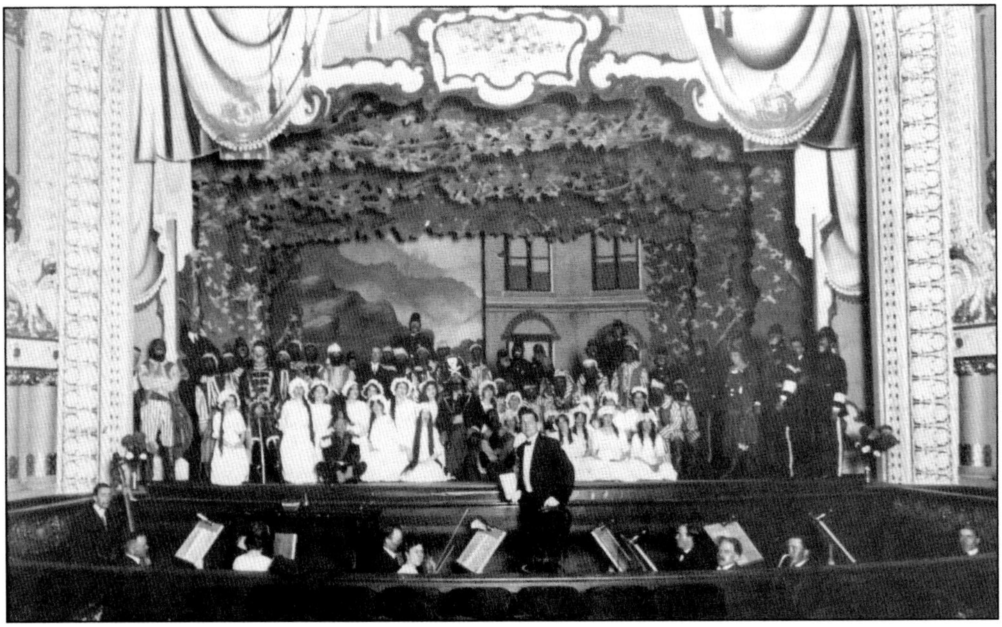

Modesto Theatre, c. 1913. This was opening night of the Modesto Theatre and its first production, *The Pirates of Penzance*, produced by the Modesto Chorale Society. Prof. Frederick J. Witcher is the conductor in the center of this *Modesto Evening News* photograph that ran February 10, 1913. The 900-seat theater was heralded as "one of the finest in the West." (Note that some cast members are in "blackface"—theatrical makeup that was prevalent at the time for white performers to give a pseudo African American appearance. While blackface is no longer an accepted form of theatrical makeup, it was in use until the 1930s in America.) The photograph below shows the theater less than a year later, after a fire, which started under the stage, destroyed the interior. Owner William B. Mensinger rebuilt the theater almost immediately.

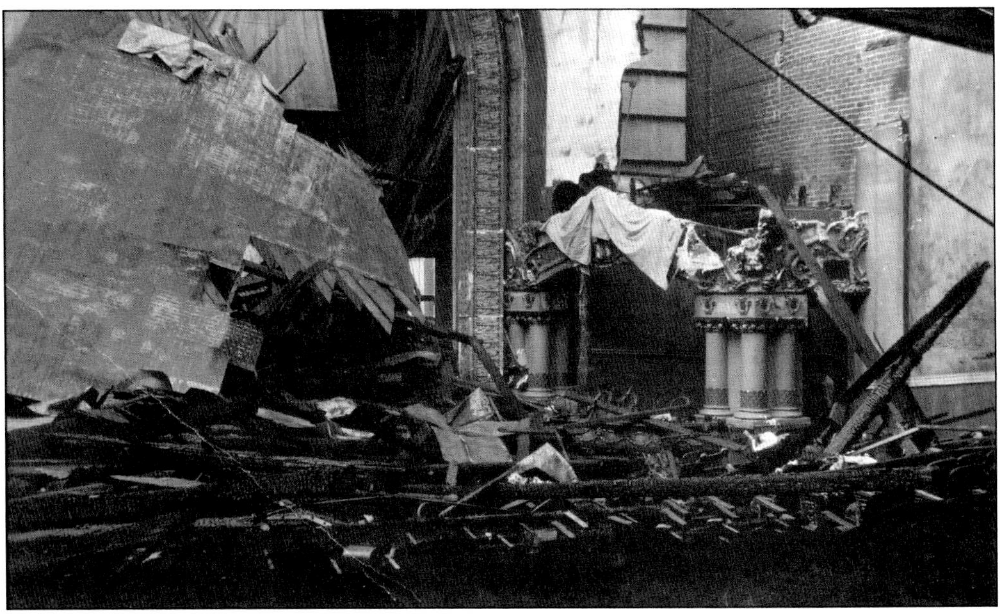

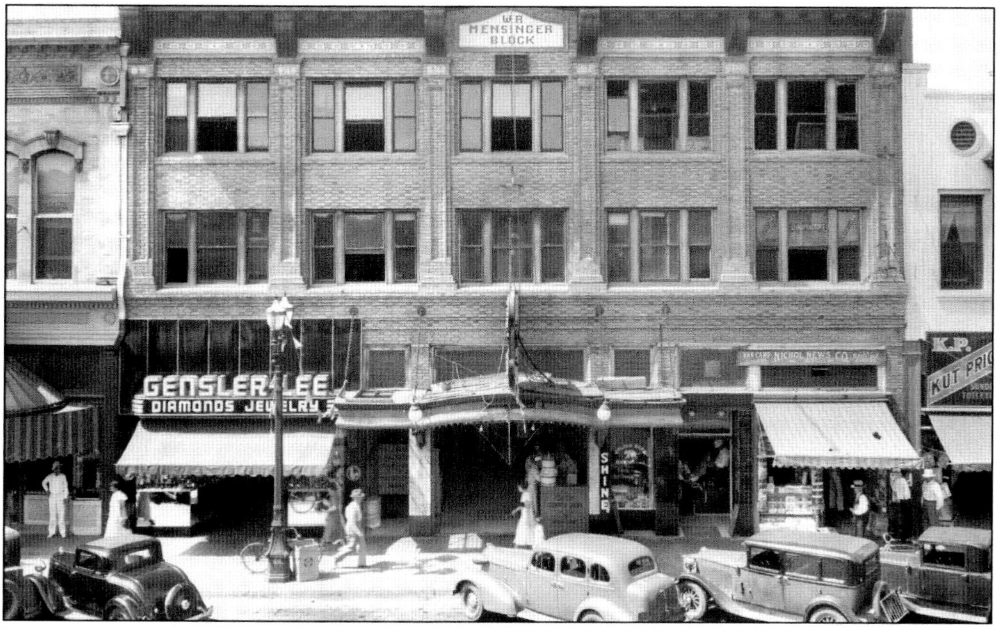

Modesto Theatre Exterior, c. 1936. This photograph of the Modesto Theatre shows the exterior of the three-story building. Used over the years for plays and movies, the building still stands in downtown Modesto, though it is empty and devoid of its theatrical trappings. In the long run, the Modesto Theatre faced too much competition from other newer theaters in the downtown area. For many years, the building served as a storefront after its closure.

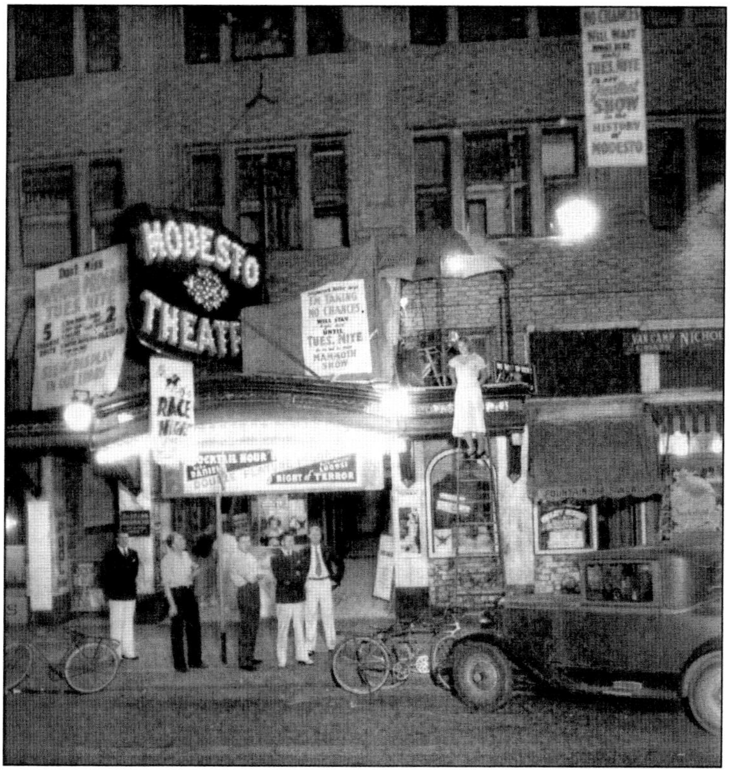

Nighttime Promotion, 1933. With a film called *I'm Taking No Chances*, it seems that the promoters at the Modesto Theatre are doing just the opposite. The theater building, which was called the Mensinger Block, is decked out in banners and lights to attract customers. A double bill is being advertised as well, with Bela Lugosi in *A Night of Terror* and *Cocktail Hour* with Bebe Daniels.

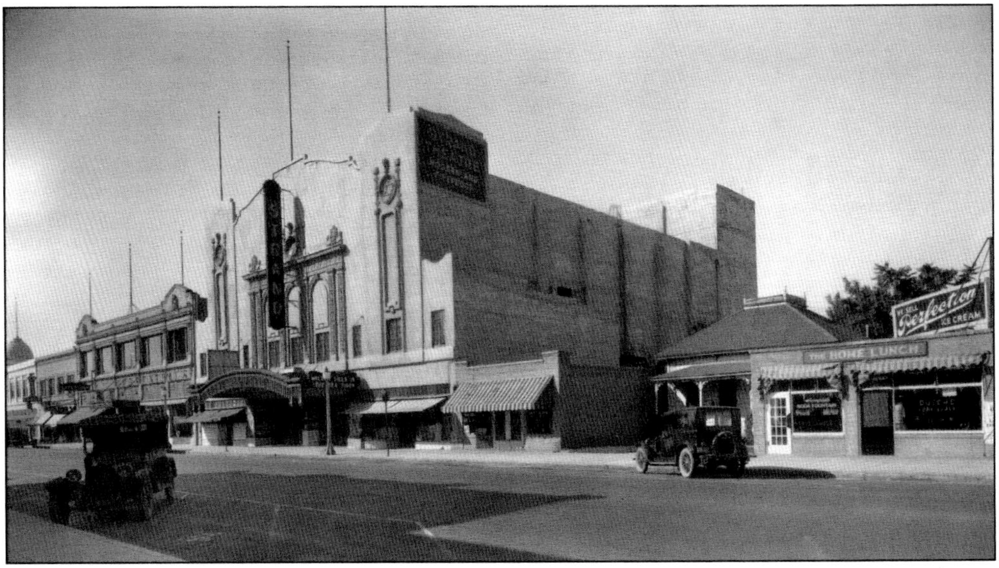

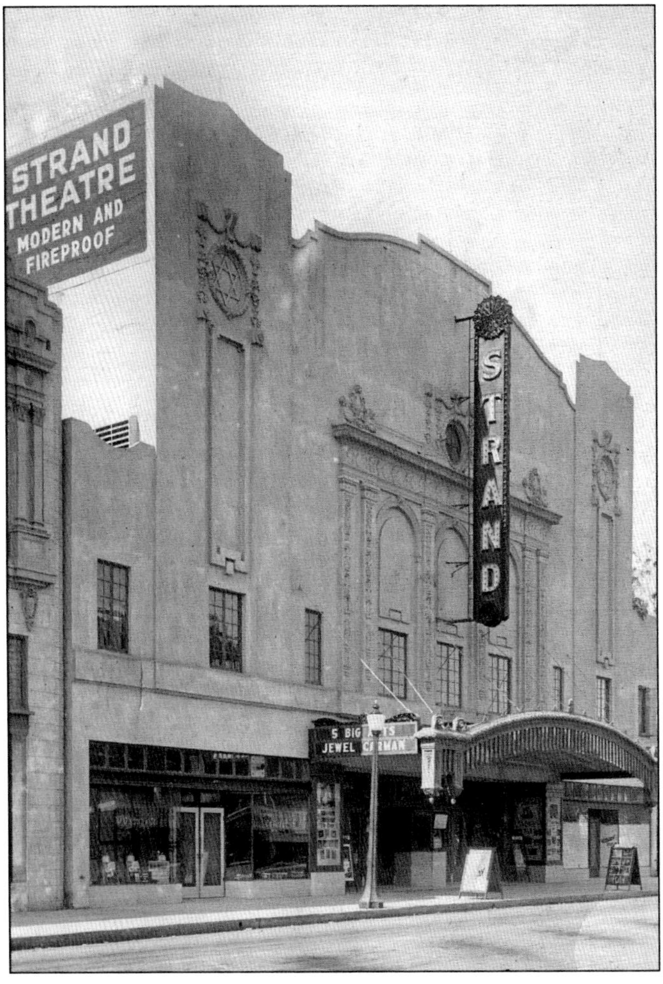

The Strand, 1920s. This was Modesto's grandest movie palace. The photograph above shows the theater at 1021 Tenth Street in 1927, with the silent movie *The Sea Witch* playing. To the left of the theater is Rosenthal's Department Store, later Montgomery Ward. The Strand cost $250,000, seated 1,500, and had plush carpeting, crystal chandeliers, and lobby murals as well as a large Wurlitzer organ. Designed and built by Reid Brothers of San Francisco, the theater offered movies, plays, and concerts. At left is another angle of the front of the building in the 1920s, advertising five big acts and a movie with Jewel Carman [*sic*]. The Strand closed in 1971 and, no longer modern or fireproof, burned in 1984. The site of the Strand is now home to the Brenden Theatres 18-screen multiplex. (Above, J. Broome, Camera Center Collection; left, McHenry Museum.)

The State, c. 1937. Designed by S. Charles Lee, famed movie theater architect, the State Theatre shows off its art deco exterior at night at right. The State was built as a movie theater without a stage. Located at 1307 J Street, it opened on Christmas Day 1934. When the theater opened with Dick Powell and Ruby Keeler in *Flirtation Walk*, the movie played continuously from 9:30 a.m. until midnight. General admission was 35¢. Of particular note was the fact that the State Theatre was air-conditioned. Banners proclaimed that the movie house was "cooled by refrigeration," a first in Modesto. As shown in the photograph below, the ticket booth was a typical freestanding kiosk. Leaping gazelles and artwork on the plaster walls highlighted the theater's interior design. (Both, J. Broome, Camera Center Collection.)

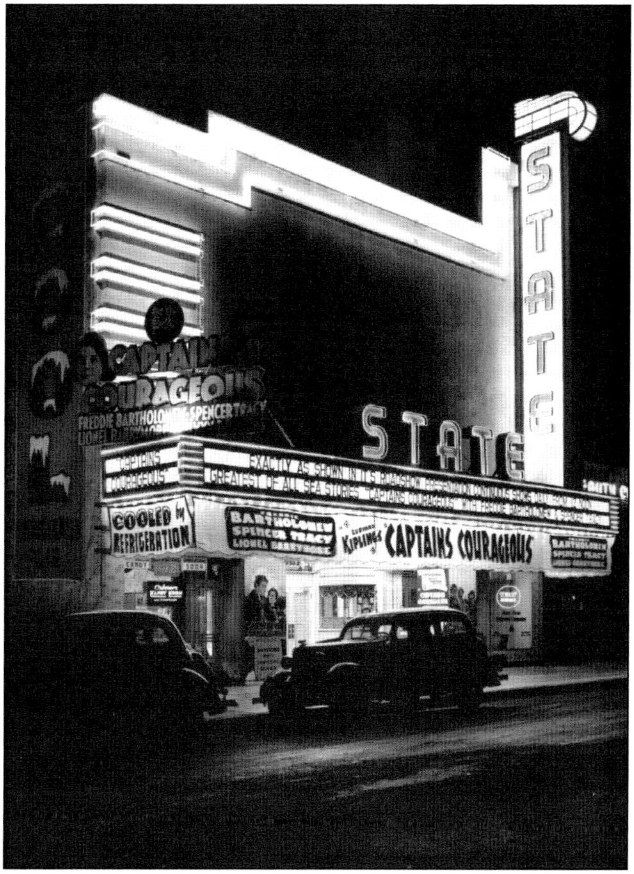

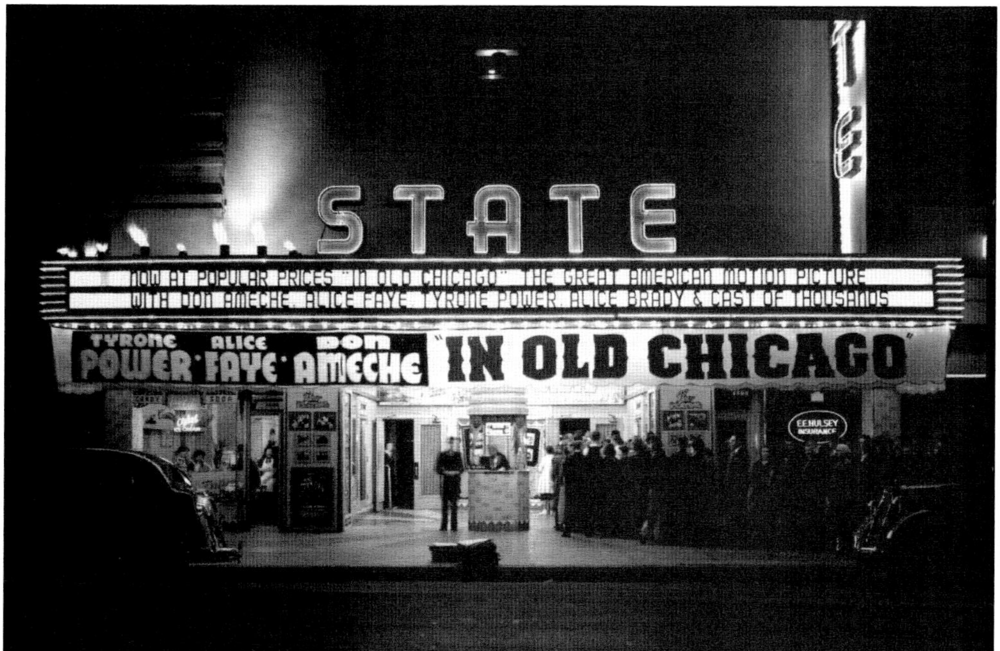

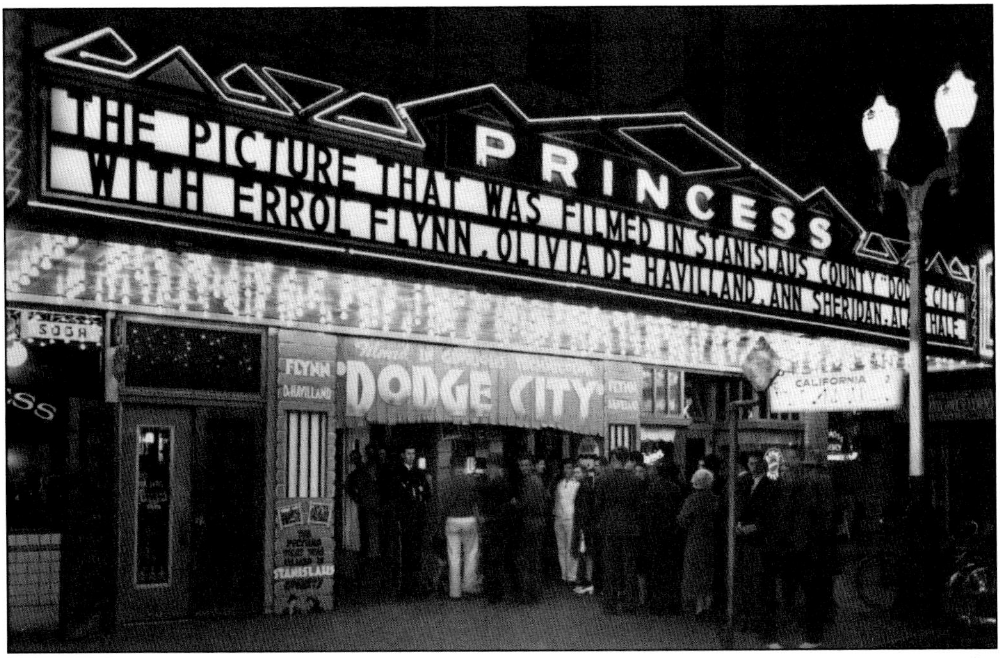

THE PRINCESS, C. 1939. While it was being built in 1924, newspaper articles referred to it as the Richards Theatre. Attached to the Hotel Covell, it was known as the National Theatre for several years before being renamed the Princess. In later years, it was the Covell Theatre and infamously featured x-rated films. This photograph shows people in line to see locally filmed *Dodge City*. (J. Broome, Camera Center Collection.)

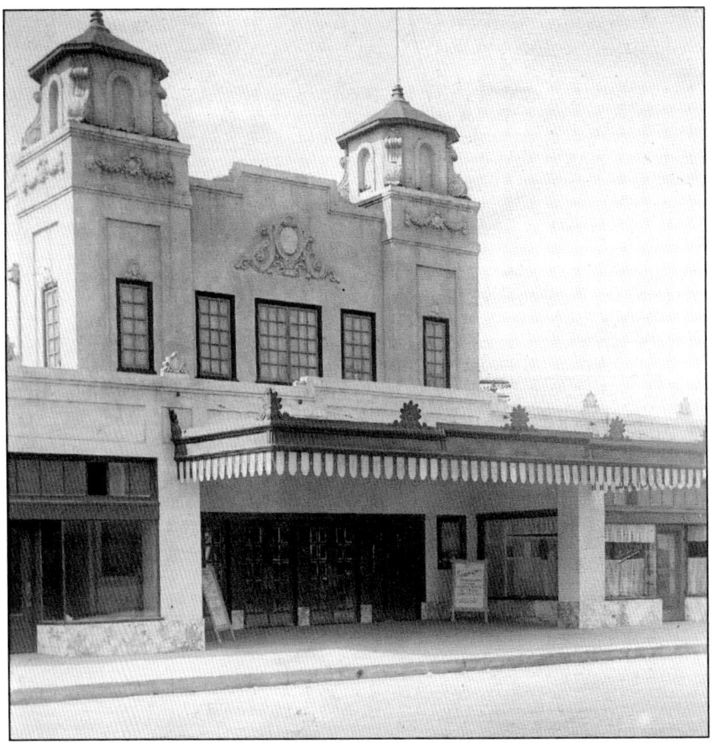

WINTER GARDEN, C. 1921. A dance hall or ballroom, the Winter Garden was a grand place for an evening out. It was the site of many dances and activities during its prime. At 1125 Tenth Street, novelty bands and orchestras played and dance lessons were hot during the Roaring Twenties along with contests. The Merry Garden and California ballrooms became as popular as the Winter Garden in later years.

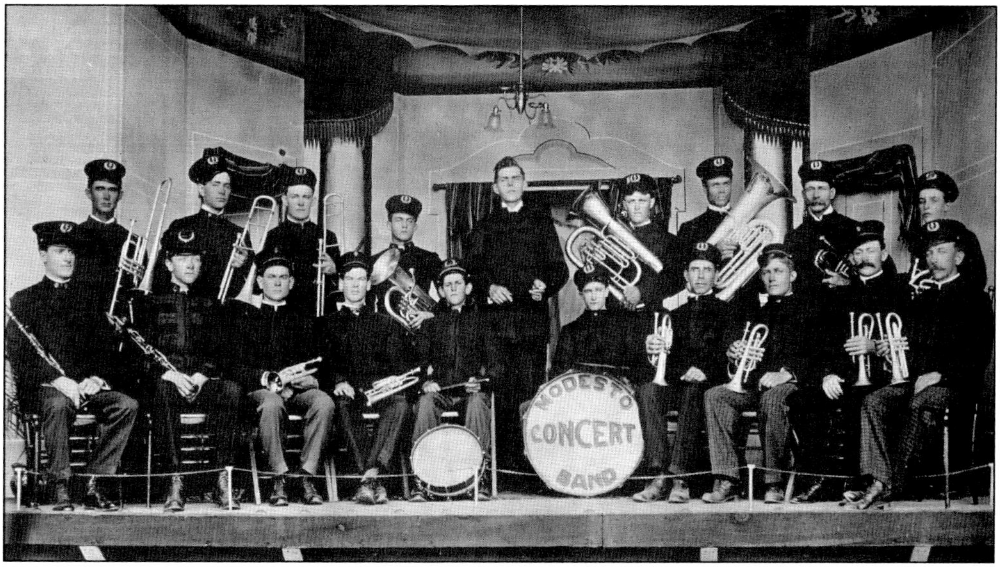

Modesto Concert Band, c. 1910. They were everywhere, music being an important commodity in turn-of-the-century Modesto. The Modesto Concert Band played in parades and for special events and provided accompaniment for dances at Rogers Hall and Plato's Opera House. There is also a newspaper report that they played at the train station when Pres. William Howard Taft came to town, accompanying him to Courthouse Park.

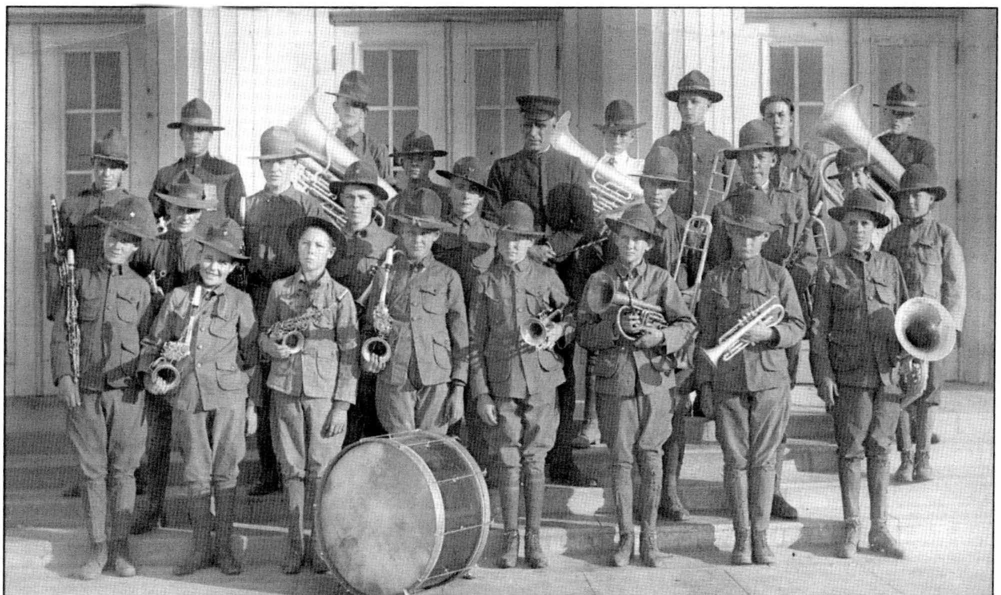

Modesto Boys' Band, c. 1921. William W. Higgins moved to Modesto in 1910 and became involved in music. In June 1919, he formed the Modesto Band, later known as MoBand. In May 1920, he recruited a group of boys to form the Modesto Boys' Band. When Higgins died in April 1922, Frank Mancini took over as director and led the Boys' Band to many band contest wins and national recognition.

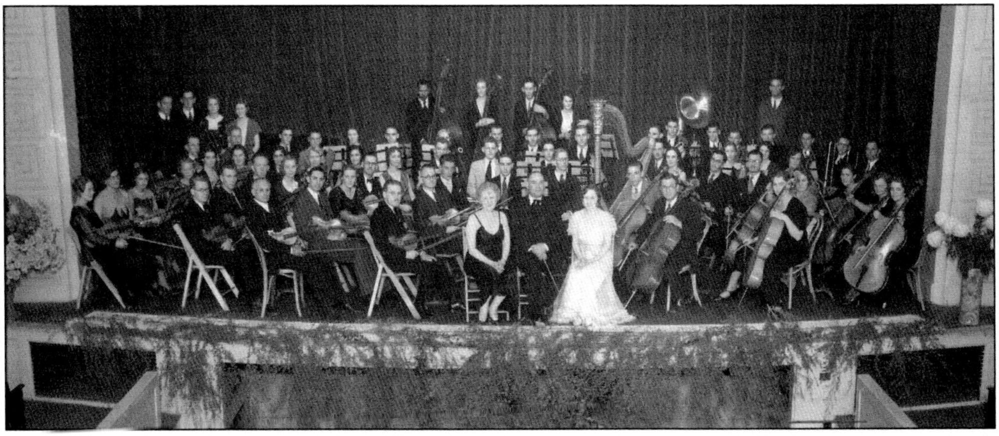

MODESTO SYMPHONY, 1930S. Frank Mancini founded the Modesto Symphony in 1929–1930 with the help of cellist Malin Langstroth and violinist Leonardo Fristrom. At 74 members strong, the symphony gave its first performance in April 1931 at the First Presbyterian Church. Mancini's successful musicianship carried over from his award-winning high school, junior college, and community bands to the symphony, which is still going strong today.

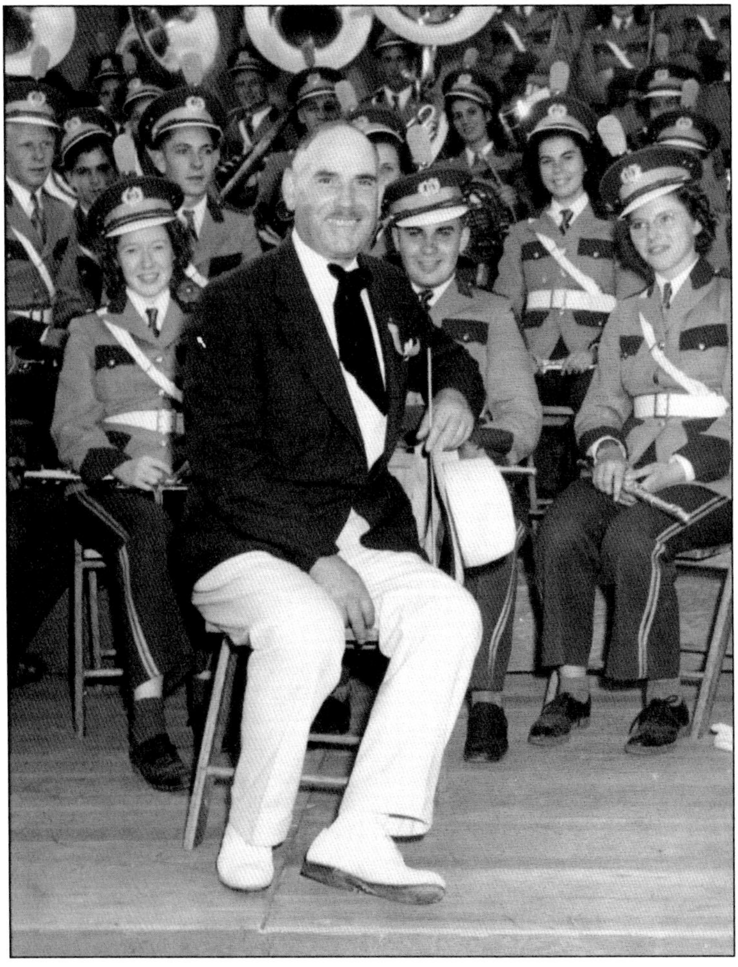

FRANCESCO ("FRANK") MANCINI, C. 1939. "Proof" Mancini is shown at the Golden Gate Exposition in San Francisco with members of the Modesto High School band. Mancini was born and educated in Italy. He was clarinet soloist and associate conductor with the Royal Italian de Vita Band before coming to the United States in 1907. In 1915, he came to San Francisco to play with John Philip Sousa's band at the Panama-Pacific Exposition.

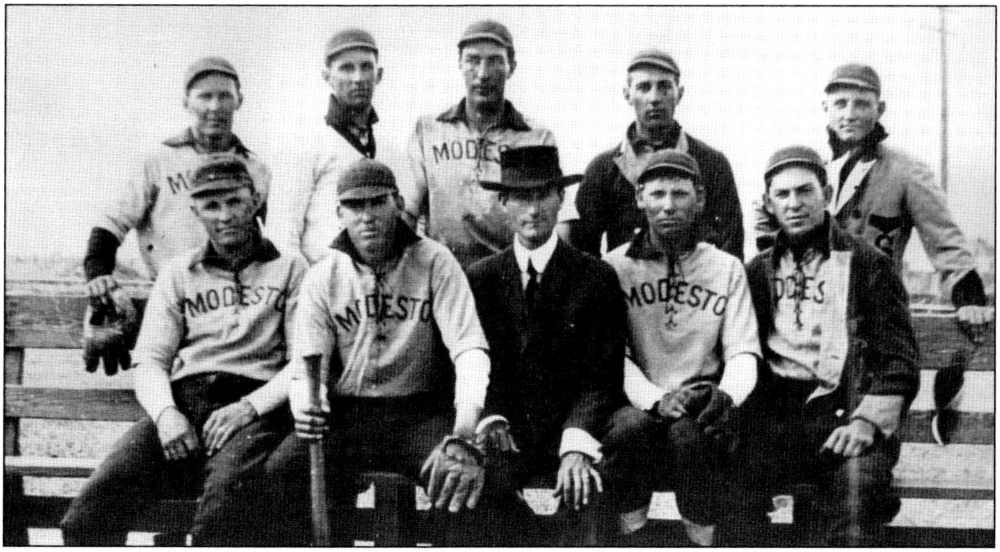

MODESTO REDS, EARLY 1900S. The two photographs on this page represent a chapter in baseball history in Modesto. The Reds were considered a semipro team and occasionally played in practice with the San Francisco Seals. The Seals would come to town for a couple of weeks to hone their skills for the next season. Modesto seems to have always had a baseball team—from 1872 (Red Caps) to the present (Nuts). The team became affiliated with various major league clubs over the years, including teams from St. Louis, Pittsburgh, Milwaukee, New York, Houston, Kansas City, Oakland, and Denver. For many years, the Modesto ballpark was called Del Webb Field, named for the owner of the New York Yankees who, at one time, played baseball in Modesto. The Modesto team was a franchise of the Yankees from 1954 to 1961.

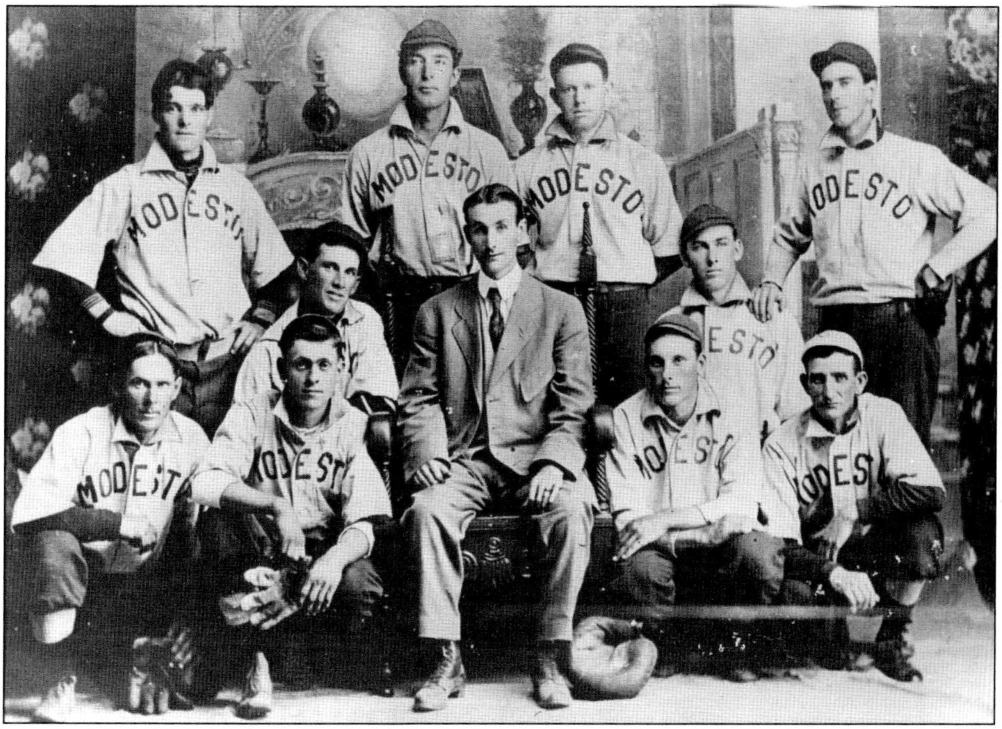

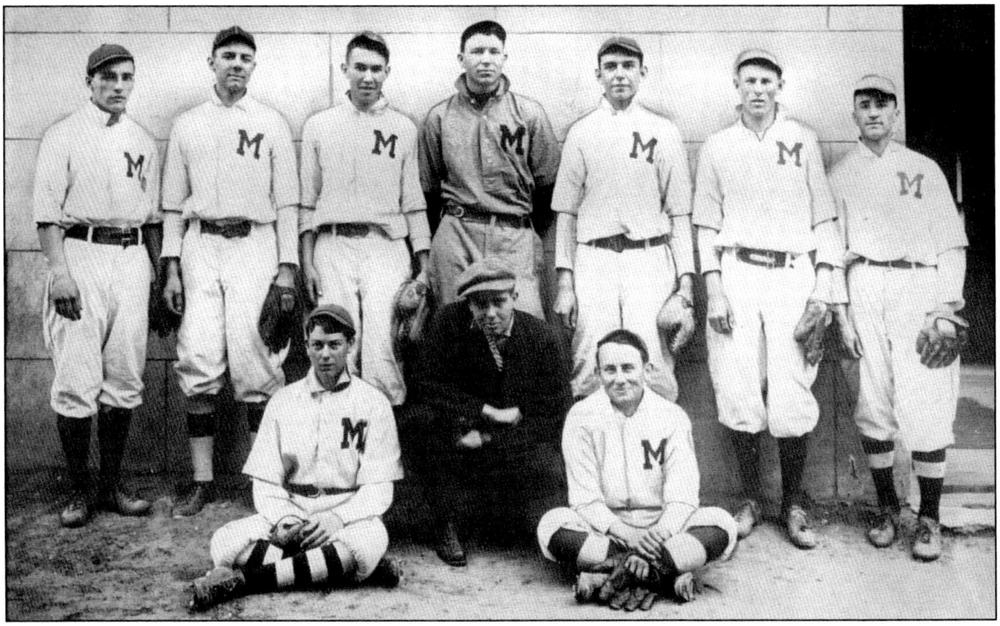

Baseball Champs, 1913. By a 5-1 score, Modesto High School's baseball team beat Palo Alto on May 31, 1913, to become champions of Northern California. Above are, from left to right, (seated) Kelton Pike, center; Everett Turner, manager; and Jack Ring, right field; (standing) Harold Johnston, left field; Earl Holtham, pitcher; Harry Talmage, catcher; C. C. Young, third base; William A Vacarro, first base; Donald Correll, third base; and Mark Bell, shortstop.

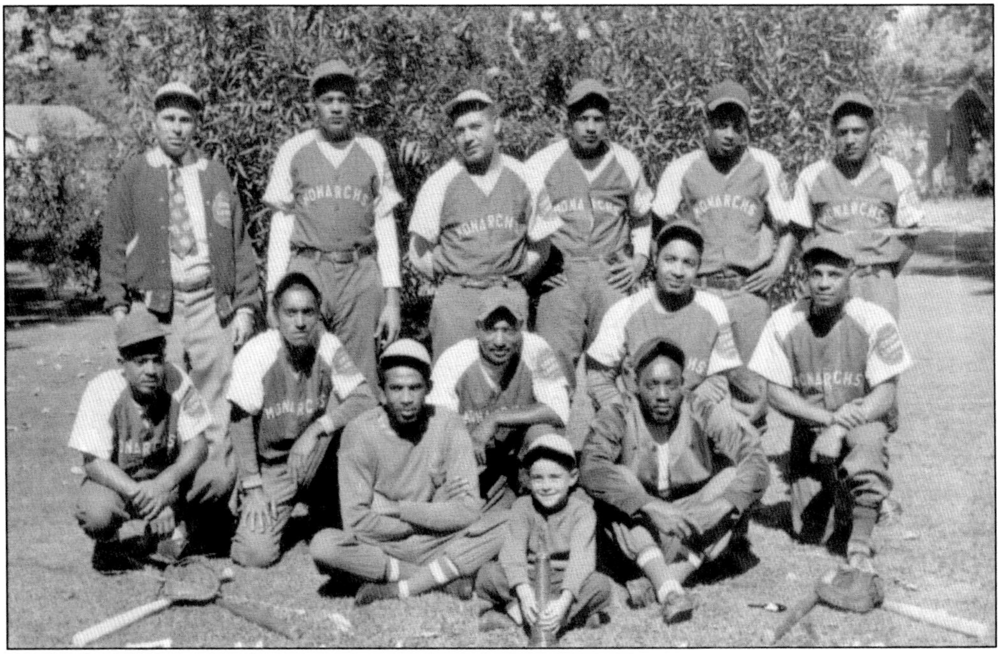

Modesto Monarchs, c. 1948. Modesto once had its own adult recreational baseball league. The Monarchs, pictured here, were made up of members of some of the first black families in Modesto. The only identified member of the group is Jesse Ard, second from the left in the first row. The Monarchs won the city championship in 1948. (Faces of Stanislaus, Gary Ard.)

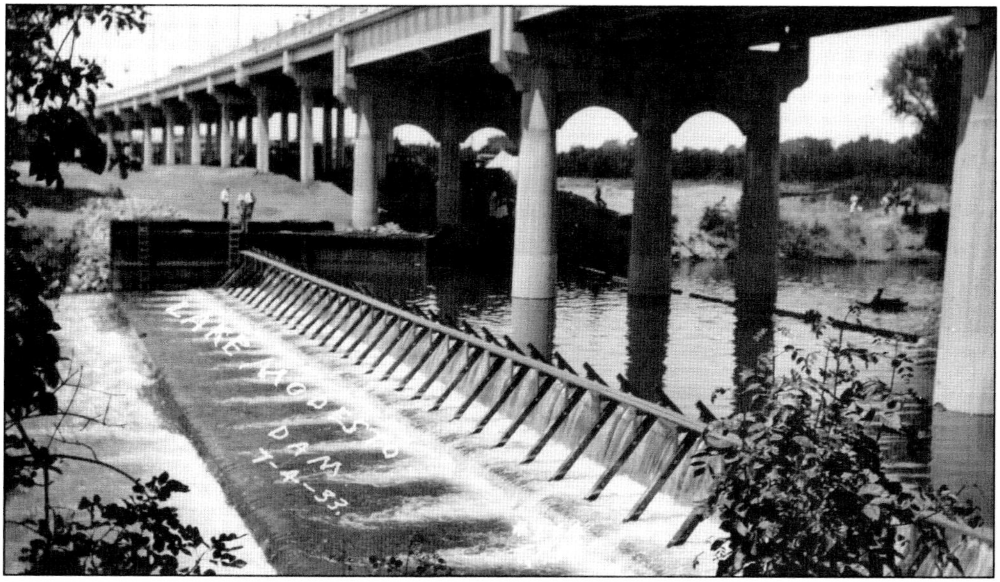

DENNETT DAM, C. 1933. A new Tuolumne River Bridge opened in 1933 and included the building of a dam to hold back the river, creating Lake Modesto, a 97-acre recreational water area. The lake extended from Legion Park to the town of Empire, according to historian Colleen Stanley Bare. The dam was named for former mayor Lincoln L. Dennett and could be raised or lowered for water flow as necessary.

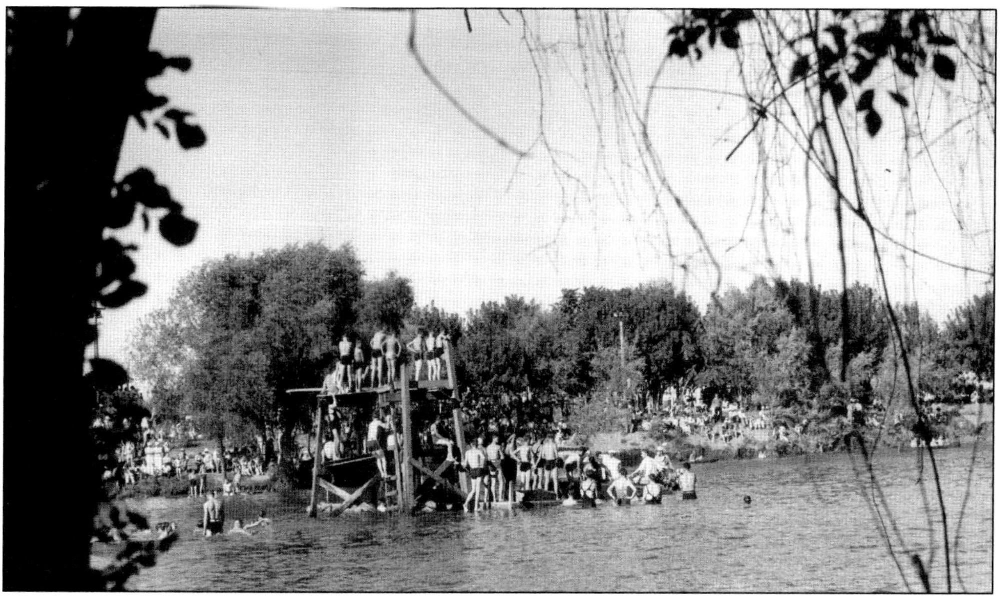

LEGION PARK, C. 1933. The Fourth of July celebration on the new lake included kayak and canoe races and swimming and diving competitions. It was an eventful day, with California governor James Rolph in town to dedicate the new Tuolumne River Bridge. Historian Colleen Stanley Bare says that the festivities surrounding the dedication and fireworks on the lake made this "one of Modesto's most unusual Independence Day observances."

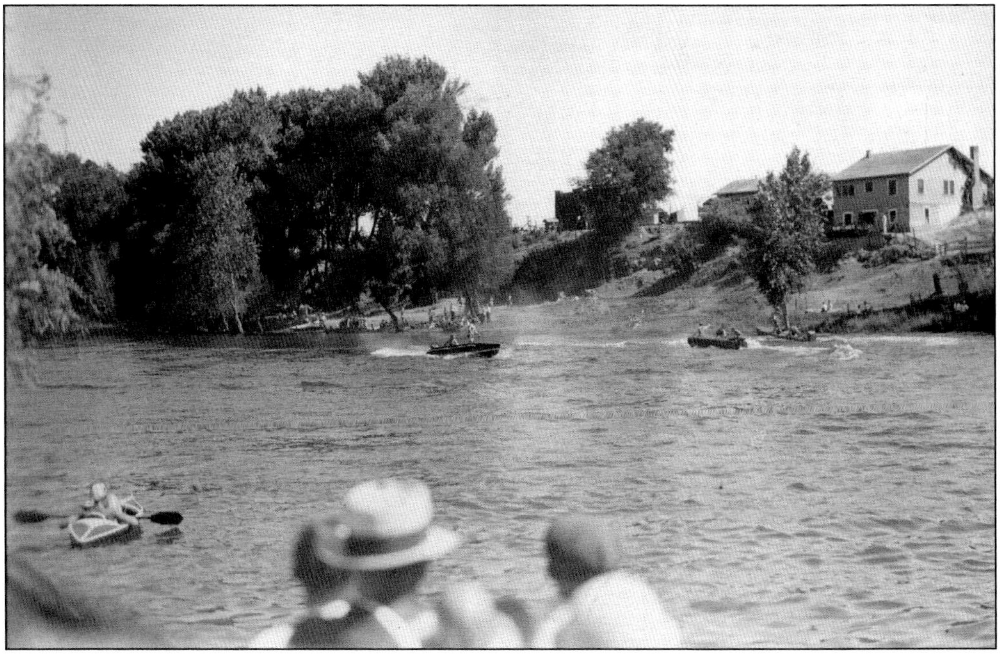

Swimming in Modesto, 1930s. Lake Modesto lasted until the 1940s, when Dennett Dam was damaged by flooding and then condemned in 1947, but those who spent hours on the water fondly remember Modesto's one-time lake. In addition to Lake Modesto, another "swimmin' hole" was Nunes Drop, located on the lateral near Virginia and Morris Avenues. Families would come to this area during hot summer days to cool off in the canal waters. Swimming lessons were given here during the 1930s, officially sanctioned by the city. During this period, swimming pools were a rare commodity for the average homeowner. Nunes Drop was popular through the 1940s, 1950s, and 1960s. (Above, McHenry Museum; below, author's collection.)

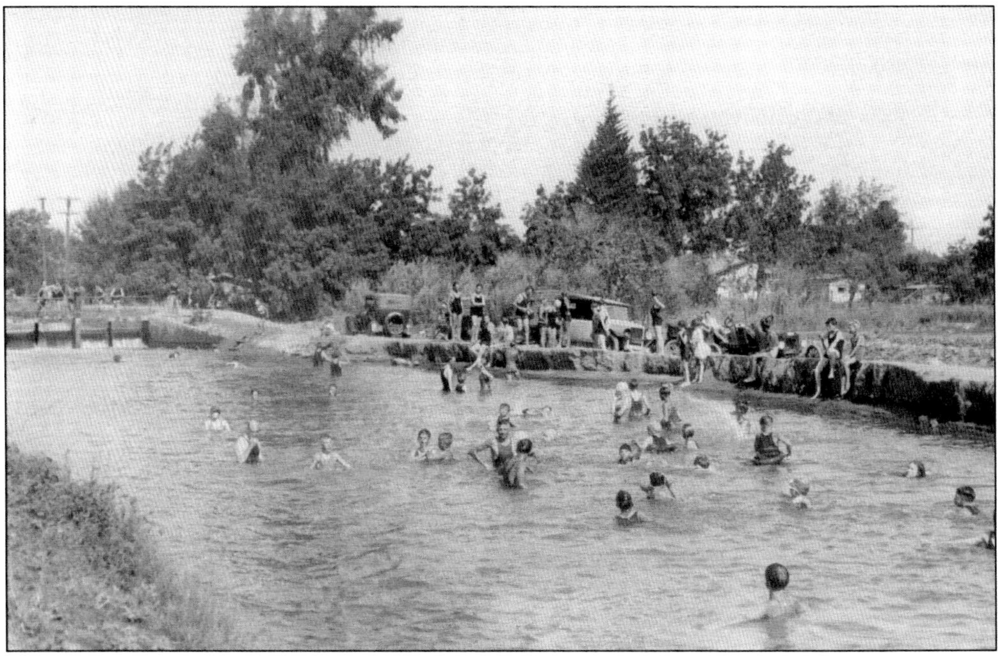

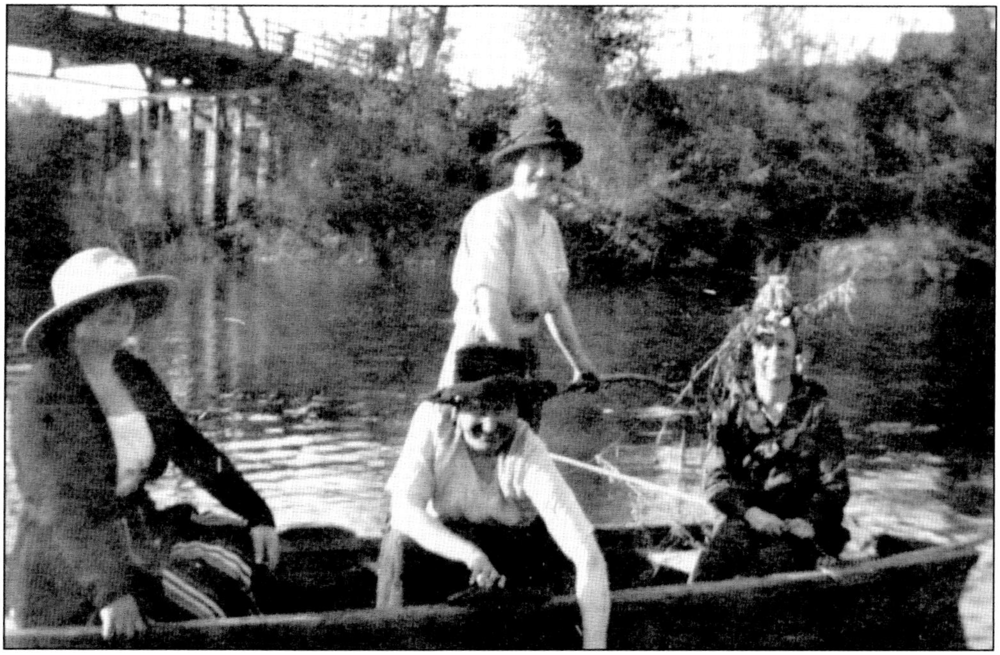

FISHING ON THE TUOLUMNE, EARLY 1900S. With the backdrop of the old Tuolumne River wagon bridge, these unidentified women are out fishing. Propriety demanded, however, that their attire remain as proper and appropriate as can be expected in the early part of the 1900s. While one of the ladies seems to be inspecting the fishing line, there is no information on whether or not fish were actually involved. (Author's collection.)

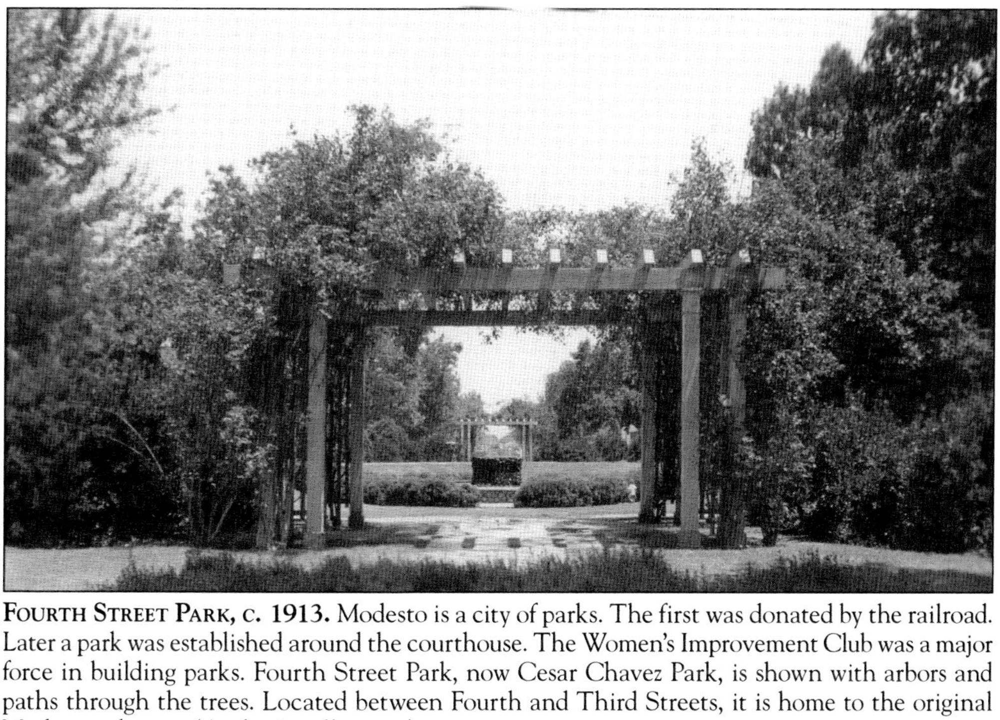

FOURTH STREET PARK, C. 1913. Modesto is a city of parks. The first was donated by the railroad. Later a park was established around the courthouse. The Women's Improvement Club was a major force in building parks. Fourth Street Park, now Cesar Chavez Park, is shown with arbors and paths through the trees. Located between Fourth and Third Streets, it is home to the original Modesto ash tree. (Author's collection.)

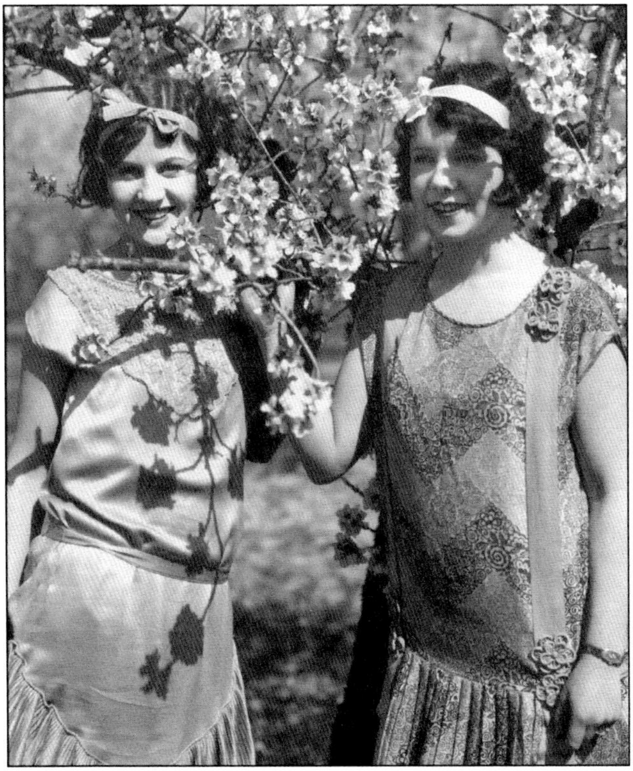

AMONG THE PEACH BLOSSOMS, C. 1930. This photograph of Doris Hilton (left) and Ruth Trail (right), standing in their stylish period dresses among the peach trees, was published in the *Modesto News-Herald*. The photograph is an obvious promotion for Modesto agriculture and other lovely delights in keeping with the time period in which it was published.

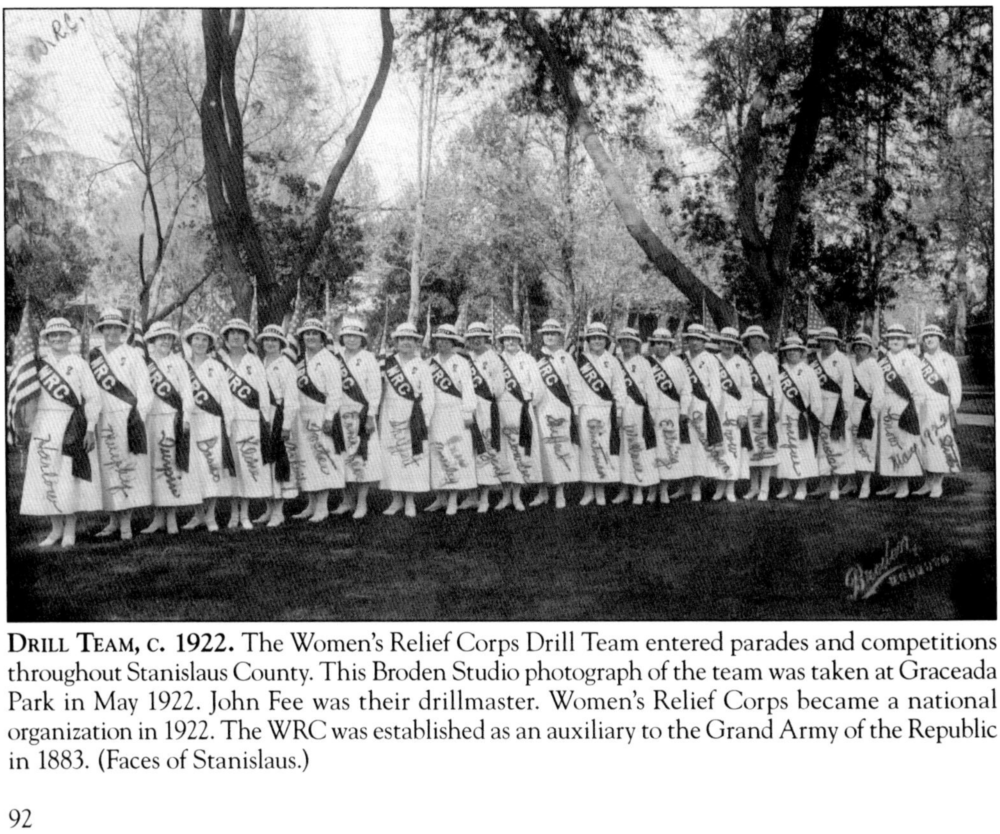

DRILL TEAM, C. 1922. The Women's Relief Corps Drill Team entered parades and competitions throughout Stanislaus County. This Broden Studio photograph of the team was taken at Graceada Park in May 1922. John Fee was their drillmaster. Women's Relief Corps became a national organization in 1922. The WRC was established as an auxiliary to the Grand Army of the Republic in 1883. (Faces of Stanislaus.)

Six

Schools, Churches, and Hospitals

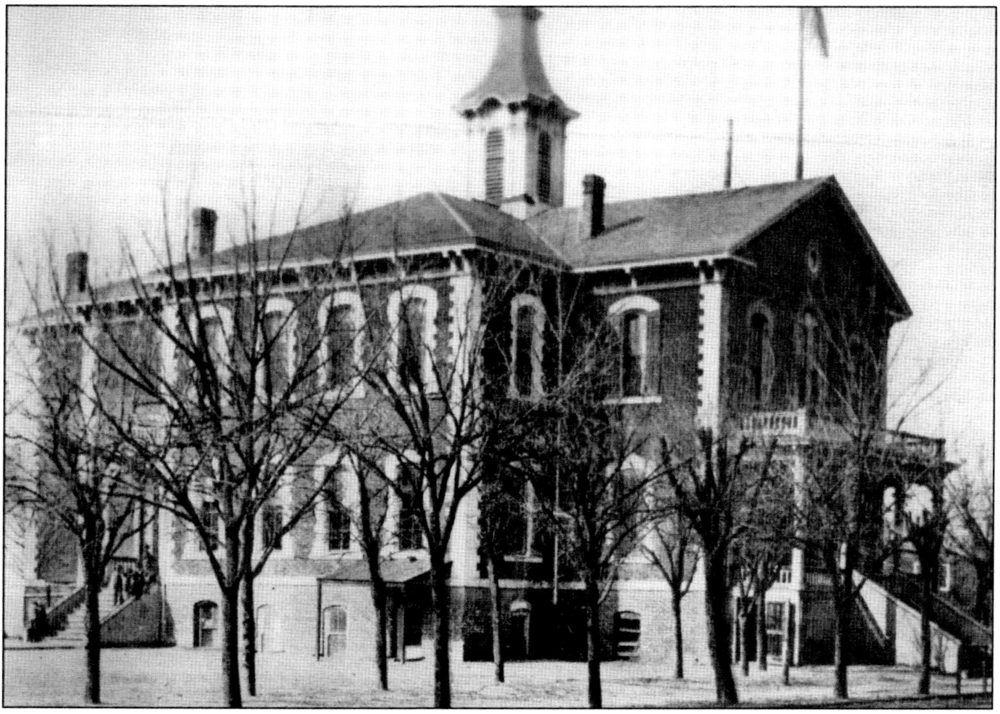

The Brick Schoolhouse, 1880s. Modesto's first school was built at Fourteenth and I Streets in 1874 on land donated by the railroad. The two-story, nine-room school, also known as the Fourteenth Street School, stood until 1909, when it was condemned and demolished. The school originally housed elementary classes but expanded to high school level with 40 students in 1883. They were taught in two upstairs classrooms.

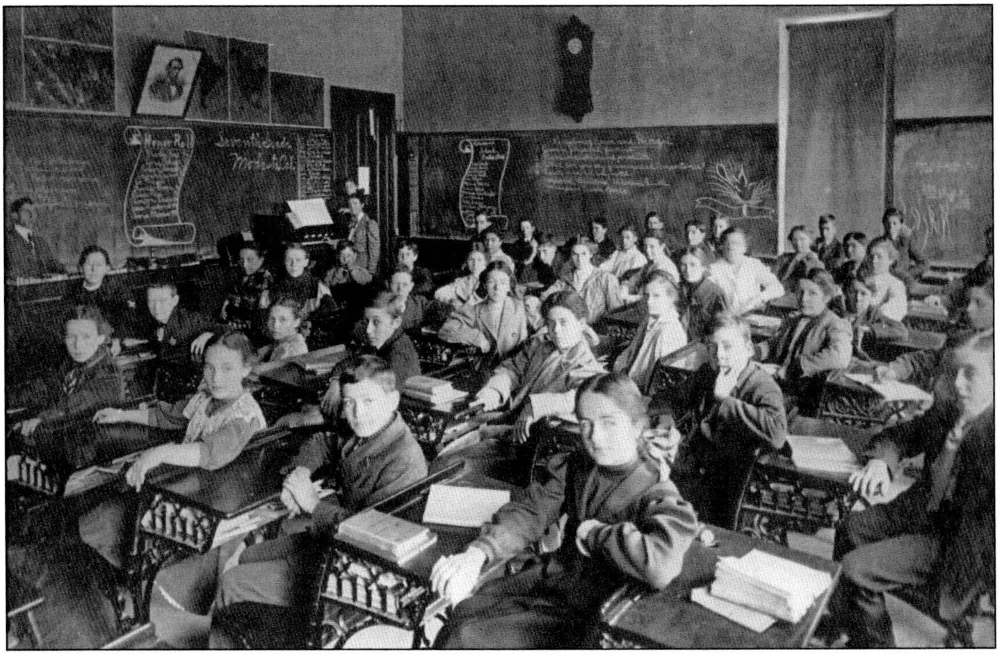

CLASSROOM INTERIOR, UNDATED. This is a seventh-grade class at the original Fourteenth Street School. There are 42 children in the classroom studying about Spain and Portugal (according to writings on the chalkboard). An honor roll is also listed on the board, along with algebra problems. The classroom also features an organ and the requisite photograph of Abraham Lincoln.

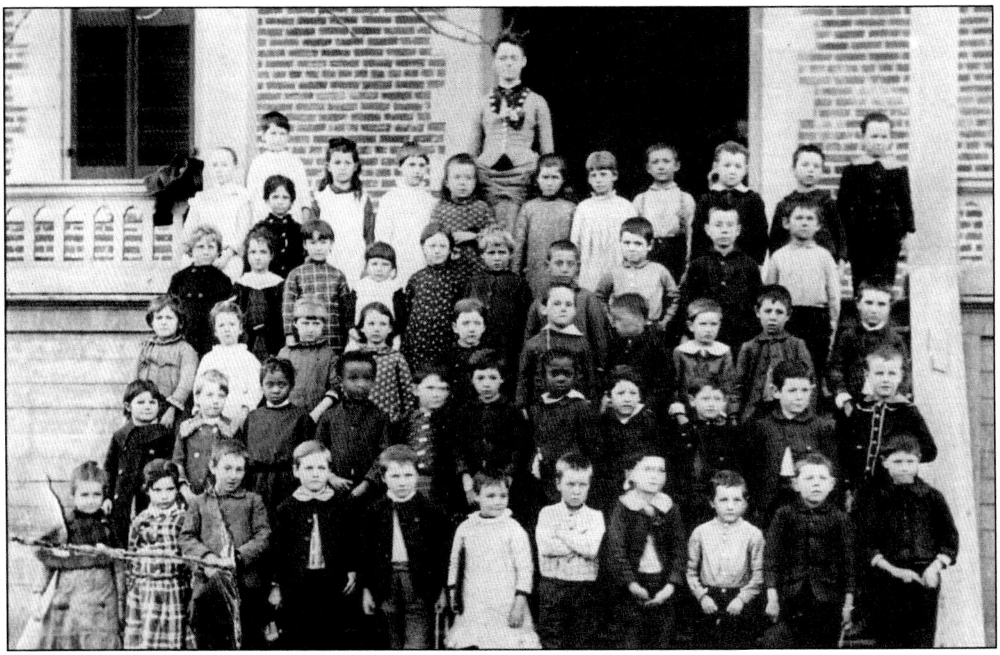

CLASS PHOTOGRAPH, C. 1908. This is another class from the Fourteenth Street School pictured in the last year of the old building's use. The teacher is identified as "Miss McInery from Fresno." None of the students are identified. It is interesting to note, however, that early Modesto classes were integrated long before integration became a political issue in America.

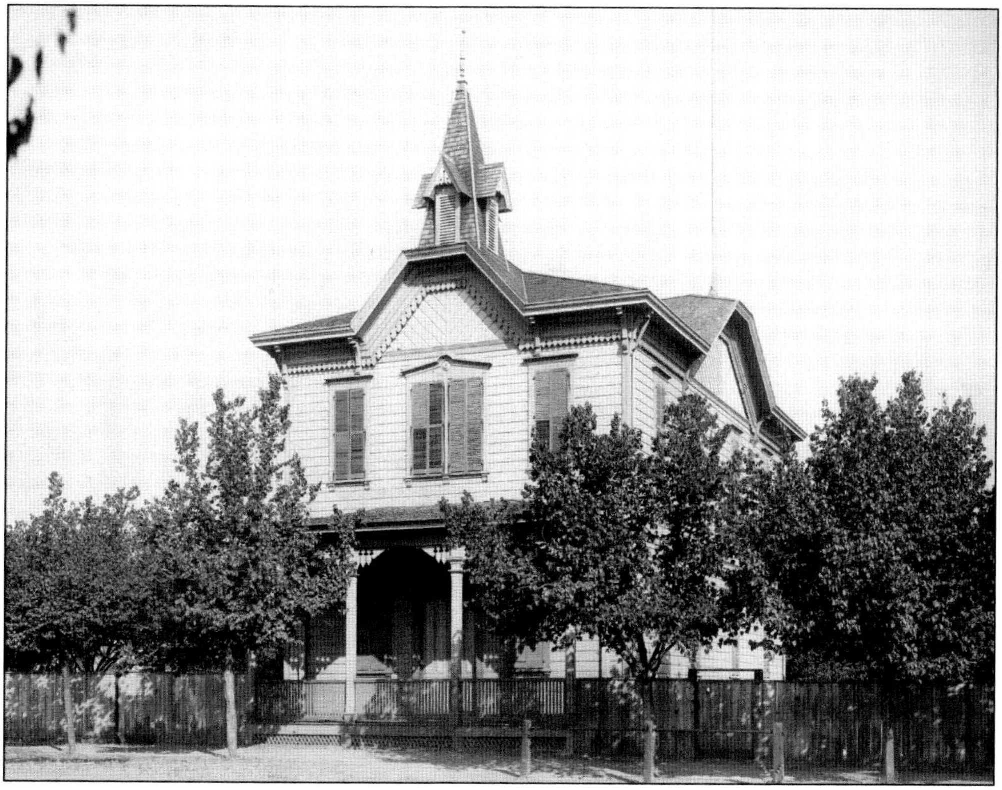

Sixth Street School, Undated. This school was established in 1889 at Sixth and I Streets. Originally an old house that had been moved from Tuolumne City, a new building took its place in 1898. The school had several different names, including Longfellow School, West Side School, and Pioneer School, according to historian Colleen Stanley Bare. The school closed in 1928.

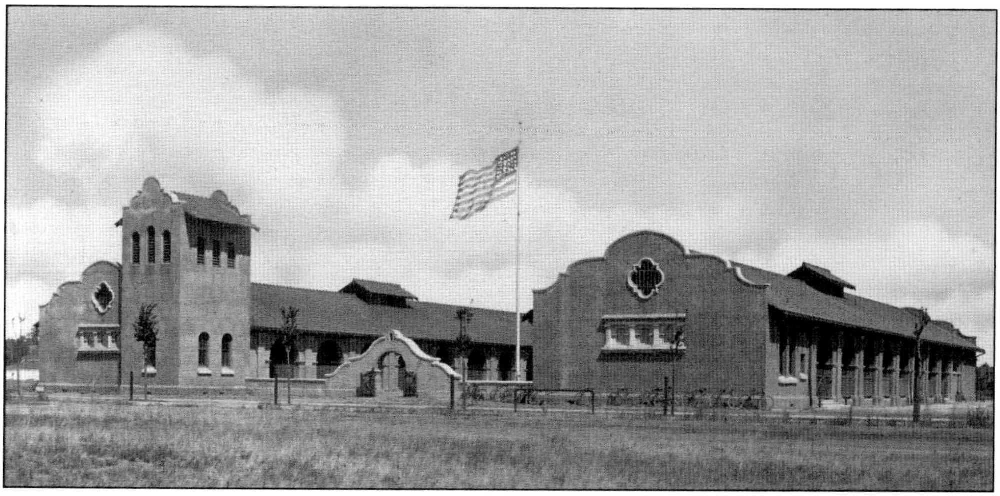

Fifth Street School, c. 1909. This school was located at the corner of Fifth and I Streets. A new school, the Sixth Street School at Sixth and I. opened in 1898, but its name was changed to Longfellow School. Younger students continued to attend the old school, described as a firetrap in a 1904 news article. The West Side/West Modesto School was phased out in 1907. Longfellow School was closed in 1928.

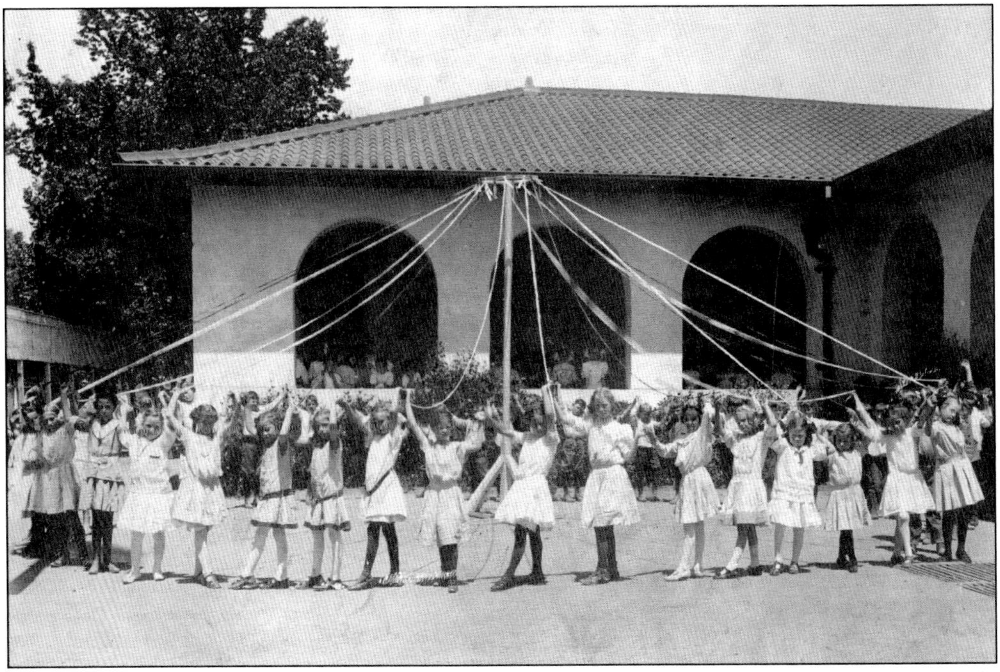

MAYDAY AT FOURTEENTH STREET SCHOOL, UNDATED. Second graders dance around a maypole outside the school. This school was renamed Capitol School in 1923 and closed in 1939. It was demolished in 1971 to make way for expansion of the *Modesto Bee*. Some of the children in this photograph are Maxine DeLappe Lonsdale (in front of pole), Margaret Jennings, Catherine Jennings, Helen Cooper McBride, Evelyn Keeley, and Florence Bates.

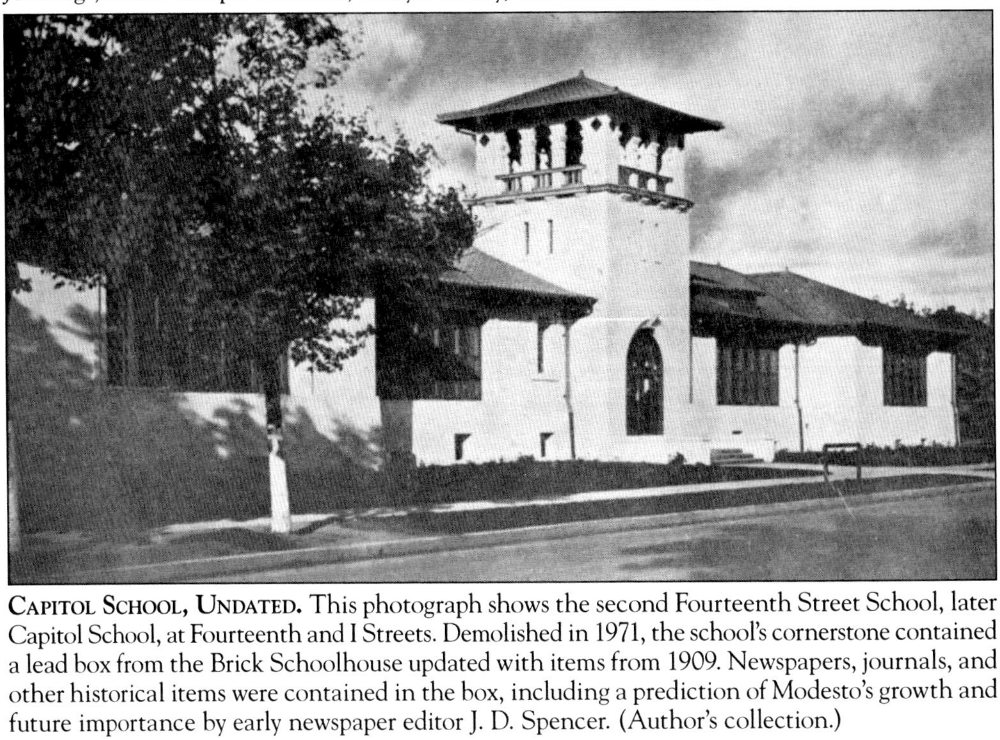

CAPITOL SCHOOL, UNDATED. This photograph shows the second Fourteenth Street School, later Capitol School, at Fourteenth and I Streets. Demolished in 1971, the school's cornerstone contained a lead box from the Brick Schoolhouse updated with items from 1909. Newspapers, journals, and other historical items were contained in the box, including a prediction of Modesto's growth and future importance by early newspaper editor J. D. Spencer. (Author's collection.)

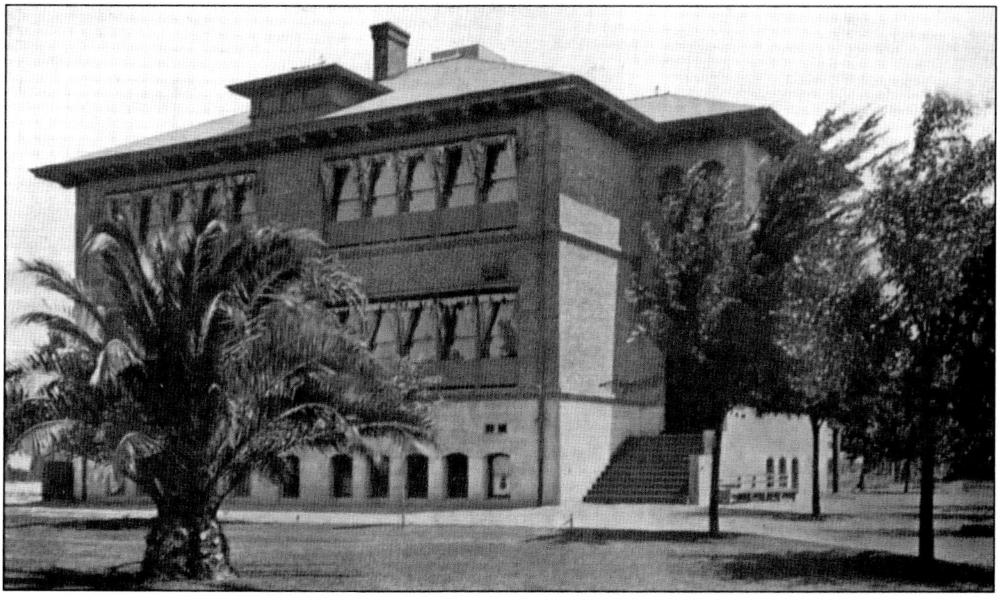

MODESTO HIGH SCHOOL, C. 1901 (ABOVE) AND 1931 (BELOW). Above, built at a cost of $19,500, plus $1,500 for the land, Modesto's first high school building opened with 81 students, including eighth graders. The two-story brick building was located at Twelfth and L Streets. Thomas Downey, who had taken over as school principal at the Fourteenth Street School in 1889, was named principal at the new school, where he served until 1915. In 1951, Modesto's second high school was named for him. In 1918, a new high school (below) was built at First and H Streets to replace the brick structure. At that time, the old school became a junior high school named Roosevelt School and stayed open until 1951. The MHS campus remains at First and H Streets today. (Above, author's collection; below, McHenry Museum Collection.)

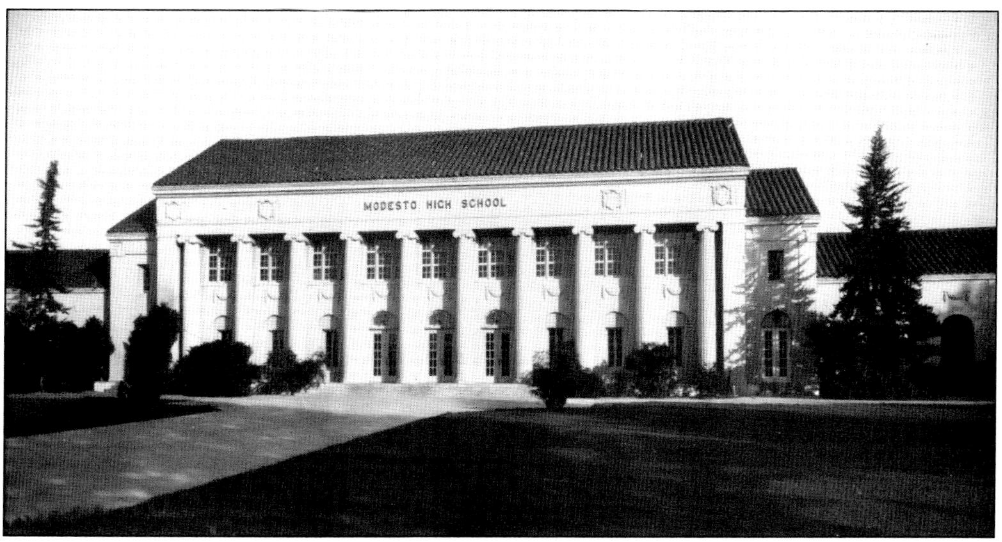

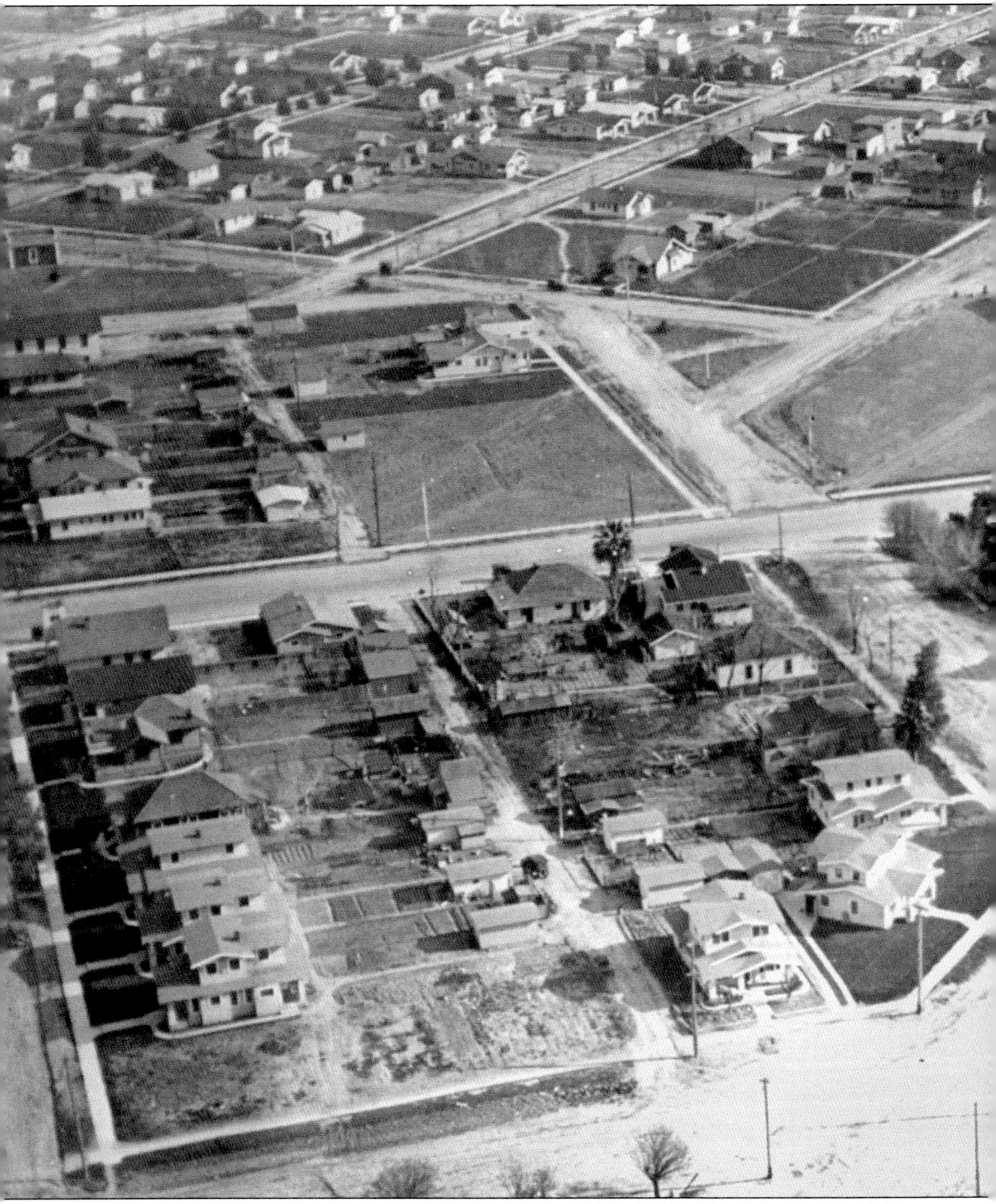

MODESTO SCHOOLS' AERIAL, C. 1919. Both Modesto High School at the top, above, and George Washington Elementary School, in the right foreground, were built at the same time. Historian Colleen Stanley Bare says that the site of the new high school was the subject of debate for several years between advocates of the west side of town or east side of town. The argument was settled when a west side resident donated land at First and H Streets. Development of the site

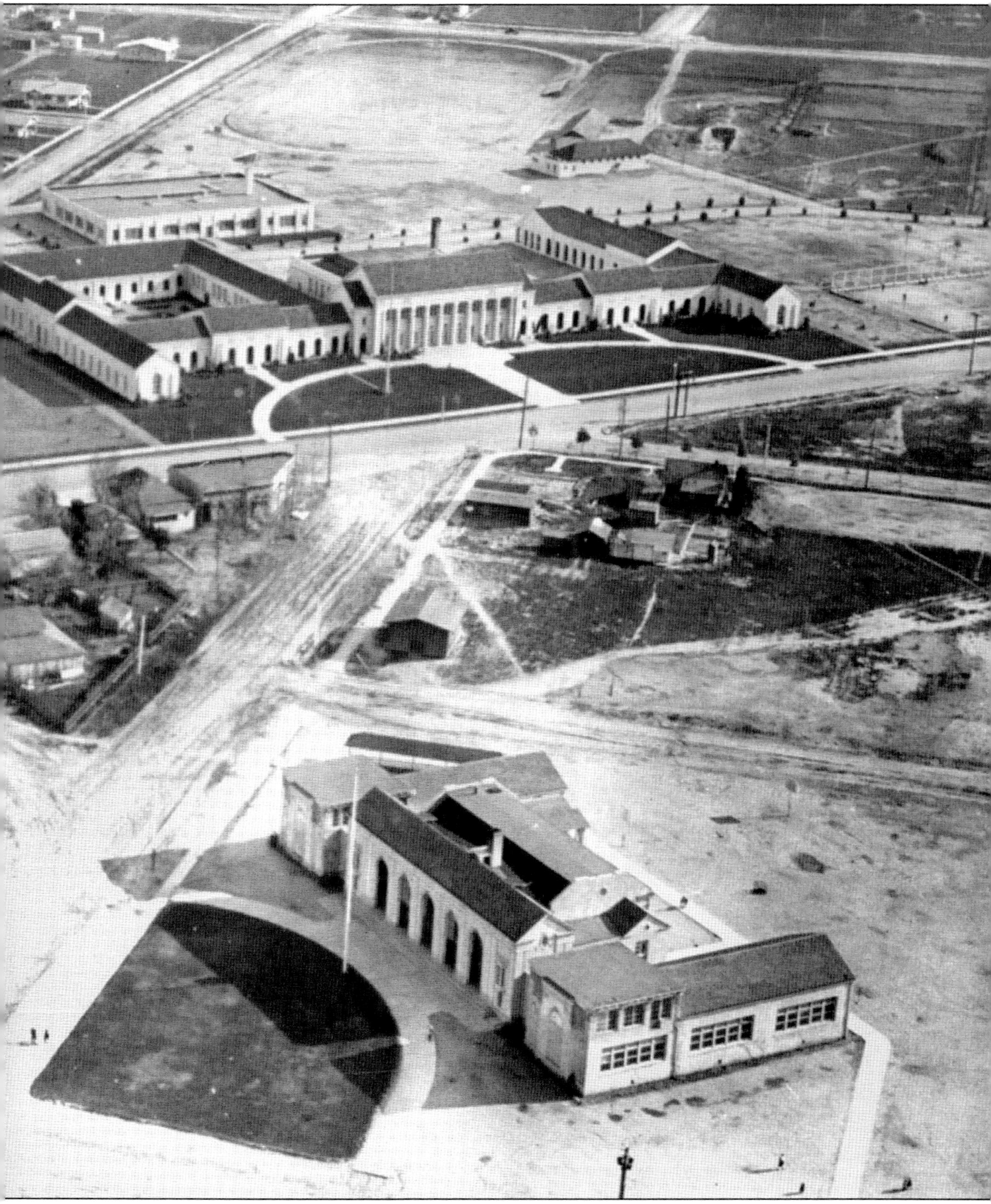

began in 1916, and the school building opened in June 1918 with 545 students. The cost of the school was $160,000. A second high school was not added for another 35 years, until Thomas Downey High School opened in 1951. Prior to that, Modesto High underwent major restoration and reconstruction in 1947.

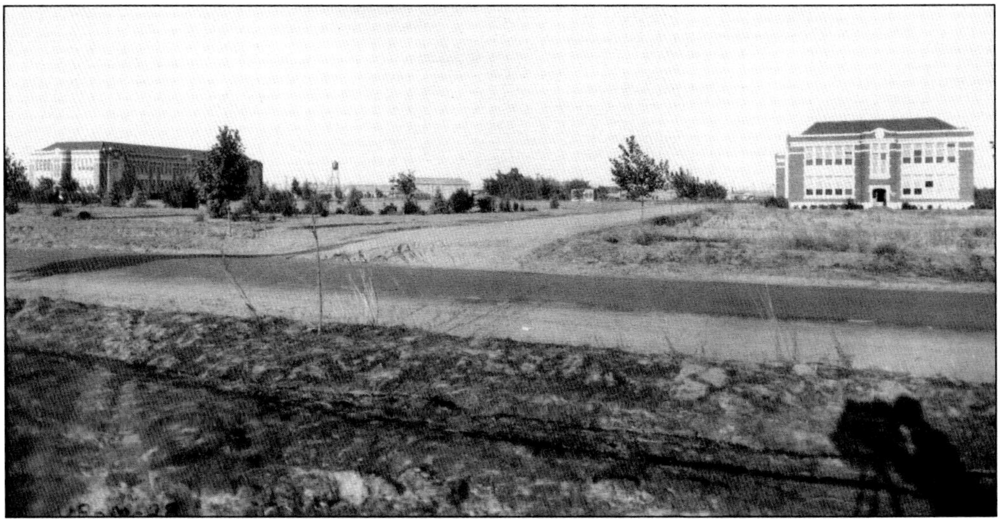

Modesto Junior College, 1920s. MJC was created under a new law that allowed junior colleges to be established separately from high school districts. It was the first such junior college in the state. Classes began in 1921 at Modesto High School as a 40-acre campus was developed on College Avenue, above Tenth Street. North and South Halls, the main classroom buildings pictured above, were completed in the mid-1920s. The photograph was taken from College Avenue. Below, one of the buildings seems to be mired in the middle of muddy roadways. This is probably South Hall, since it was the first completed in 1923. The first president of MJC was Charles S. "Jim" Morris.

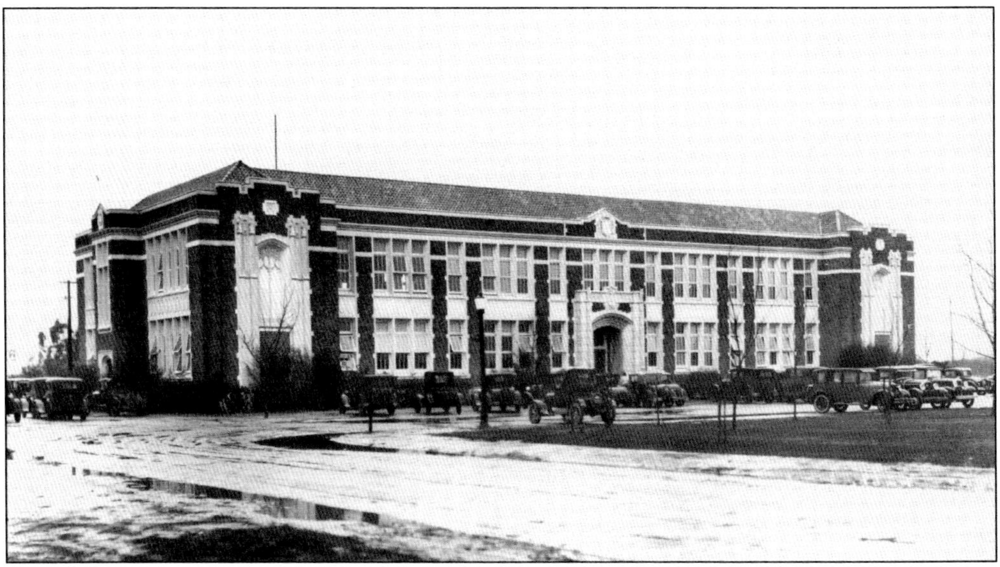

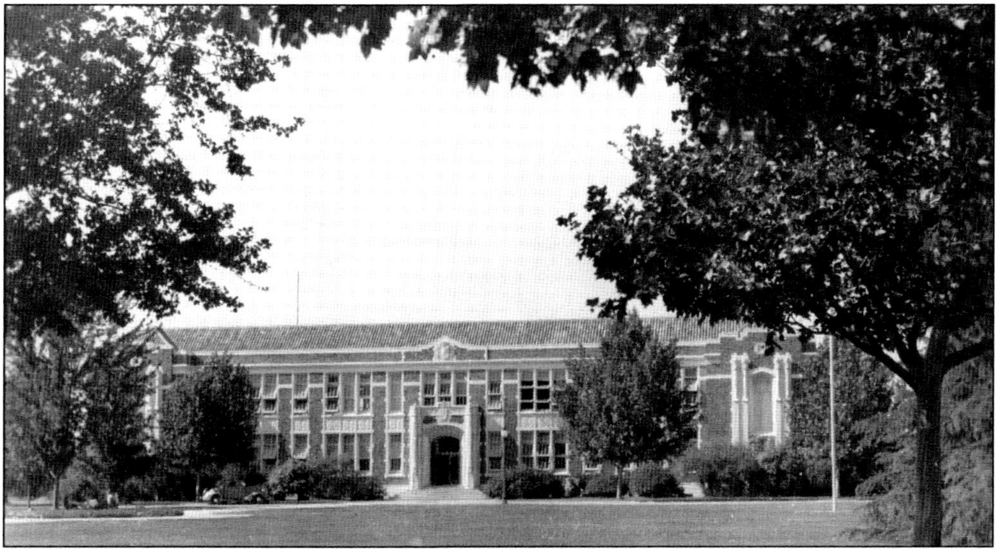

North Hall, 1930s. This photograph of MJC's North Hall provides a more finished look. The trees and grass still distinguish the college campus today, having grown in to provide a parklike setting. Landscape architect Howard Gilky designed the MJC campus as well as Mills College and Modesto High School, according to historian Colleen Stanley Bare. Both North and South Halls were demolished in the 1970s.

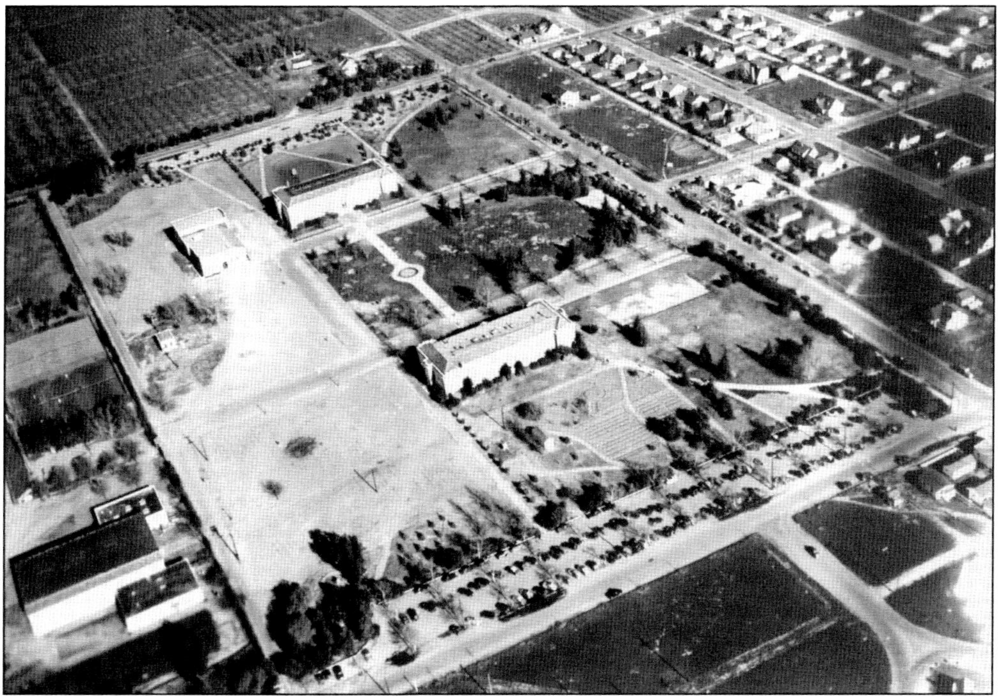

MJC Aerial View, 1920s. This view of the MJC campus taken from the air shows the basic layout of the 40-acre campus and three completed buildings—North and South Halls and the gymnasium—as well two or three smaller structures. Homes are being built to the east of the campus. The area in the lower left corner is an industrial tract. There is still plenty of farmland surrounding the school.

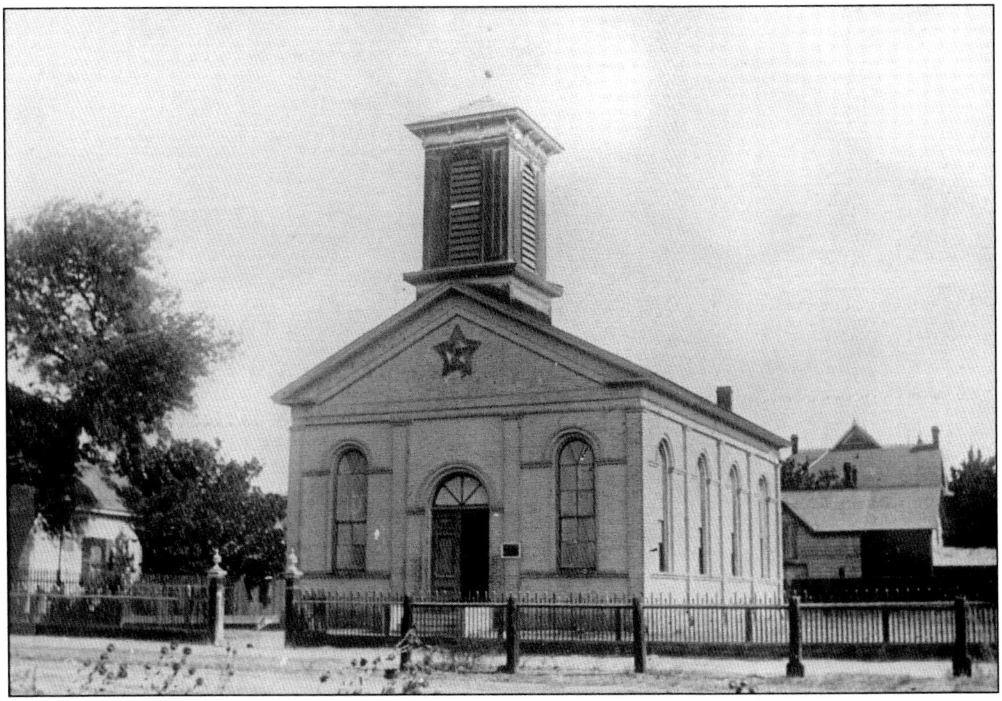

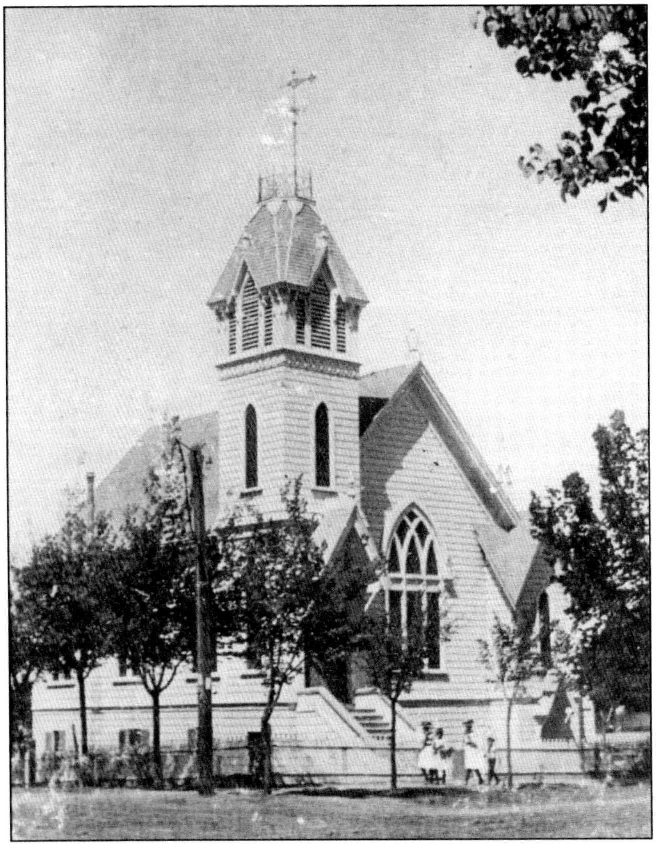

First Churches in Modesto, c. 1873 (Above) and 1881 (Left). The above photograph is the First Christian Church on Eleventh and G Streets as it looked in 1873, the year the brick building was completed. In 1904, it was torn down to build a new frame structure (opposite page), and it was renamed the Church of Christ. At left is the First Presbyterian Church in 1881, located at Fourteenth and I Streets, completed the year of the photograph. This church was used until 1910, at which time a new building was constructed on the same spot. The very first church built in Modesto was the Congregational Church in 1872 on I Street between Twelfth and Thirteenth Streets, later occupied by the German Lutherans, according to historian Colleen Stanley Bare.

EARLY CHURCHES, C. 1873 (RIGHT) AND 1925 (BELOW). Two additional photographs of early Modesto churches are seen on this page. The photograph at right is the First Methodist Episcopal Church, built in 1873. This church was located on three lots at Thirteenth and H Streets and was replaced in 1890 by a larger church in the same location. The photograph below shows the larger 1904 building for the Church of Christ (First Christian Church) as it looked in 1925. Modesto has welcomed many different denominations, including the Church of Jesus Christ of Latter-day Saints, first located at Fourth and F Streets in 1928, as well as the German Baptist Brethren in the Wood Colony, plus the Beth Shalom Synagogue on Sherwood Avenue.

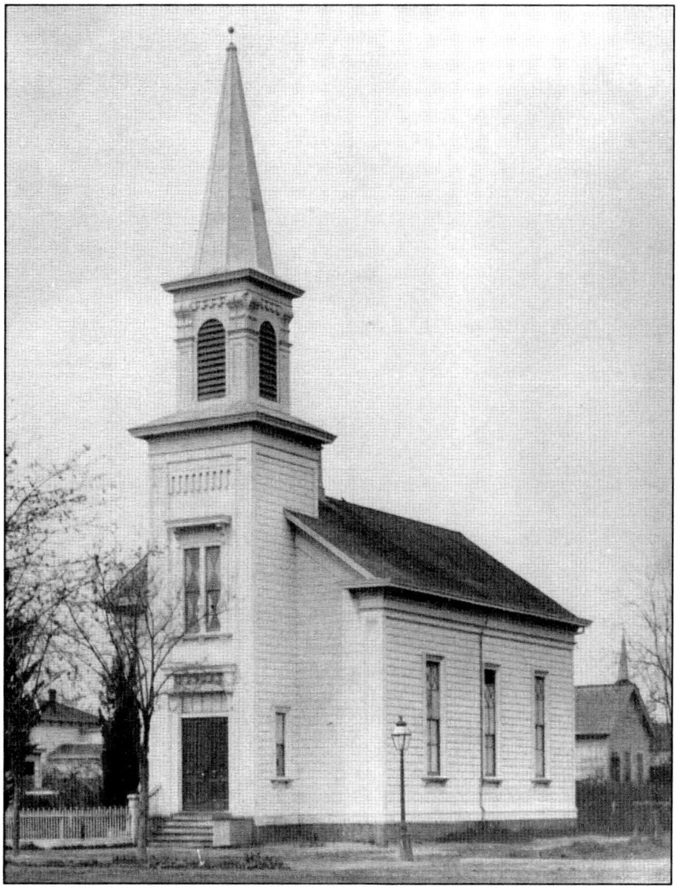

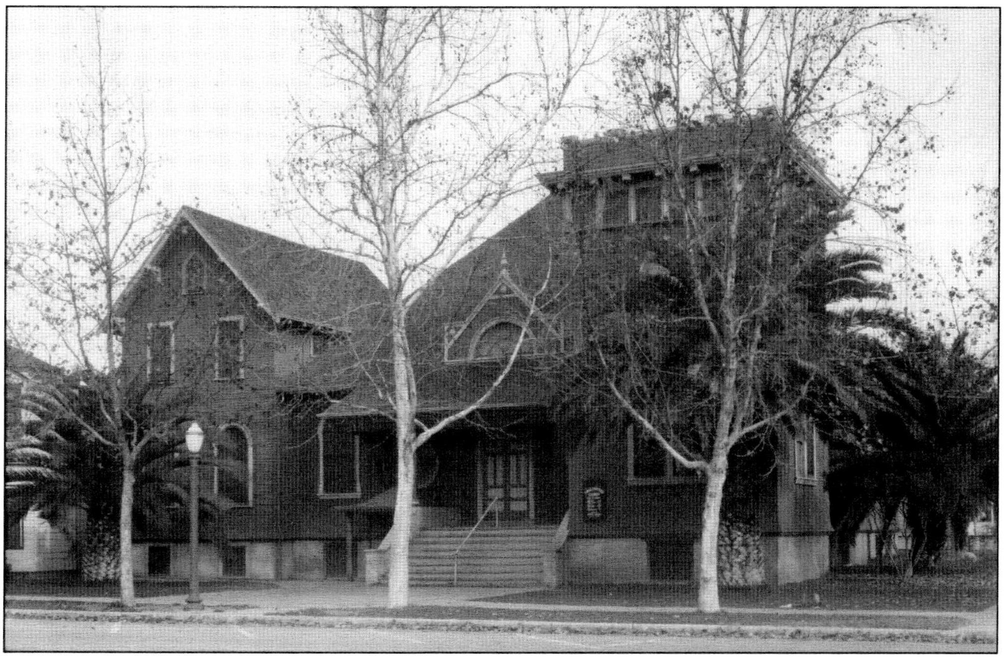

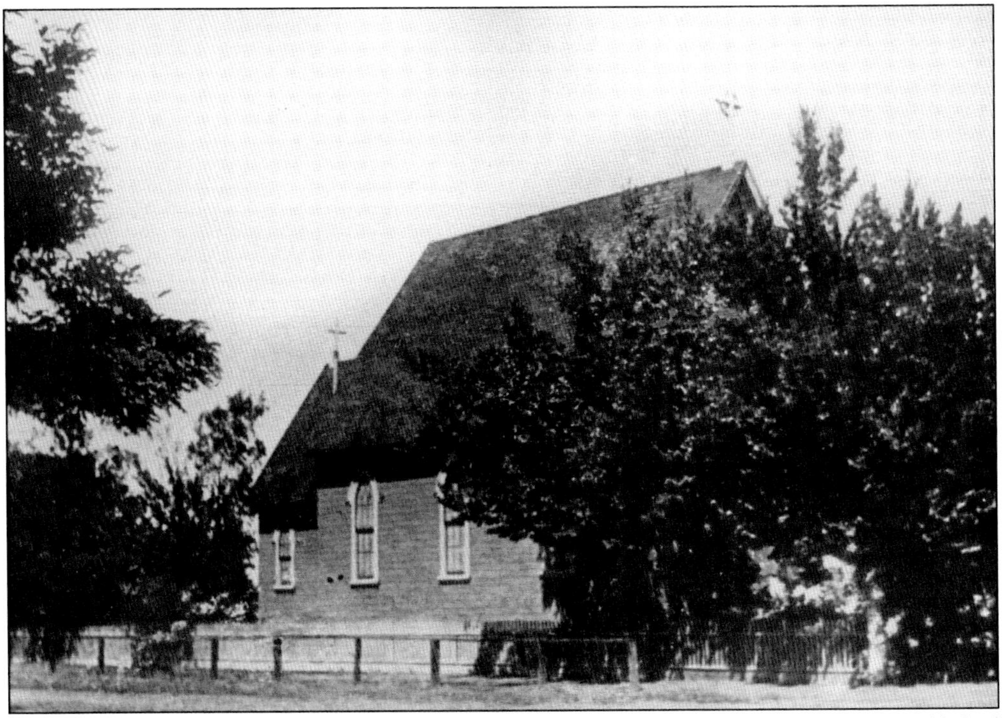

CATHOLIC CHURCHES, C. 1878 (ABOVE) AND C. 1913 (BELOW). St. Stanislaus parish was established in 1875, and the church above was built three years later. The church was located at Eighth Street between J and K Streets. Visiting priests served the parish until 1881, when a permanent priest, Fr. Patrick Walsh, was appointed. The mission-style church building in the photograph below was constructed in 1913 at Seventh and J Streets. This church has continually served St. Stanislaus parish since that time. Most recently it has been reserved as a chapel for weddings and funerals, since a much larger church building was completed on Maze Boulevard, near St. Stanislaus Catholic School. Two other Roman Catholic churches serve Modesto: Our Lady of Fatima on Granger Avenue and St. Joseph's Church on Oakdale Road.

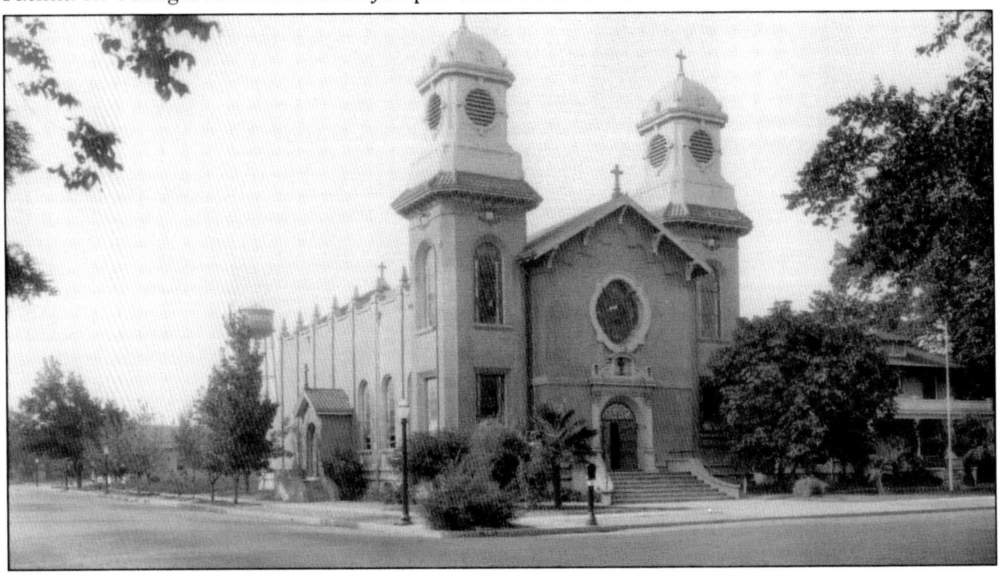

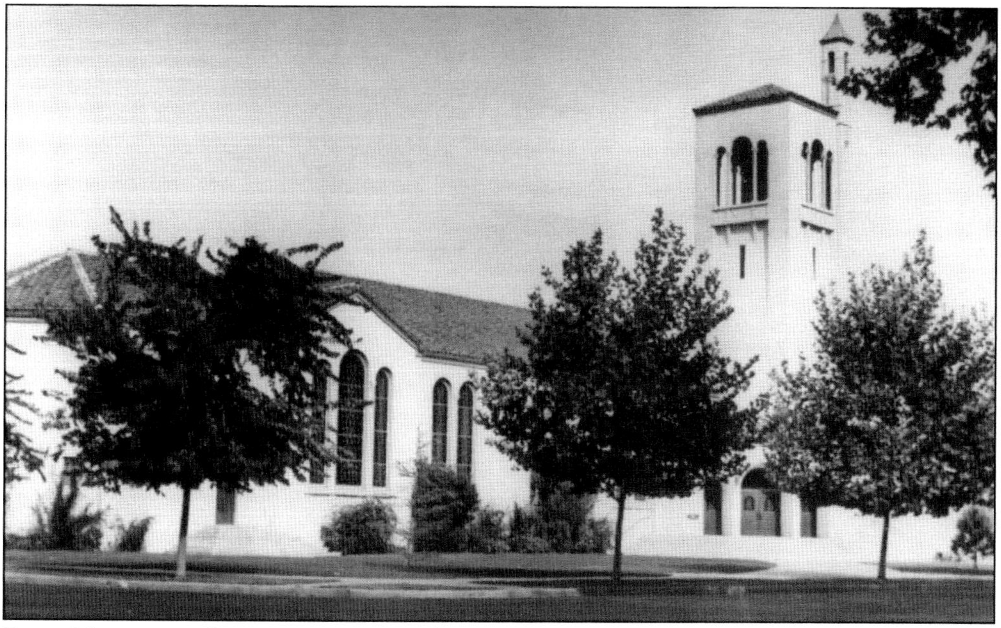

First Methodist Church, c. 1932. This imposing structure is the descendant of the First Methodist Episcopal Church, originally built in 1873 at Thirteenth and H Streets. Another building was constructed in 1890, but this structure replaced it on Sixteenth and I Streets in 1932. Many churches were demolished because of stringent city ordinances in the mid-1960s, but First Methodist Church was brought up to code and remains in use.

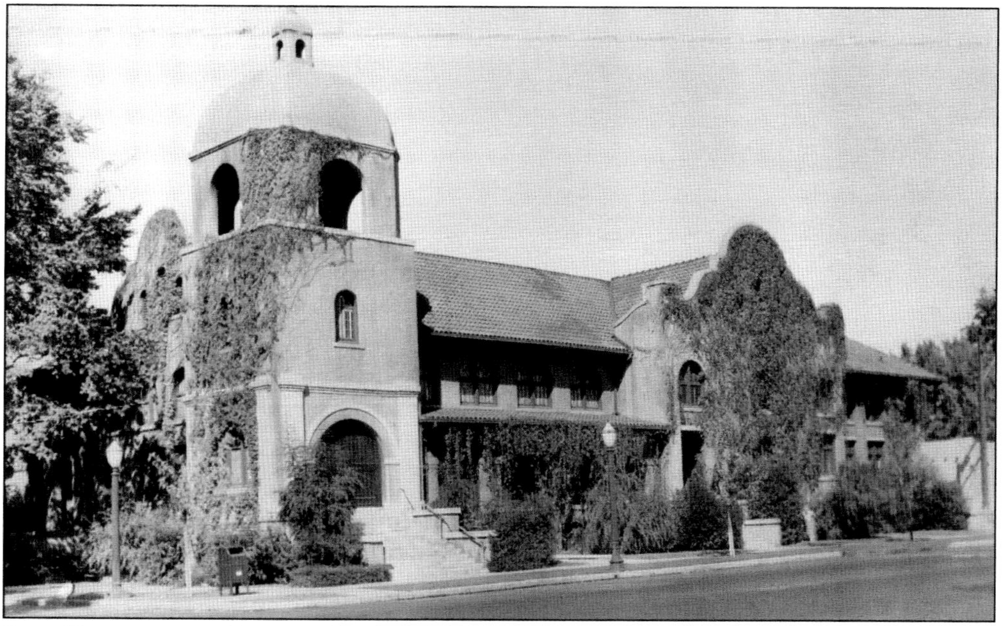

First Presbyterian Church, Undated. First Presbyterian Church members originally met in Rogers Hall until a church could be built at Fourteenth and I Streets in 1881. The church had been organized in 1879. This impressive building, designed in a mission style so prevalent in Modesto, had plenty of room for worship services and also contained recreational facilities. Built in 1911, it was directly across the street from the McHenry Library.

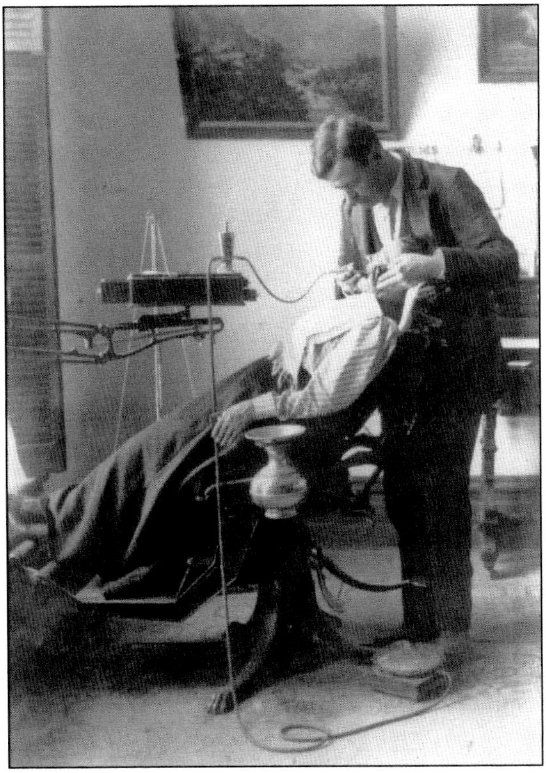

EARLY DENTISTRY, 1890S. Dr. M. L. Cooper, a highly regarded dentist in early Modesto, was said to be 10 years ahead of his time. The photograph shows that he also had the most advanced equipment, including the cuspidor. He was known for poetic attempts to balance accounts: "McKinley is in and I know you are flush so please call early and avoid the rush," Cooper wrote. (Faces of Stanislaus, Helen McBride.)

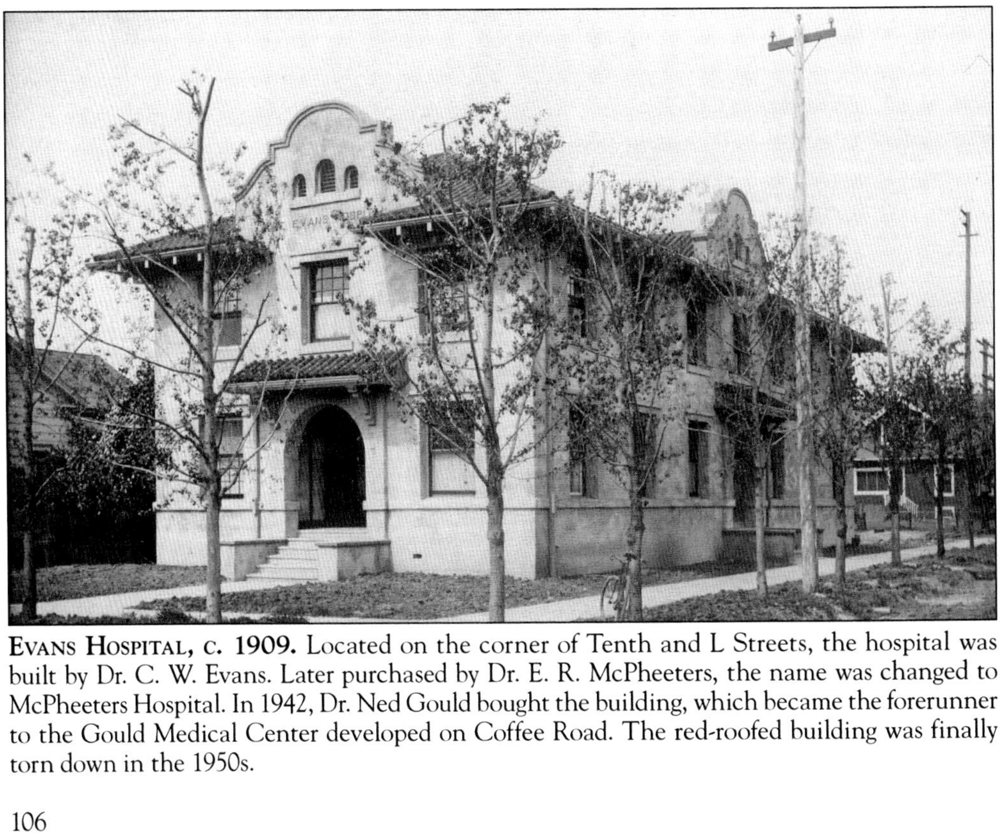

EVANS HOSPITAL, C. 1909. Located on the corner of Tenth and L Streets, the hospital was built by Dr. C. W. Evans. Later purchased by Dr. E. R. McPheeters, the name was changed to McPheeters Hospital. In 1942, Dr. Ned Gould bought the building, which became the forerunner to the Gould Medical Center developed on Coffee Road. The red-roofed building was finally torn down in the 1950s.

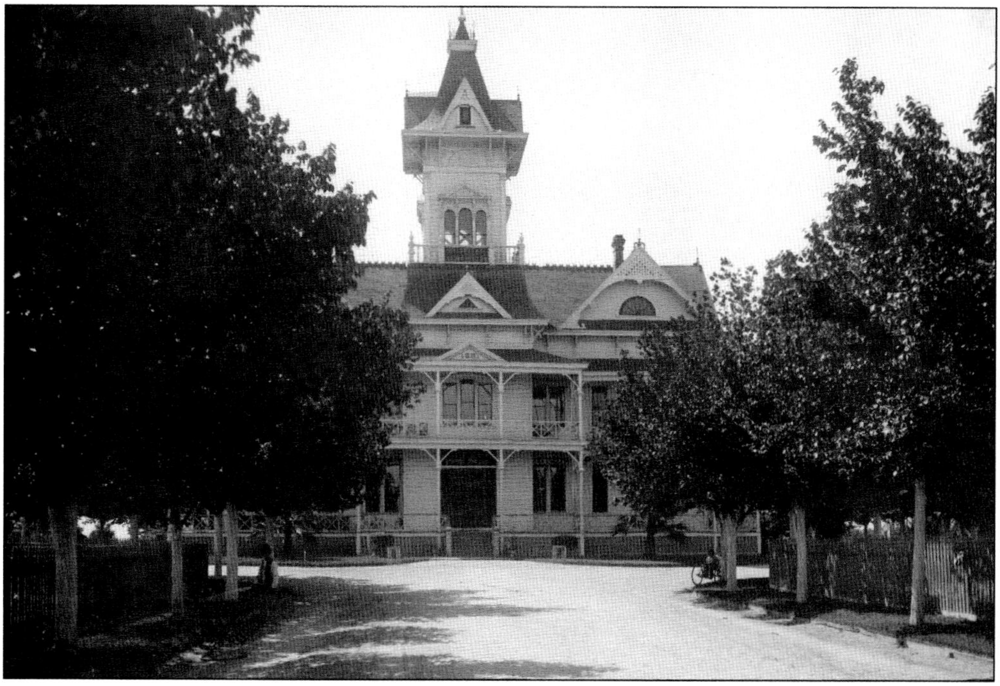

County Hospital and Almshouse, c. 1891. This stately Victorian structure was home to the Stanislaus County Hospital until 1950. An almshouse was a public institution for homeless and aged persons without means. As such, the county hospital provided care for the indigent. It remained in operation in other facilities well into the 1990s.

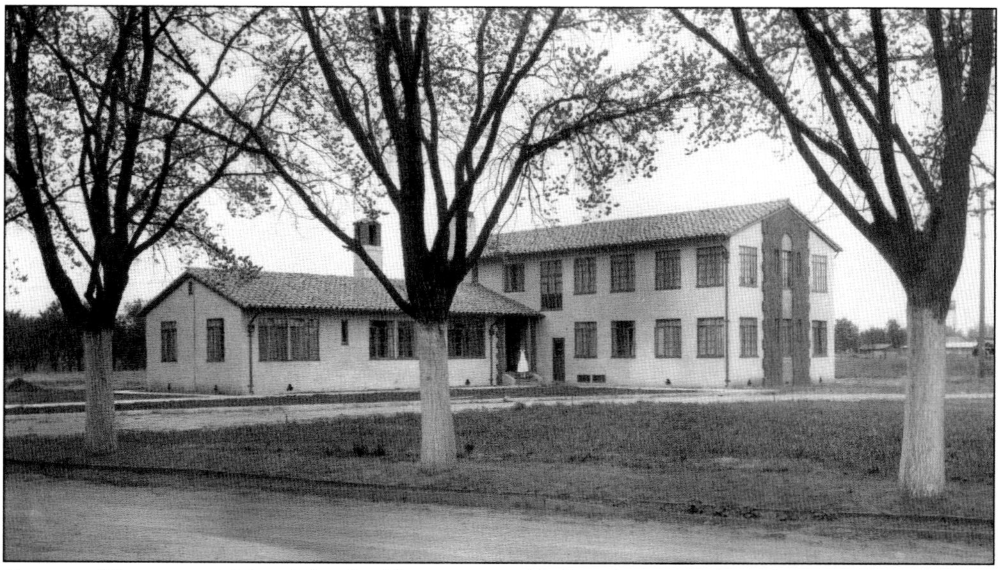

County Hospital, 1930s. New buildings were added to the grounds at the Stanislaus County Hospital to expand its capacity. Eventually, after the 1891 structure was torn down in 1950, new facilities were built, creating a modern and efficient hospital called Scenic General. Other county health care facilities were also located at the Scenic Drive site. The county hospital closed in the 1990s.

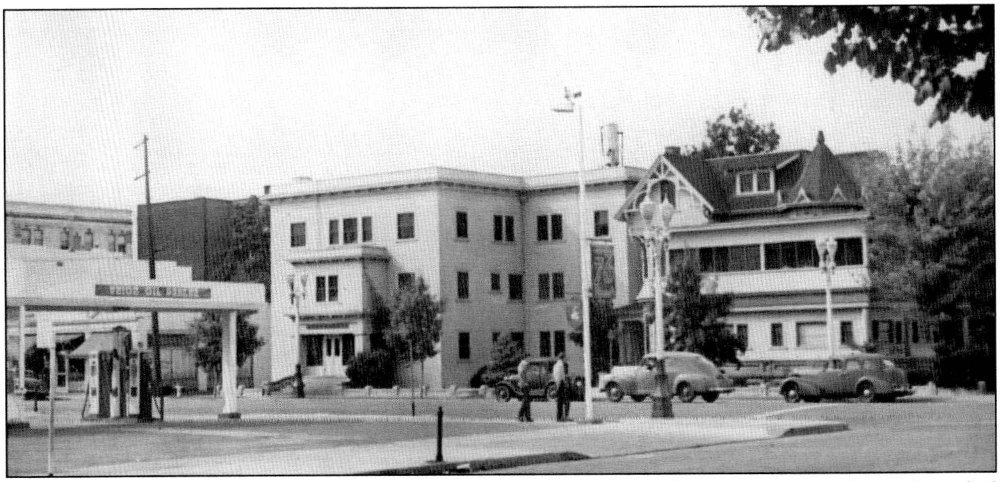

Robertson Hospital, c. 1945. Located at 1115 J Street, Robertson Hospital was founded by Dr. J. C. Robertson. In this photograph, the Hotel Covell can be seen on the extreme left. The hospital is in the center, and the offices of Robertson, Husband, Edmond, and Treadwell, Physicians and Surgeons, are on the right in what was once the home of Dr. C. W. Evans. This building was closed in 1950.

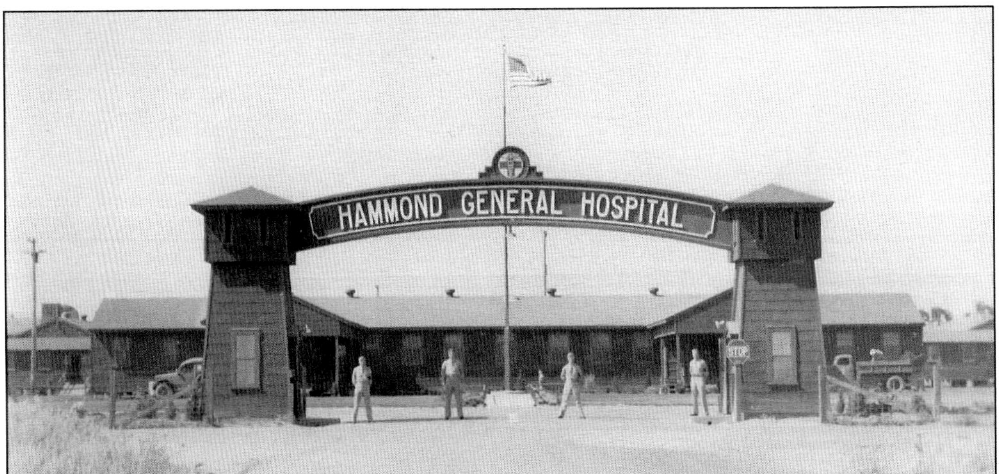

Military Hospital, c. 1942. Hammond General Hospital, the largest military hospital on the West Coast, was built in Modesto. Named for Civil War general William Alexander Hammond, the 3,000-bed facility was located on Blue Gum Avenue. After it closed in 1945, it became Modesto State Hospital and later Modesto Junior College's West Campus. Over 24,000 injured soldiers were treated at the facility during World War II.

Seven

CHANGING TIMES

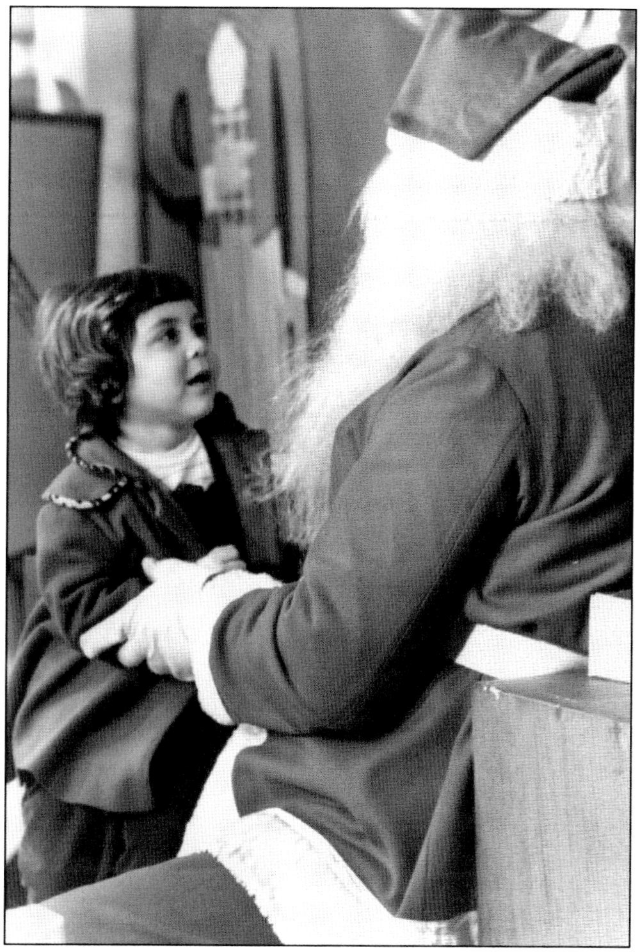

YES, VIRGINIA, C. 1949. The author's sister, Virginia, at the age of two and a half, visits Santa at Sears Department Store in downtown Modesto. Prior to the start of the 1950s, Modesto still retained its small-town feel. With the coming of the 1950s and 1960s, drastic changes would occur downtown, as the city began the systematic removal of Modesto's historic past. (Author's collection.)

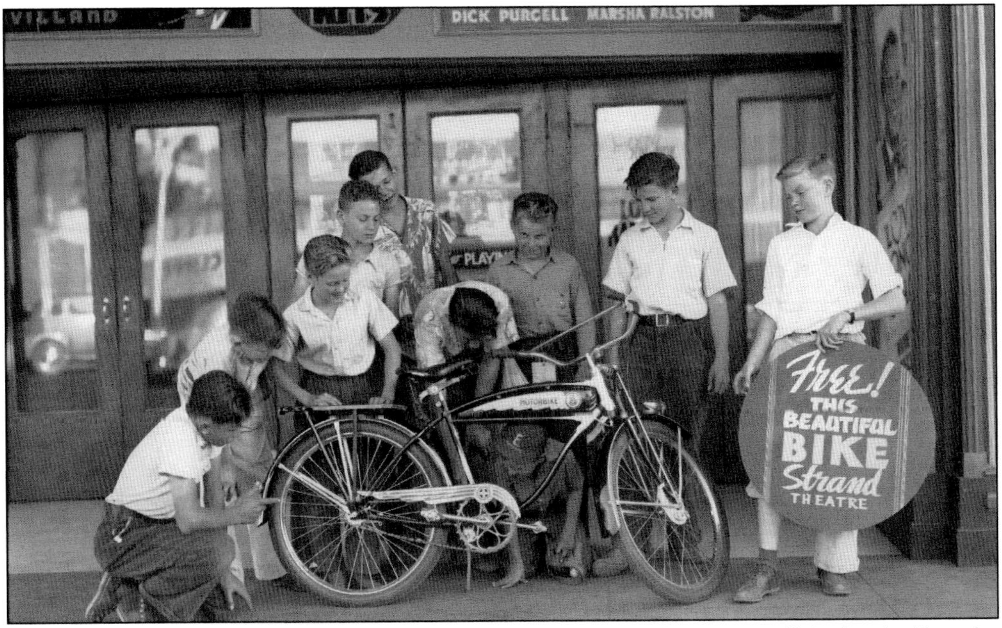

Free Bike at the Strand, 1940s. This unidentified group of boys can still find a thrill in the opportunity to win a free bicycle. Each one of the nine youngsters is eyeing the features of the Schwinn Motorbike being given away at the Strand Theatre in downtown Modesto. This was part of a promotion that took place during the weekly serials that unspooled each Saturday at the movie theater.

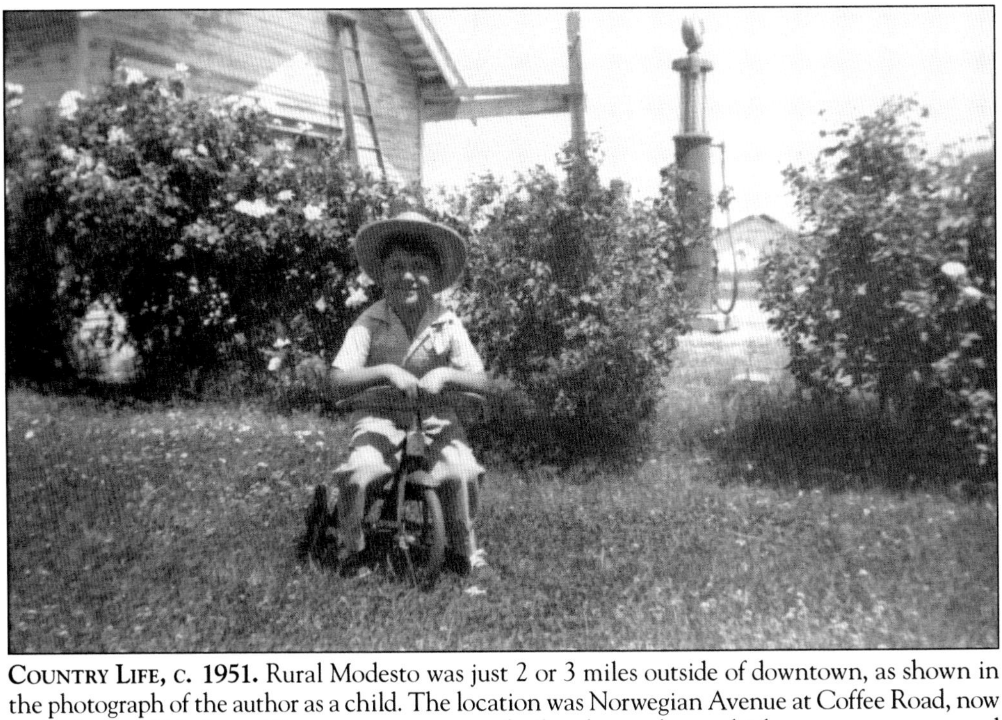

Country Life, c. 1951. Rural Modesto was just 2 or 3 miles outside of downtown, as shown in the photograph of the author as a child. The location was Norwegian Avenue at Coffee Road, now in the heart of Modesto. The property contained a farmhouse, barn, chicken coops, garage, and that old-fashioned, glass-topped gas pump used for a trucking business. (Author's collection.)

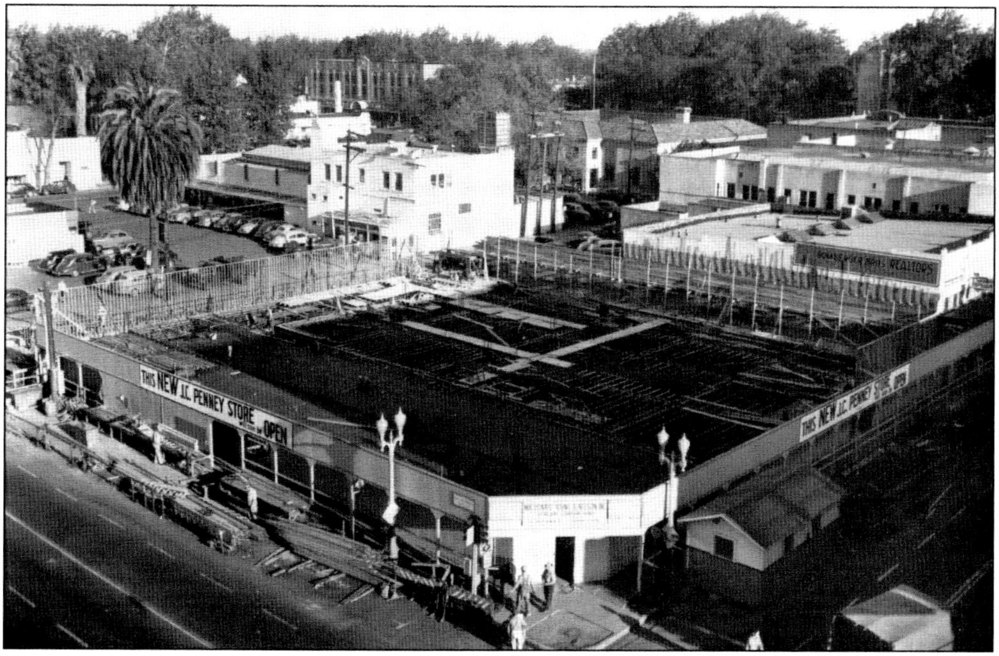

J. C. PENNEY, C. 1947. A new department store was not so unusual at this time in downtown Modesto. This construction photograph was taken from an upper floor at the Hotel Covell. Built at a cost of $750,000, the new store would be managed by J. C. Penney's nephew, Richard E. Penney. Richard had worked at the old Modesto store since 1939. He also served as an MID director.

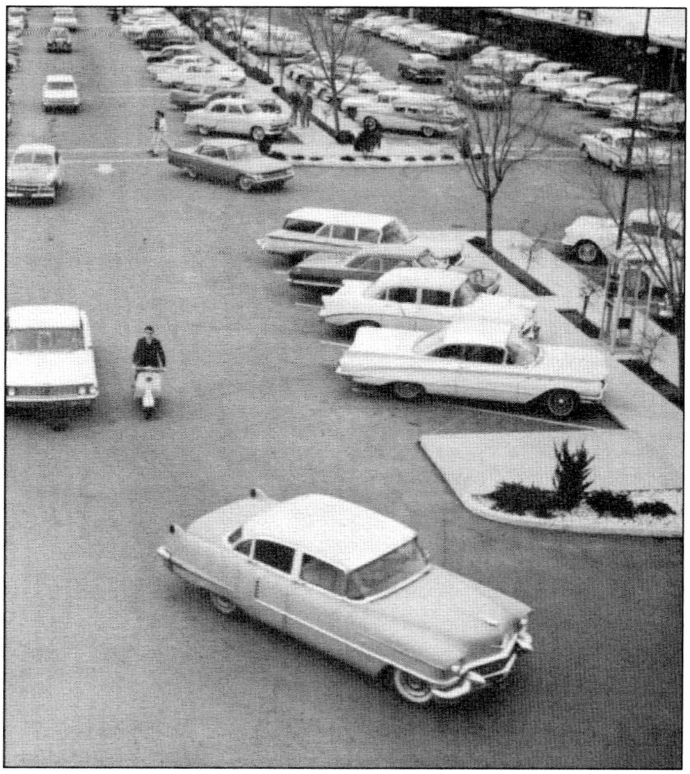

MCHENRY VILLAGE, 1950S. Cars pack the parking lot at McHenry Village, Modesto's first shopping center located outside the downtown area. No one could understand why businesses would locate "way out in the country." When the center opened in 1953, it marked the beginning of the shift of retail stores away from downtown. It also marked the beginning of development on prime agricultural land. (Author's collection.)

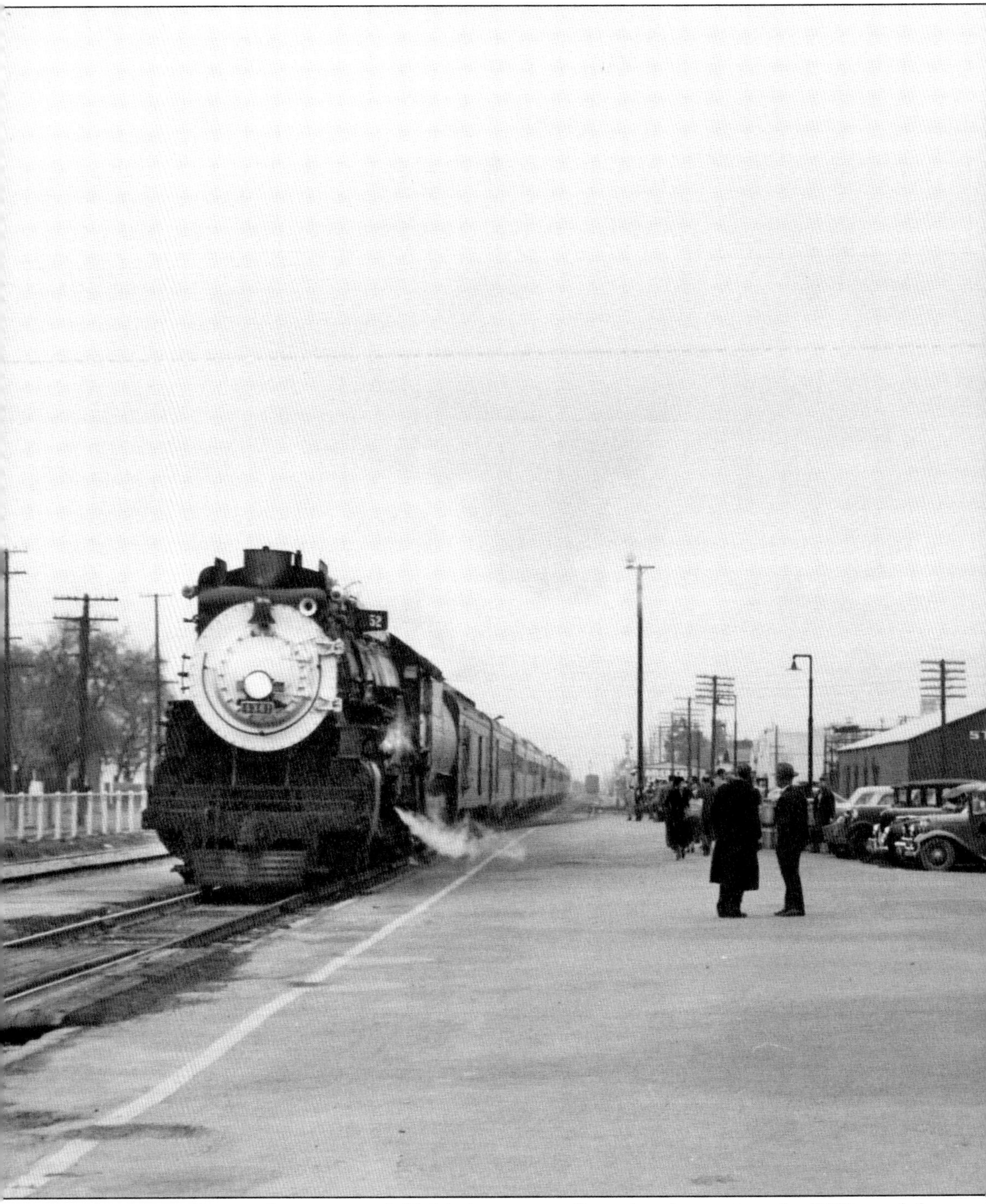

Southern Pacific Station, c. 1947. Modesto was still a railroad town into the 1950s, and the Southern Pacific Railroad Station continued to offer passenger service on such historic trains as the *San Joaquin Daylight*. Southern Pacific preferred freight rather than passengers and ended much of its passenger service in the 1960s and 1970s. Amtrak took over in 1971, and passenger service moved to the Santa Fe and Union Pacific lines, which run east of Modesto. In this photograph,

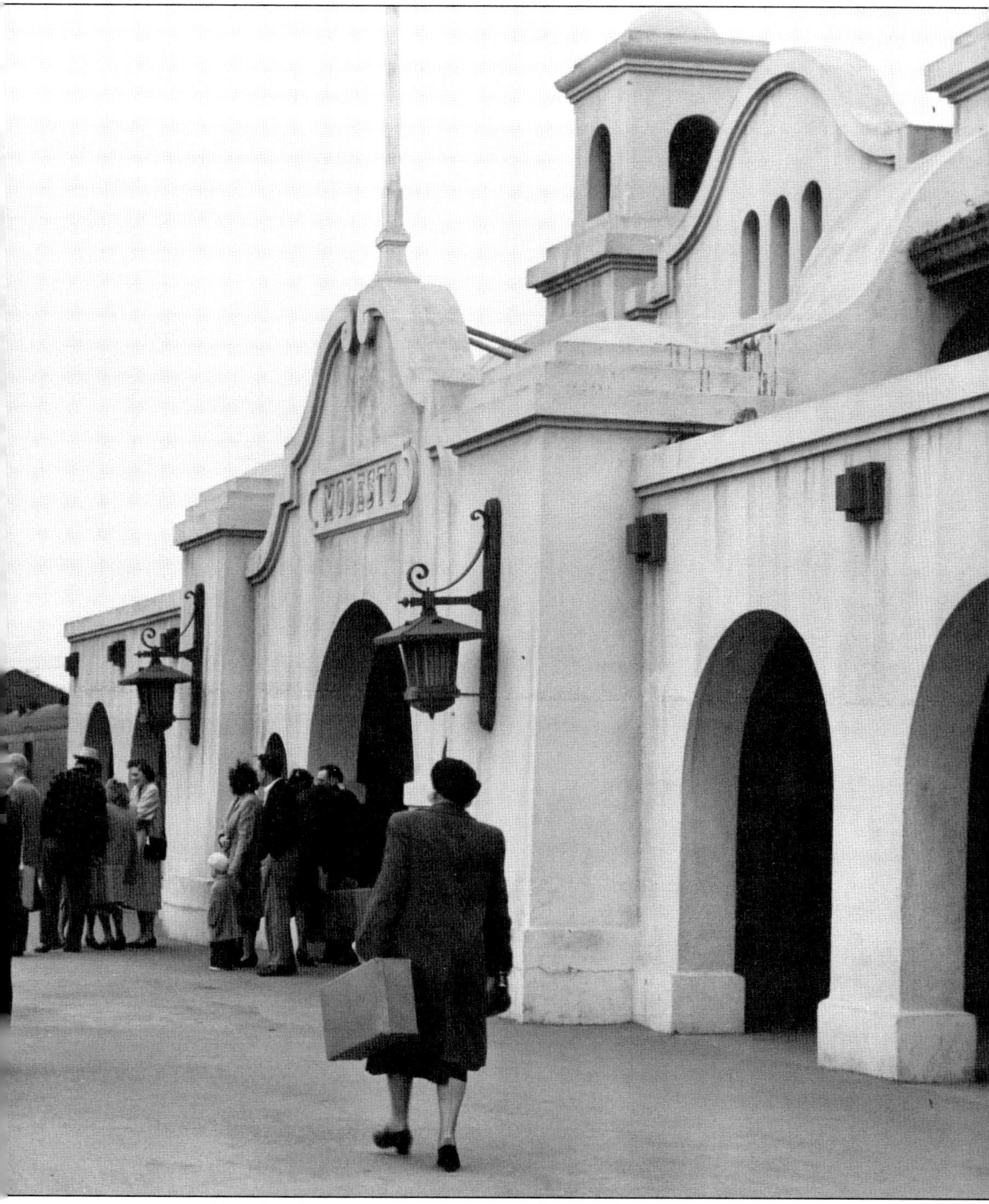

passengers wait to board as the train comes to a stop in front of the station. The Southern Pacific Station, opened in 1915, is now the transportation hub for Modesto's bus system and Greyhound. It no longer provides train service. A new Amtrak station was built in east Modesto and offers bus service into Modesto.

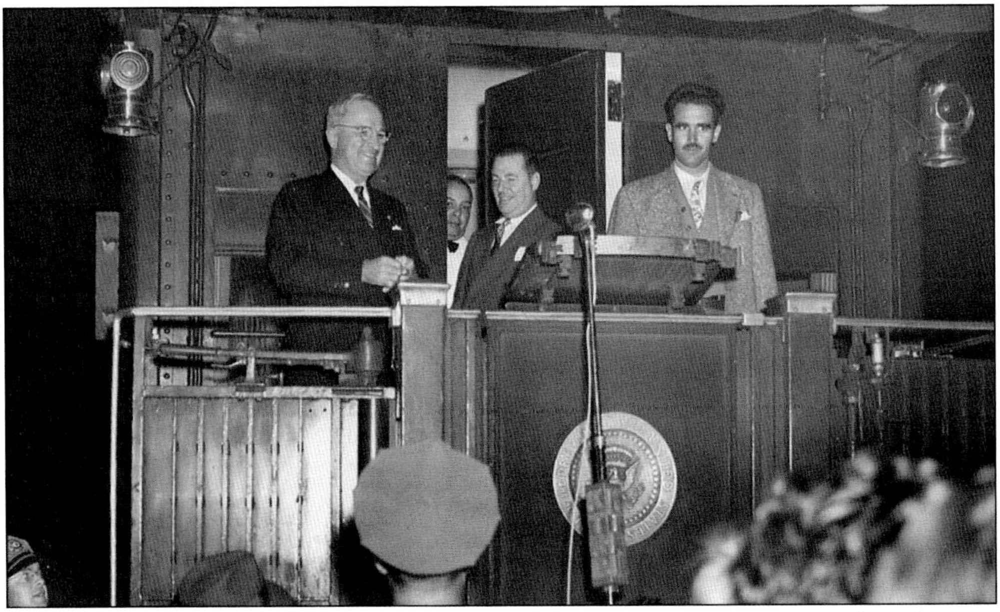

WHISTLE-STOP, C. 1948. The Central Valley of California was an important area for politicians during this period of time, so it was no surprise when they would pay a visit to Modesto, no matter how briefly. The two photographs on this page were taken during the 1948 presidential campaign. Above, Pres. Harry S Truman speaks to an enthusiastic crowd of 1,500 at the train station on September 23 at 6:00 a.m. Below, his Republican rival, Thomas E. Dewey, also stopped in town to give a speech on the "Dewey Victory Special." As presidential historians recall, this is the race where Truman was trailing in the polls yet defeated Dewey by a substantial margin. Note that local radio station KTRB is aggressively on the spot, covering the news event. (Both, Modesto Radio Station Museum, Lee Roddy.)

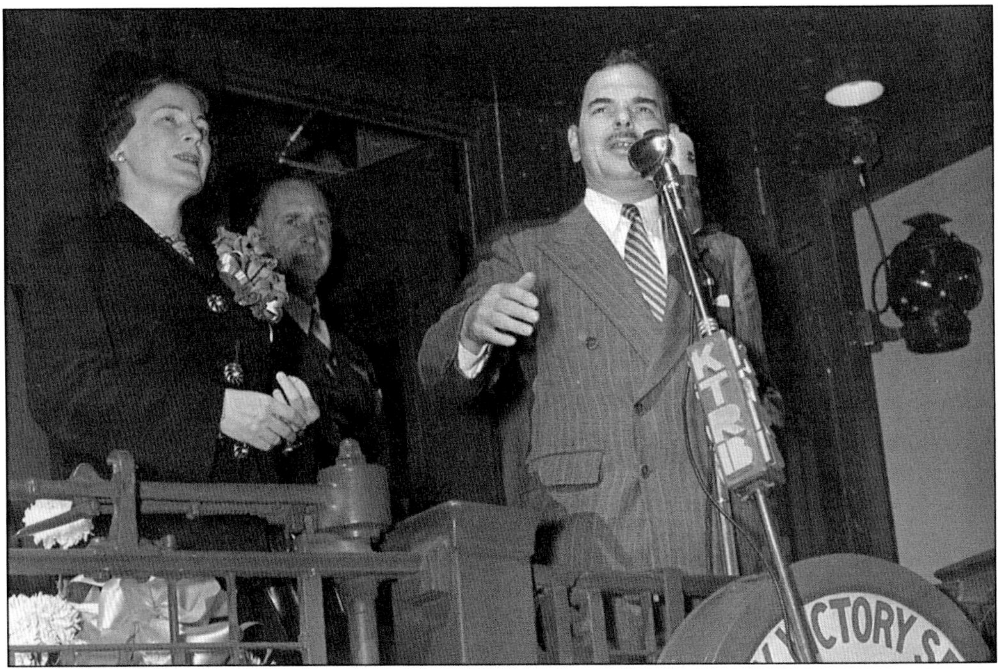

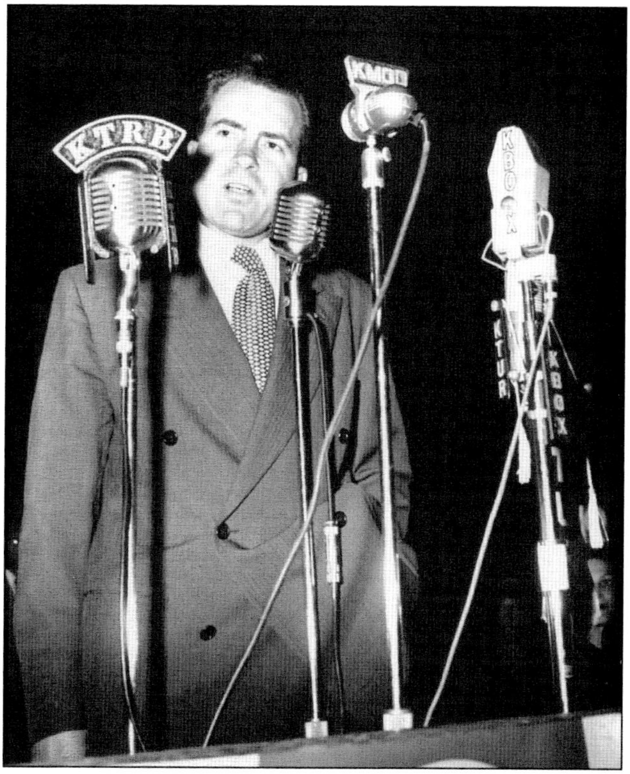

Nixon Visits, c. 1952. In October 1952, Richard M. Nixon made a second visit to Modesto to speak at Courthouse Park while running for vice president. He visited in 1950 while running for congress. This time around, all of the area radio stations are represented by the microphones at the podium: KTRB, KBOX, KTUR, and KMOD. Nixon talked about Truman's "terrible blunder" in Korea. (Modesto Radio Museum, Bill Slater.)

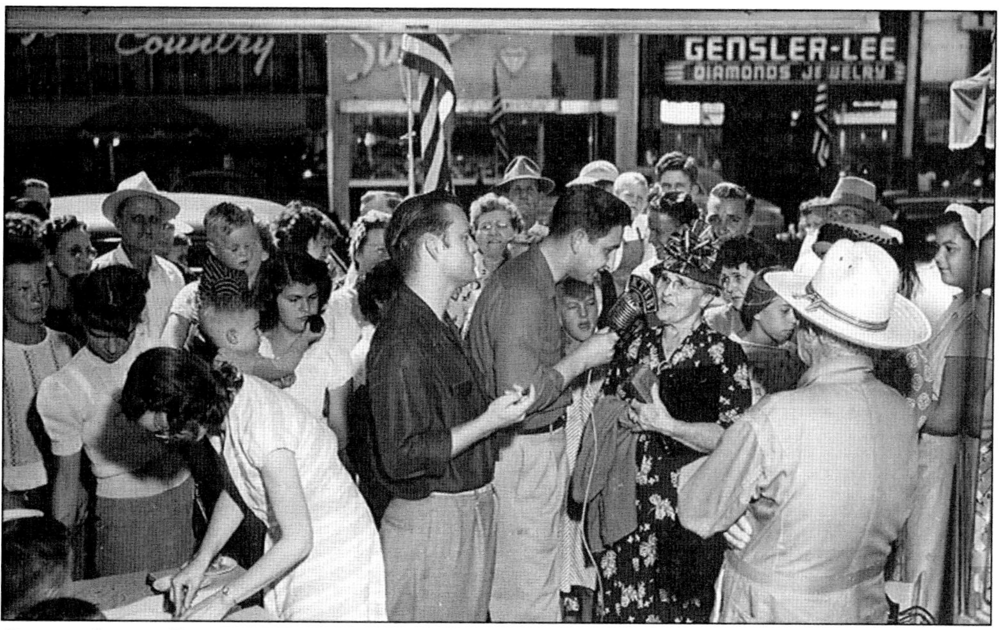

On the Street Interview, 1950s. KTRB had been in existence since 1933 and was a powerful broadcasting voice in Northern California. Milt Hibdon (with microphone) and Lee Roddy (at his right) took the show on the road with interviews throughout the community. In this photograph, they are on Tenth Street interviewing a crowd of Modestans. (Modesto Radio Museum, Lee Roddy.)

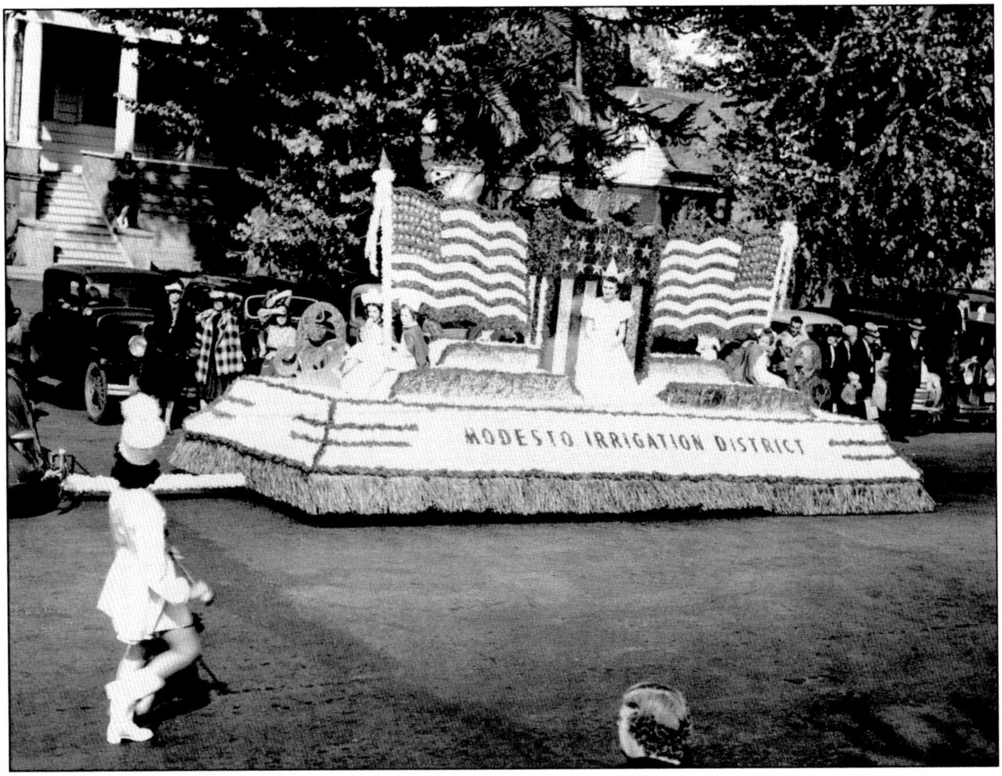

MID Parade Float, 1940s. It would not be a parade without floats, and it would not be the Modesto Fourth of July Parade without a patriotic float from the Modesto Irrigation District. Modesto's annual parade has sometimes been threatened by lack of sponsors and cancellation, but it is still part of the celebration. (Author's collection.)

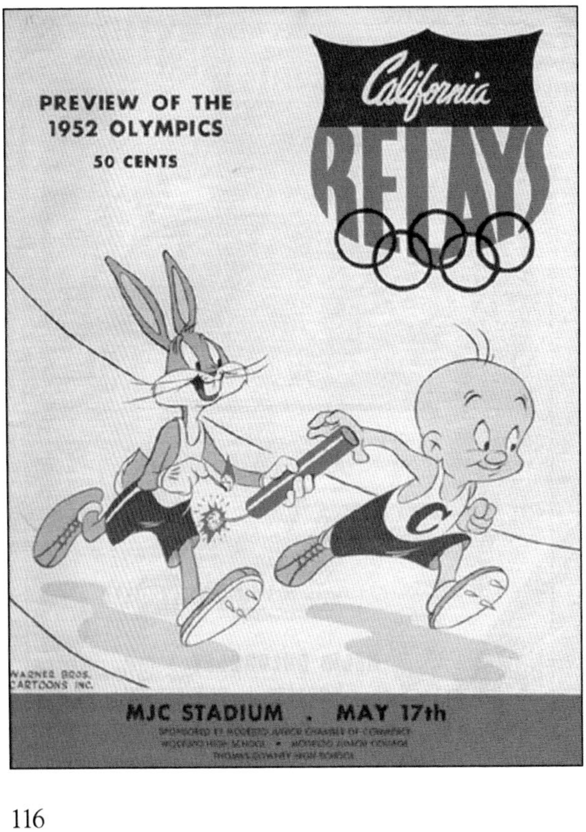

California Relays, c. 1952. This program cover for the California Relays made use of Warner Brothers cartoon characters. The relays began in 1942 and were held at the Modesto Junior College Stadium. An annual event in Modesto until 2008, the relays were a catalyst for track and field participants going on to bigger competitions. Many world records were shattered at the Modesto competitions. (Author's collection.)

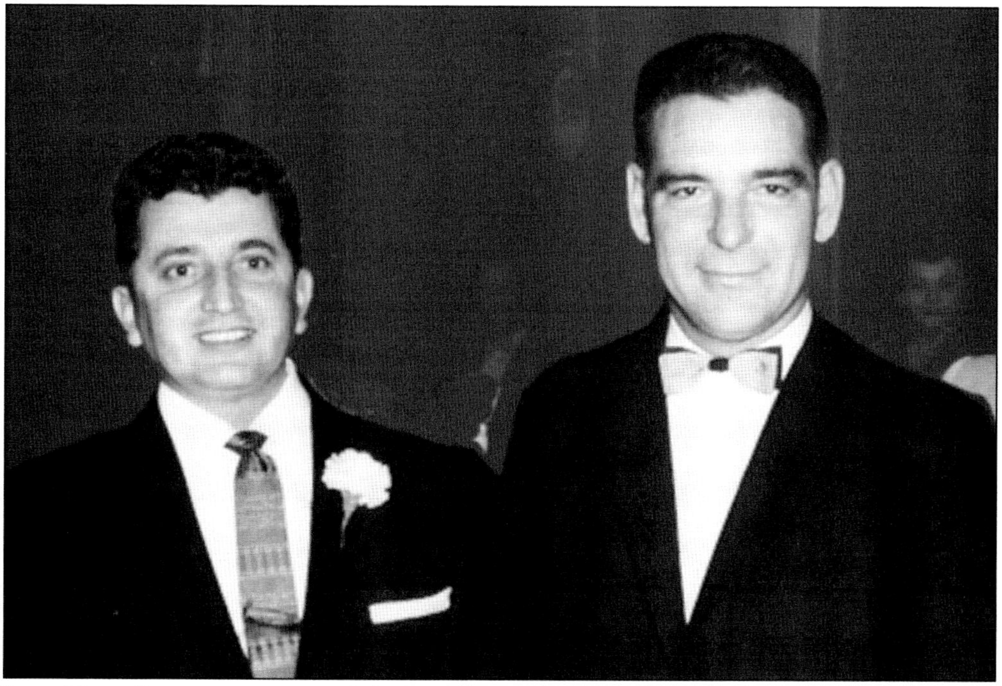

SAVE MART SUPERMARKETS, C. 1952. In 1952, cofounders Mike Piccinini (above left) and Nick Tocco (above right) opened their first Save Mart Supermarket in Modesto (below) on Crows Landing Road. Known for innovation, Save Mart was one of the first supermarkets to offer customers prepackaged meats, yard and garden supplies, plants, fresh-cut flowers, and gift items, all creative concepts for the time. These products and services were new for the 1950s and relatively unheard of for the area until Save Mart introduced them. In 1956, a corporate office was established adjacent to a newly constructed Save Mart shopping center in Modesto. In conjunction with the corporate office, three subsidiary companies were established: Yosemite Management, providing accounting and management services; Yosemite Properties, providing property management support; and Yosemite Advertising, providing graphic art material. In 1973, a warehouse facility was established in Modesto and named Yosemite Wholesale. (Both, author's collection.)

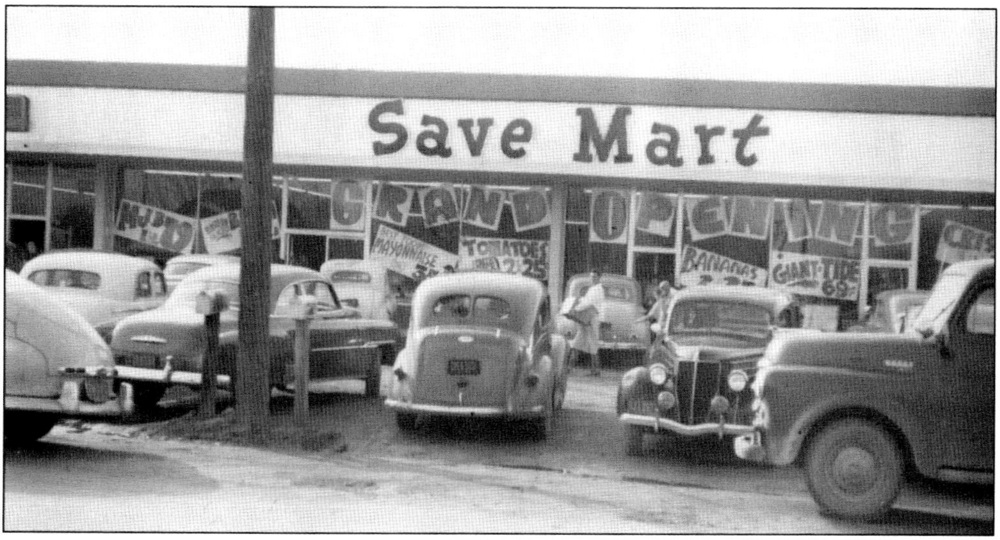

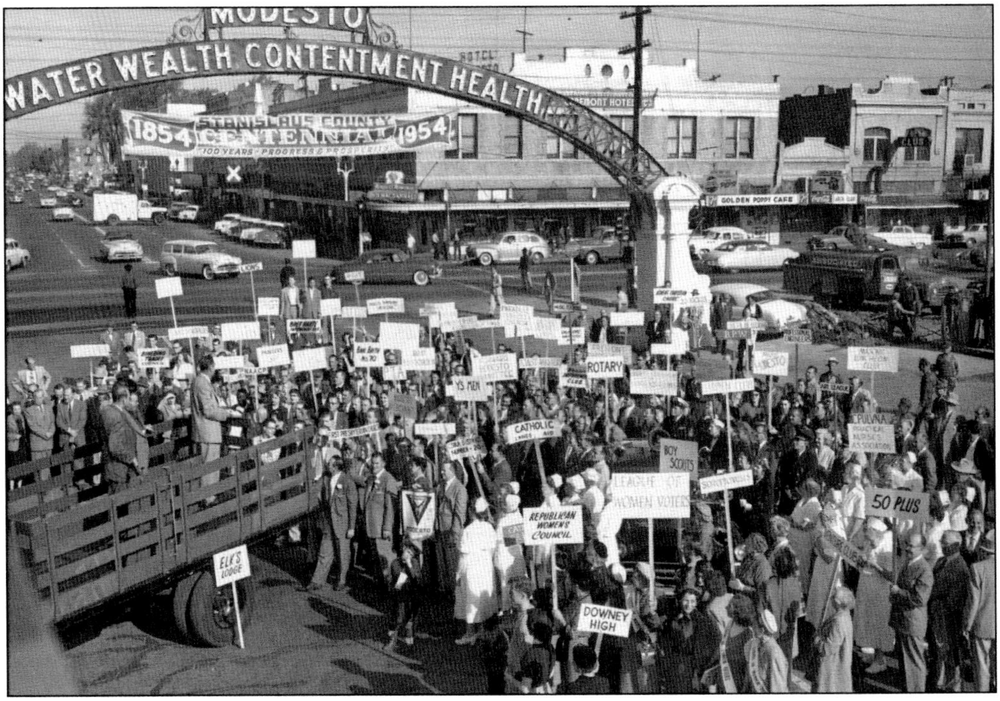

STANISLAUS COUNTY CENTENNIAL, C. 1954. Celebrating the county's 100th birthday, area groups and service clubs got together under Modesto's famed arch and stood for a photograph. The clubs represented include everything from political organizations such as the Republican Women's Council to the Rotary, Masonic Luncheon Club, and the NAACP. Representatives of the organizations all found time to pose for this historic moment. (J. Broome, Camera Center Collection.)

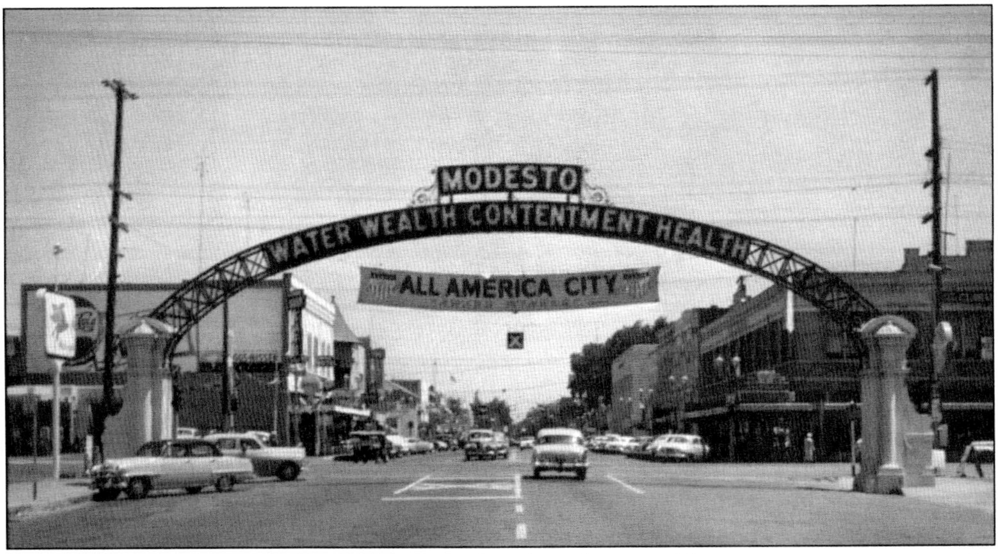

ALL-AMERICA CITY, C. 1954. The All-America City Award is one of the most prestigious community recognition awards. Started in 1949, the award honors cities and towns of all sizes where community members, government, businesses, and nonprofits work together to address critical local issues. Modesto won the award in 1954 and then again in 1972. It is among more than 500 communities named All-America cities since the award's inception. (Author's collection.)

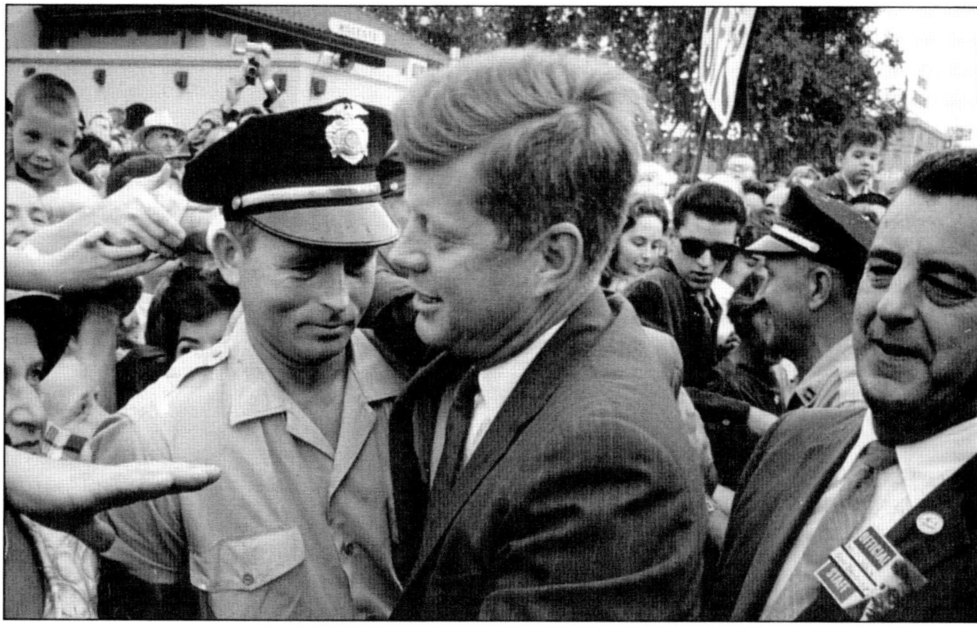

JFK Whistle-Stop, c. 1960. September 8, 1960, Sen. John F. Kennedy, campaigning for president, stopped in Modesto. He spoke about the valley, saying, "The work that you have done in harnessing the land and water and the power I think shows what can be done with the resources of the entire United States." He then stepped off the train into the crowd to shake hands. (J. Broome, Camera Center Collection.)

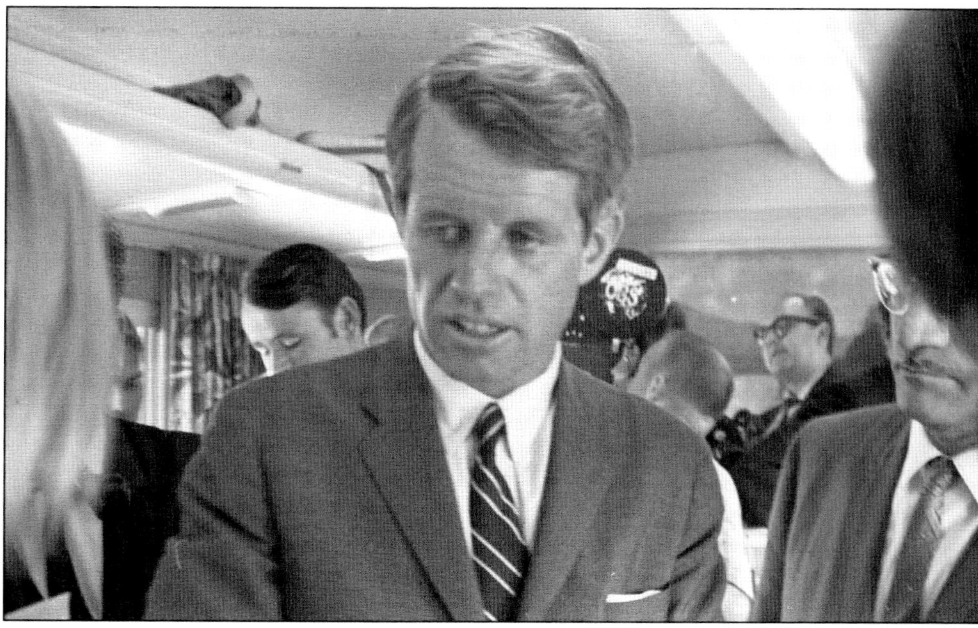

RFK on Board, c. 1968. This slightly blurry photograph of Robert F. Kennedy was taken on board his whistle-stop train between Stockton and Modesto. It was May 30, 1968, and on June 4, he would win the primary and lose his life. A huge throng of people, wanting to be part of history, watched RFK as he spoke at the Modesto Southern Pacific Station. (Author's collection, David J. Fox.)

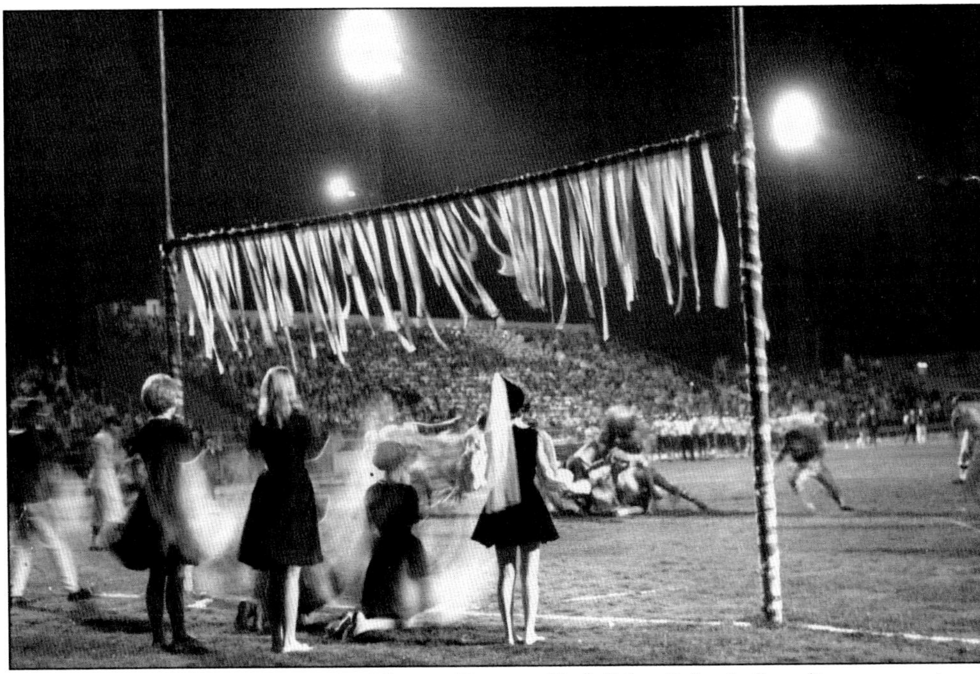

Downey High Football, c. 1966. Thomas Downey High School's football stadium was equipped with lights and bleachers in the 1960s and soon became the site of most of the area high school football games. In this photograph, one of the Downey mascots and the cheerleaders wait for the Knights to score. After the Friday or Saturday night game, it was on to cruising in downtown Modesto. (Author's collection.)

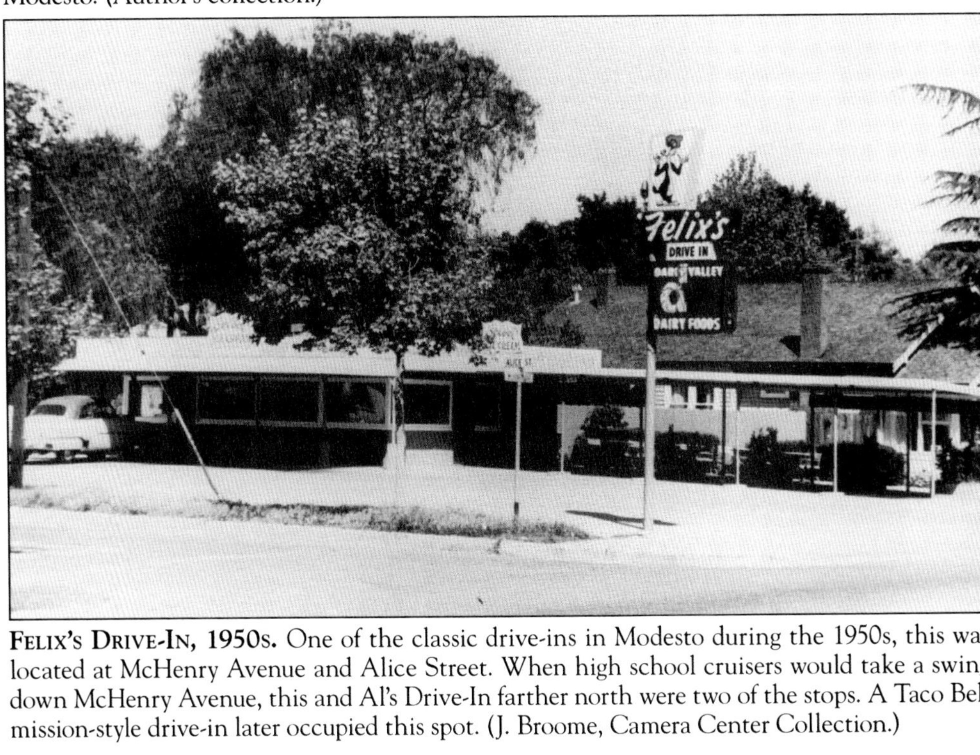

Felix's Drive-In, 1950s. One of the classic drive-ins in Modesto during the 1950s, this was located at McHenry Avenue and Alice Street. When high school cruisers would take a swing down McHenry Avenue, this and Al's Drive-In farther north were two of the stops. A Taco Bell mission-style drive-in later occupied this spot. (J. Broome, Camera Center Collection.)

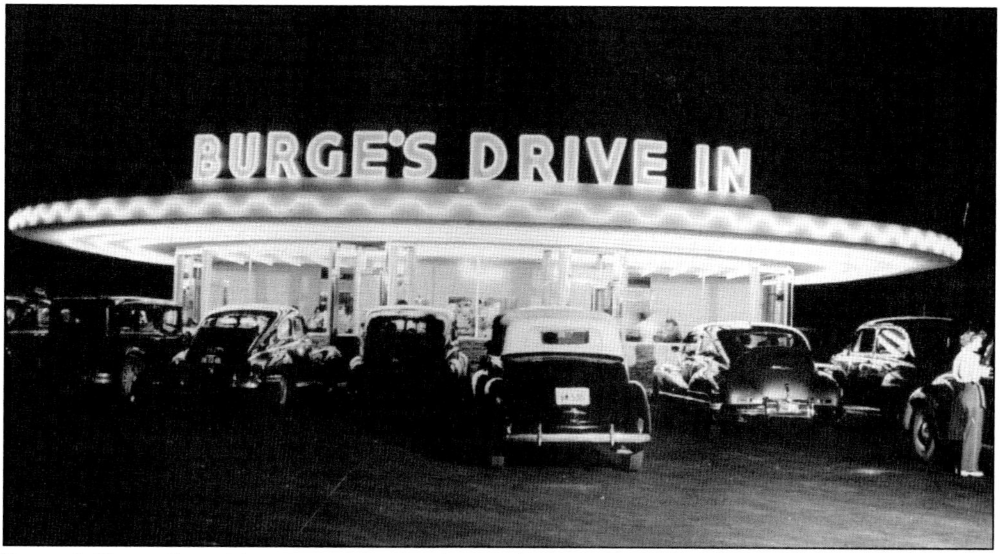

Burge's Drive-In, 1950s. It was a great place to hang out. One description of Burge's Drive-In, located at the corner of Ninth and O Streets, tells the story of how there was not enough room to park all the cars in a row, so they would park behind each other. When the first car wanted to leave, the drivers of the other cars would amiably move out of the way and then pull back in—talk about a simpler time. The carhops knew all the teens and others who showed up for the burgers and soft drinks and knew what they liked. Inside, patrons could sit at a table where they could pick out their favorite tunes on the jukebox. Burge's was Modesto's little touch of heaven for the better part of two decades. (Both, J. Broome, Camera Center Collection.)

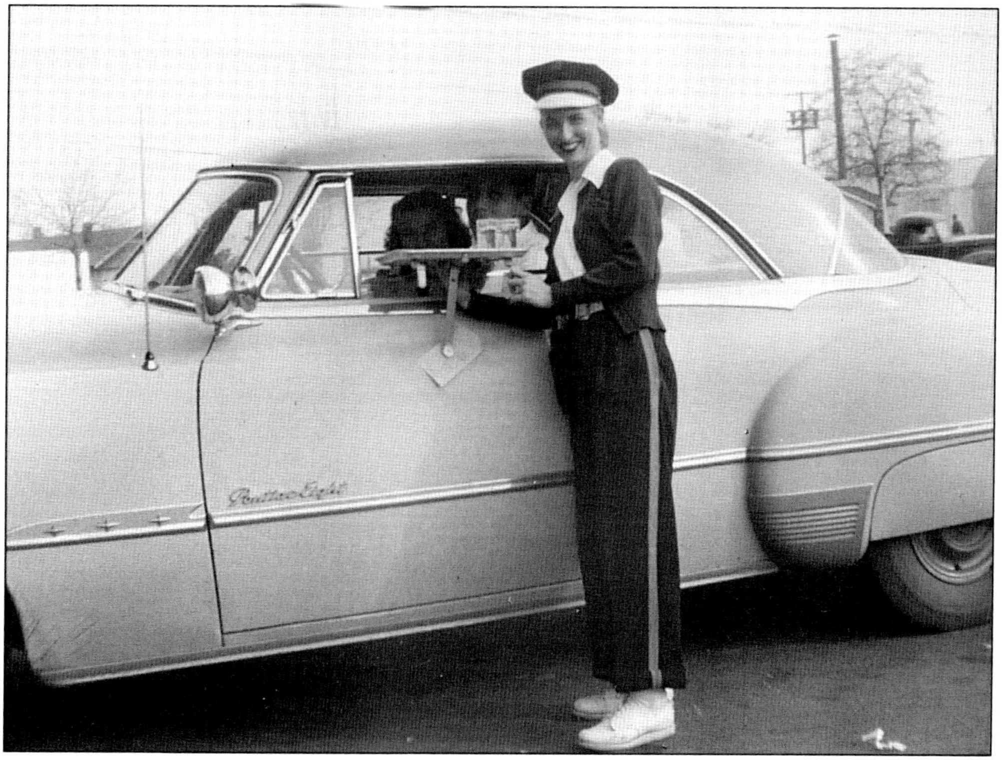

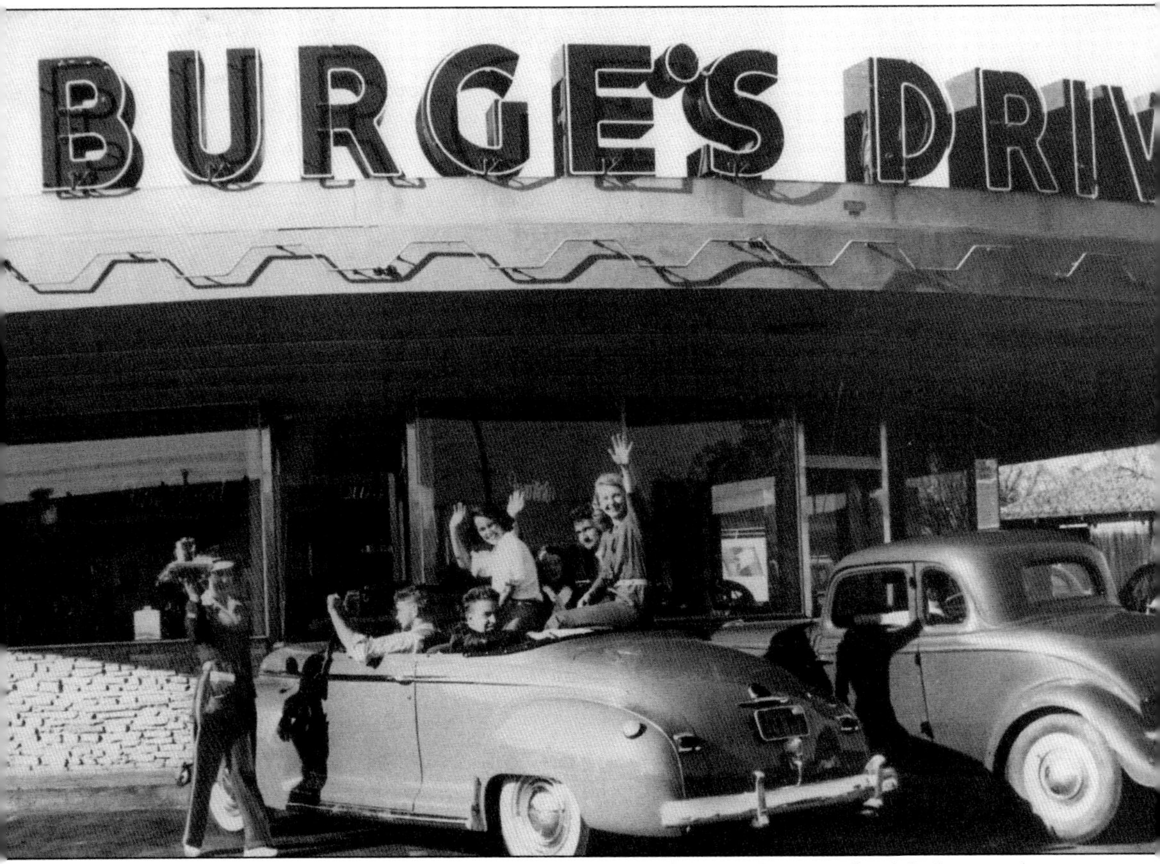

TEENAGE HANGOUT, 1950S. Everyone assumes that Mel's Drive-In existed in Modesto at the time depicted in George Lucas's *American Graffiti*. But it didn't. There were a few drive-ins that fit the description, none of them Mel's. The photograph above is a daytime shot of Burge's Drive-In, which sometimes had roller-skating carhops. It was located on Ninth Street at O Street. Grady Williams remembers Burge's: "Dragging the main was from Lucky parking lot down Tenth to a left turn on 'O' Street to Burge's, where you turned around and backtracked to repeat the process. The city, due to congestion and hoping to discourage cruising, made Tenth a one-way street. The route became Tenth and Eleventh—a long time ago." As depicted in the 1973 film, Modesto was the place to be toward the end of the school year. The city embraced the *American Graffiti* concept but not enthusiastically.

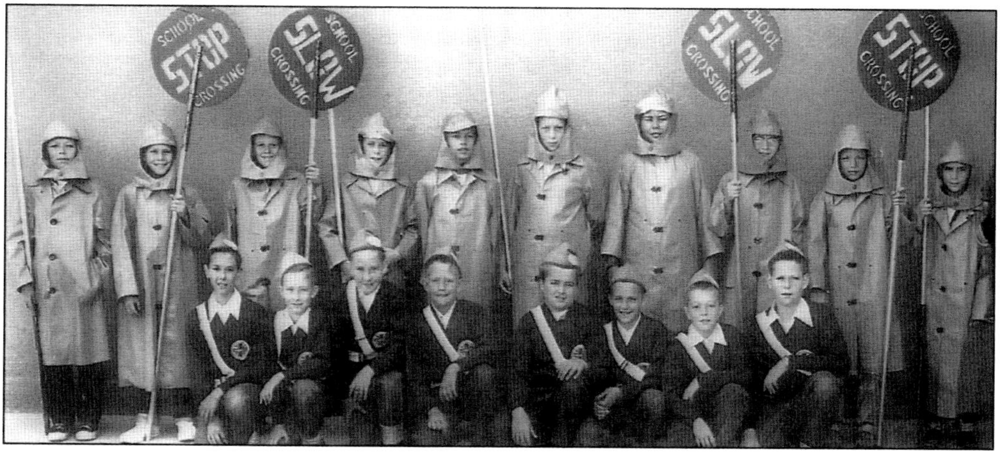

FILMMAKER GEORGE LUCAS, 1950S (ABOVE) AND C. 1977 (BELOW). The lineup of crossing guards above includes youngsters from John Muir School. The most notable among them is the last person in the top row at right, George Walton Lucas Jr. Born in 1944, Lucas attended Roosevelt Junior High School and Thomas Downey High School. He was unable to attend his high school graduation in 1962 because of injuries suffered in a severe automobile accident. After attending MJC, he found his calling in films and eventually used his last year at Downey High as the basis for his first commercially successful film, *American Graffiti*, in 1973. In 1977, he made a $10-million film called *Star Wars* and changed filmmaking forever. The photograph below shows Lucas as he looked during the filming of the science fiction fantasy, when he was 33 years old. (Above, J. Broome, Camera Center Collection; below, author's collection.)

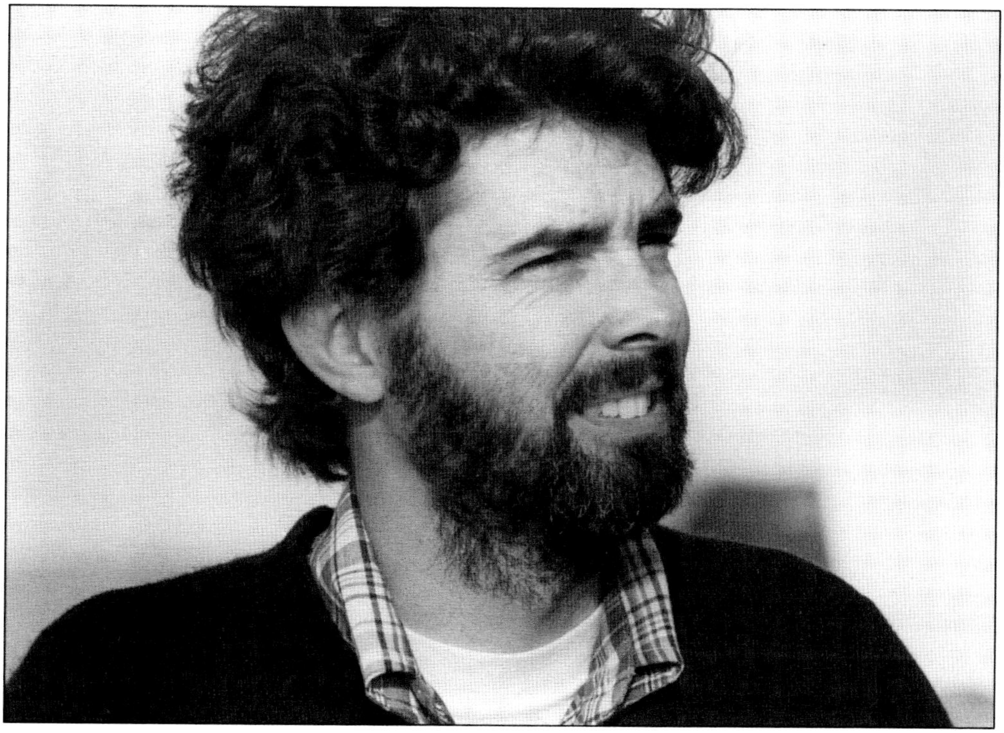

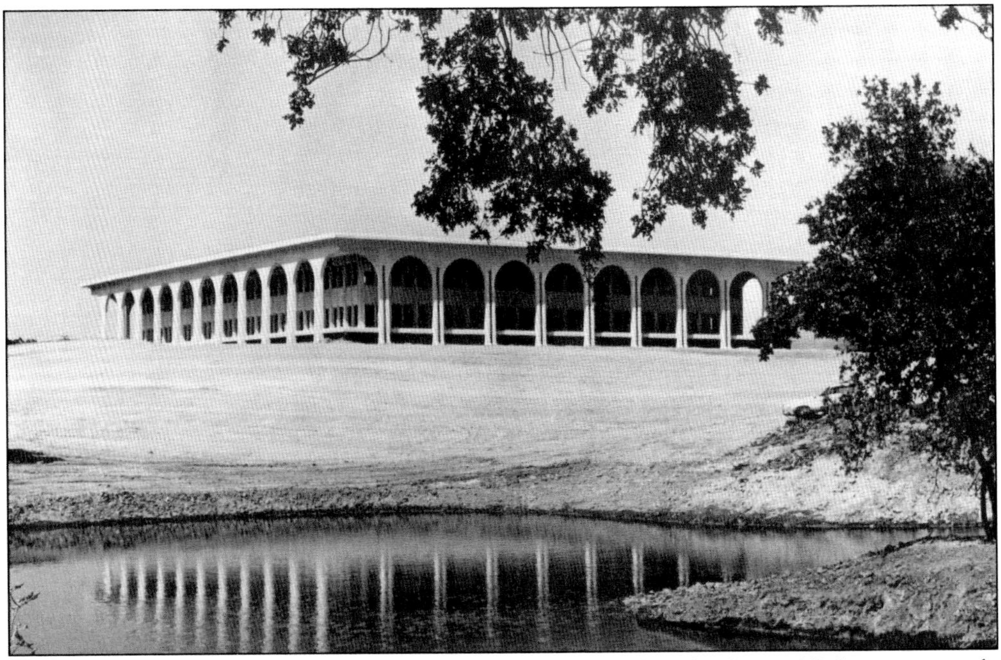

E. AND J. GALLO WINERY, 1970S. A new administration building for the world's largest privately held winery coincided with Ernest and Julio Gallo appearing on the cover of *Time* magazine. They were the first Modestans to receive the honor (George Lucas has since been on the cover several times). Below is the winery's underground cellar. Gallo began in 1933 shortly after the end of Prohibition. Ernest went to the McHenry Library to find a book about wine making but was told there were none (a decade of Prohibition had seen to that). The librarian remembered some pamphlets in the basement, and Ernest found one on fermentation and one on the care of wine. They were exactly what he needed. He said, "These old pamphlets probably saved us from going out of business our very first year—as did those new wineries that produced undrinkable wines."

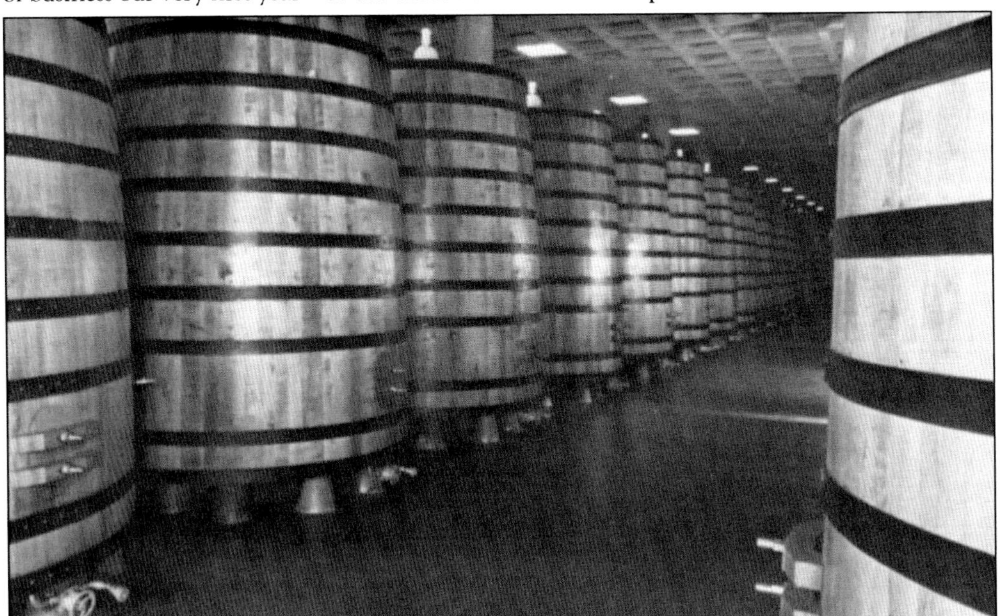

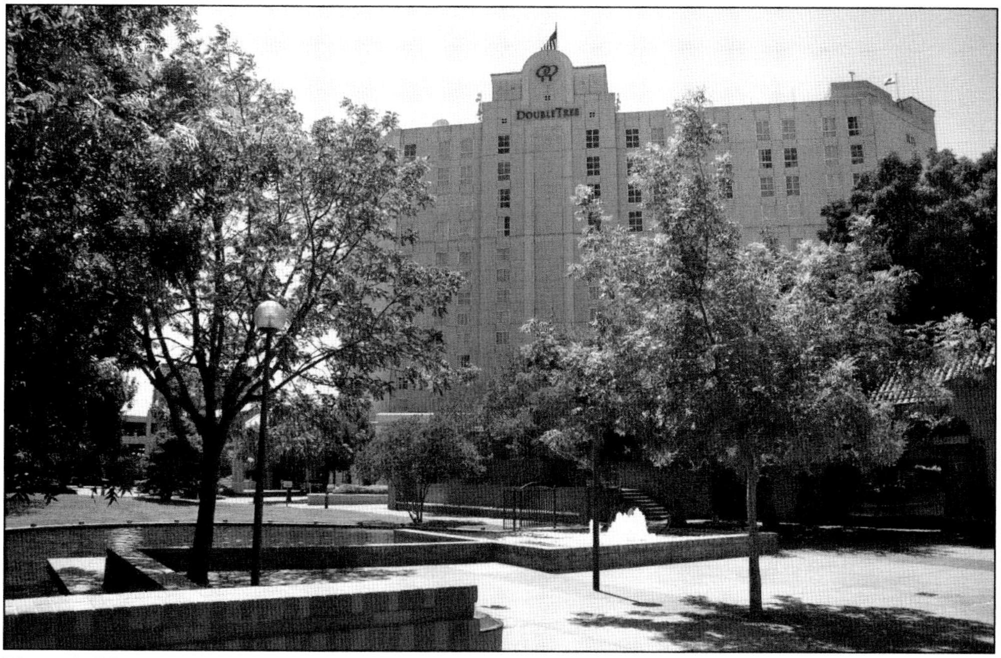

TODAY'S MODESTO, C. 2009. Downtown Modesto no longer boasts four or five major hotels but does have the Doubletree Hotel on Ninth Street. The 14-story hotel-office tower, originally the Red Lion Hotel, was built as part of a redevelopment project completed in 1988. The parklike grounds are in front of Modesto Centre Plaza, a 43,000-square-foot conference center. The project opened on March 3, 1988, with "Bob Hope In Person." (Photograph by the author.)

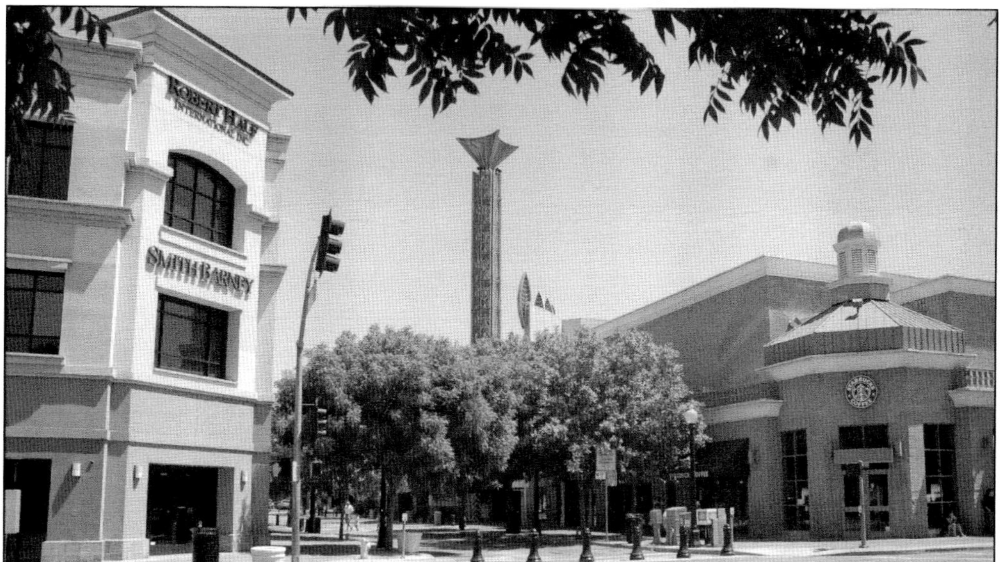

TENTH STREET PLAZA, C. 2009. Looking south down what was Tenth Street at K Street, the plaza features the 18-screen Brenden Theatre building, located approximately where the Strand Theatre once stood. The plaza is used for outdoor music and lunchtime gatherings. Restaurants, shops, businesses, and city and county offices at Tenth Street Place are all part of the development. The theater building, with its tall tower, was the first to open in 1999. (Photograph by the author.)

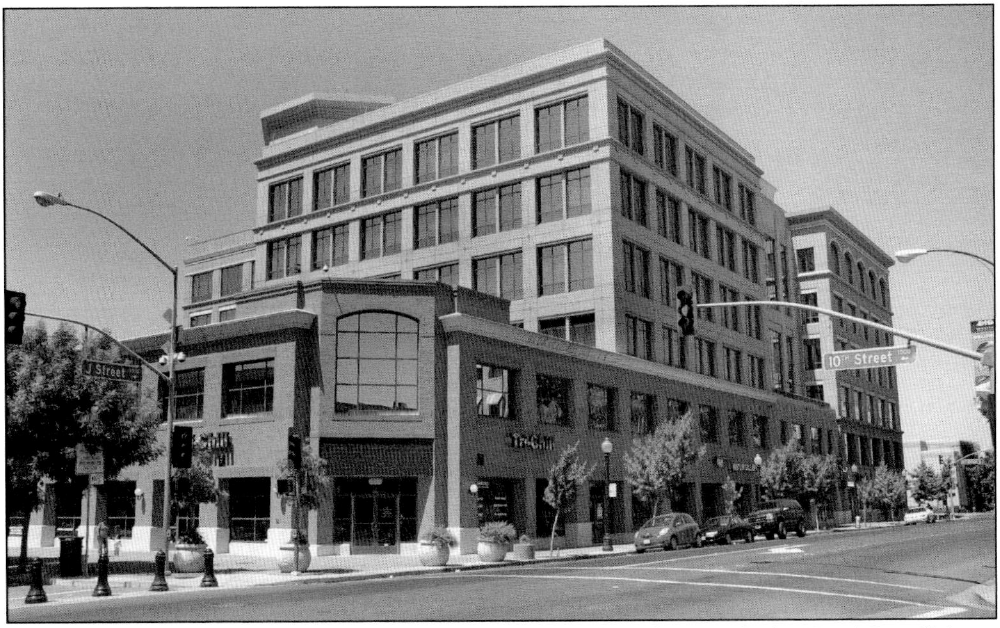

Tenth and J Streets, c. 2009. Once graced by the Hotel Hughson with the Hotel Covell down the street, this corner is now home to Tenth Street Place. The building houses both Modesto City Hall and Stanislaus County offices. Bricks from the Hotel Covell were recycled for use in the plaza located in front of the building on Tenth Street. The development brought new life to downtown Modesto with restaurants adding to the mix of businesses. (Photograph by the author.)

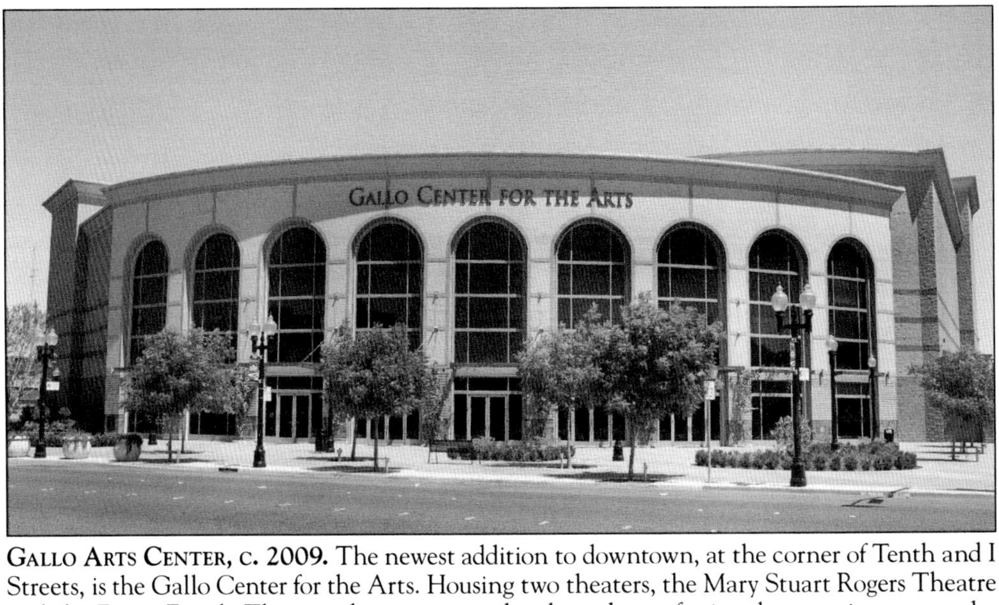

Gallo Arts Center, c. 2009. The newest addition to downtown, at the corner of Tenth and I Streets, is the Gallo Center for the Arts. Housing two theaters, the Mary Stuart Rogers Theatre and the Foster Family Theatre, the arts center has brought professional entertainment to the community, assisted by an endowment from the Ernest Gallo Foundation. The Modesto Bank Building was once located on this corner. (Photograph by the author.)

BIBLIOGRAPHY

Bare, Colleen Stanley. *Modesto Then and Now.* Modesto, CA: McHenry Museum Press, 1999.

———. *The McHenry Mansion, Modesto's Heritage.* Modesto, CA: McHenry Mansion Foundation Press, 1985.

Elias, Sol P. *Stories of Stanislaus.* Modesto, CA: self-published, 1924.

Gallo, Ernest and Julio, with Bruce B. Henderson. *Ernest and Julio: Our Story.* New York, NY: Times Books, 1994.

Gauvreau, Robert. *Modesto: Images of Yesterday, Images of Today, A Rephotographic Survey.* Modesto, CA: McHenry Museum Society Press, 1984.

Gooch, Kathleen M. *Stanislaus County: An Illustrated History.* Northridge, CA: Windsor Publications, 1988.

Legacy of Healing: A 60-Year History of Gould. Modesto, CA: Sutter-Gould Medical Foundation, 2009.

Osborn, Billy J. *Modesto: An Informal History.* Lincoln, NE: iUniverse, 2003.

Nash, John D. and Mary M. *In A Goodly Land, Latter Day Saints of the Stanislaus.* Fresno, CA: Linrose Publishing Company, 1997.

Pollack, Dale. *Skywalking: The Life and Films of George Lucas.* New York, NY: Harmony Books, 1983.

Ray, Herndon Carroll. *Stanislaus County 1854–1954: A Century of Growth.* Modesto, CA: Stanislaus County Superintendent of Schools, 1955.

Stanislaus County Blue Book. Modesto, CA: self-published, 1935.

Tatum, Robert Daras, and Loley Myers. *Old Times in Stanislaus County.* Pittsburg, CA: Highland Publishers, 1994 and 1996.